車輪蘇州月餅

夾肉小燒餅椰絲雪

菊花酥燒餅燒餅肉

夾肉小燒餅椰絲雪

燒餅咖哩餃鮮肉酥

CHINESE COOKING

酥車輪蘇州月餅

夾肉小燒餅椰絲雪

菊花酥燒餅塊菊

夾肉小燒餅椰絲雪

燒餅咖哩餃鮮魚肉酥

CHINESE COOKING

NIM CHEE LEE

Portland House
New York

Editor: Jeni Fleetwood

This 1987 edition published by Portland House,
distributed by Crown Publishers, Inc.,
225 Park Avenue South, New York, New York 10003

ISBN 0-517-64454-1

Printed by Jarrold Printing, Norwich

h g f e d c b a

CONTENTS

INTRODUCTION

Chinese food is one of the most popular cuisines in this country. Everyone loves going out for a Chinese meal, sharing and enjoying together all the tasty and various dishes.

However, when it comes to actually cooking Chinese food, many people think it is simply beyond them, believing the ingredients hard to find, the dishes themselves awkward and time-consuming to make and the techniques impossible to master. Yet there is no more mystery to Chinese cooking than to any other cuisine. With the help of this book, by taking recipes in simple step-by-step stages, you will be surprised how quickly you too can learn to master this exciting cuisine and share with your family and friends some of the world's most delicious food.

Preparing Food

The Chinese spend some time preparing food before cooking – marinating meat, slicing vegetables and soaking dried food. Since cooking is so quick, it is worth getting into the habit of preparing all the ingredients in advance and laying them out by the stove, so that no time is lost when it comes to actually cooking. No special equipment is needed for preparing food, although traditionally a cleaver is used for most jobs, from quartering a chicken to crushing garlic. However, if you do not own one of these, a heavy knife works just as well.

Vegetables are almost always cut in small pieces, often sliced diagonally or cut in thin strips. This lets them cook quickly while retaining their crunch, and helps them absorb the flavor of the other ingredients and seasonings. Cutting vegetables in small pieces also makes eating with chopsticks a lot more simple.

Meat is also cut up before it is cooked – especially for stir-fried dishes. Usually it is cut in thin matchsticks, about ⅛ inch thick, but can also be cut in rectangular slices, about ¼ inch thick and 1 inch wide. Meat is also frequently marinated, often in a mixture of soy sauce, rice wine and oil. This helps tenderize the meat and adds flavor. When marinating, always use a non-metallic container, preferably a glass or earthenware one, since metal can react with the marinade, giving an unpleasant taste to the food.

Garlic and ginger can be prepared in various ways, but usually they are either thinly sliced, cut in fine threads or minced. Garlic can be crushed with a garlic press if liked – this is also a quick and easy method for making ginger juice.

Cooking Techniques

In China, fuel was – and in parts, still is – expensive and even scarce. Consequently cooking had to be quick and very efficient and most Chinese cooking techniques pivot on this important principle. Furthermore, the emphasis on crispness and texture in Chinese dishes means that food rarely needs cooking for long periods. Texture is as important as taste to the Chinese, so vegetables, particularly green ones, carrots and shoots,

are normally just "flash" cooked and meat is thinly sliced and marinated to ensure minimum cooking.

Stir-frying is, to the Chinese, the perfect method of cooking, and the wok the perfect piece of kitchen equipment. Food, which has been thinly sliced, is cooked in the hot oil over a high heat. Normally the meat is added first – as the meat cooks, it is pushed up the side of the wok and the prepared vegetables are added. None of the ingredients take long to cook and often a stir-fried meal can be cooked and ready in under 5 minutes.

If possible, always use a wok when stir-frying. Heat the empty wok over a high heat until smoke rises. This prevents food sticking. Gently add the oil, swirling it halfway up the side to coat. Then add the ingredients in the order of the recipe, remembering to stir and turn the food over with the metal scoop to ensure the food cooks and browns evenly.

Deep-frying is also very popular in Chinese cookery, particularly when food is cooked twice – first steamed or stir-fried and then deep-fried. Traditionally a wok is used for deep-frying. However, for most people, it is probably more convenient to use a deep-fat fryer. The oil should be heated to 350°F or until a cube of bread browns in about 60 seconds. The food should then be carefully lowered into the oil, either using a wire basket, a metal slotted spoon or, for dumplings or fritters, metal tongs. Make sure to turn food over midway through cooking so that it browns evenly.

Steaming is another extremely efficient way of cooking. While one dish is being simmered in a saucepan, two or three others can be arranged in steamers and stacked over the top of the pan, so that they cook gently in the steam. Steaming means that food loses none of its fine flavor or color and it also ensures that delicate food retains its shape. Consequently, steaming is a very popular method for cooking fish.

Bamboo baskets are the most common type of steamers used in Chinese cooking. These are inexpensive and widely available from Oriental markets. However an aluminum steamer or even a colander will work just as well. Either way, the food should fit comfortably in a single layer inside the steamer. The steamer itself should fit neatly over the top of the saucepan.

To steam food, unless you are steaming food over another dish, pour 2 inches of water into a saucepan and bring to a boil. Arrange the food in the steamer and place this over the saucepan. Cover with a lid and steam as directed in the recipe. If you are steaming food over a high heat or for a long period, always make sure the saucepan does not boil dry. If necessary, top up with a little extra boiling water from time to time.

Chinese Meals

Rice is regarded as the main course of a Chinese meal (except in the northern wheat-producing regions of China). Savory dishes are seen as the flavorings to or accompaniments for rice – quite the reverse of the Western idea that meat or fish forms the main dish of a meal.

One of the most notable aspects of a Chinese meal is that there is no set order of courses. The soup may be served first, if wished, but it is usual practice for people to help themselves to more during the meal. The food is eaten from bowls, rather than plates – during the meal people will help themselves to a little of one dish at a time, along with the rice. Chopsticks are traditionally used for picking up the food. These were invented by the civilized Chinese centuries before Europeans first thought of using the fork.

If you are serving a dish which has to be picked up in the fingers (spareribs for instance), finger bowls of water for washing may be needed. These look attractive with flowers, or slices of lemon floating in them. You may need extra napkins for drying your fingers afterward. In a Chinese restaurant, steamed towels may be brought to you, but these are difficult to organize in a Western home.

In Chinese restaurants, food is always kept warm at the table on a small warmer or hot tray. If you don't have one of these, you can improvise by placing two flat candles in a shallow dish and standing a wire cake rack on the top to support dishes of food.

In Chinese homes, the meal is usually eaten fast – and silently. After the meal China tea – without milk, sugar or lemon of course – is served, when the company will relax and chat. The tea is drunk in small handleless cups and the correct way to hold these is with the thumb underneath the ring at the bottom and the index finger on the rim, so that you do not burn your fingers.

Menu Planning

Once you become proficient at Chinese cooking, you will want to plan your own full-scale Chinese meals.

The general practice in China is to serve one savory dish per person, in addition to the rice dish. If wished, a soup, an appetizer or perhaps a noodle dish can also be included in the meal.

When choosing the savory dishes, you should aim to include a good balance of texture, color, flavor and aroma – the important elements of Chinese cooking. It is also important to choose an interesting range of meat, poultry, fish, shellfish and vegetable dishes, and to make sure that they have been cooked by different culinary techniques. If you follow these basic guidelines, you will find menu planning fun and rewarding. For further ideas, look at the menu suggestions given on pages 384 and 385.

Chinese Ingredients

The authentic nature of this book naturally means that many of the recipes call for Chinese ingredients. Some of the vegetables listed may at first be unfamiliar to you, but an illustrated key on pages 392 and 393 will help you to identify just what you are looking for! The glossary on pages 386 to 391 will help you to get to know other Chinese ingredients featured. Where possible, better-known Western substitutes are suggested, but bear in mind that if you use these substitutes, the taste of the dish will be different, and less authentic.

It is worth making special sorties into those areas of the many big cities where the Chinese communities live, and searching through the food stores for special ingredients. Do not be afraid to ask for assistance: the Chinese people are famous for their friendliness and will be only too willing to help. So, do not be put off by a recipe because of the alien nature of the ingredients; remember that these ingredients are common everyday ones to the Chinese, and that you will find the great majority of them in almost any Oriental market or grocery.

FISH AND SHELLFISH

Fish is eaten throughout China – along the coastline there is an abundance of sea fish and shellfish, while inland there is an equally plentiful supply of river fish.

China's native fish, such as yellow fish, garoupa and milkfish, are difficult to find in the West, but many Chinese dishes also feature the more familiar types of fish – haddock, mackerel, halibut and trout to mention a few. The recipes selected for this chapter concentrate on the more widely available species.

Where shellfish is concerned, many of the varieties that are plentiful in China are commonly seen in the West. Some of China's most famous and memorable dishes feature crab, lobster, scallops and jumbo shrimp and for a special meal or celebration party, Sautéed Shrimp (p. 13), Baked Creamy Clams (p. 15) or Shrimp Salad (p. 21) would all make stunning and delicious appetizers. Do note, however, that most Chinese shrimp recipes call for green shrimp. These uncooked shrimp, in the shell, are becoming increasingly available from markets and fish counters at large supermarkets and they can also be bought, frozen, from Oriental markets.

菜泥蝦片

Shrimp and Spinach Broth

(SERVES 4)
INGREDIENTS

1½ cups green jumbo shrimp
1 teaspoon grated fresh
   gingerroot
1 lb. spinach
⅓ cup vegetable oil
½ cup clear soup stock (see
   p. 261)
2 tablespoons all-purpose
   flour, mixed with a little
   cold water
½ cup milk
½ teaspoon white pepper

SEASONING
1 teaspoon salt
1 teaspoon sugar
1 tablespoon heavy cream

Shell and de-vein the shrimp (see Step 1, p. 55) and rinse in cold water. Pat dry on paper towels, then cut in half lengthwise with a sharp knife or cleaver (see small picture 1, right). Place the grated ginger in a bowl, stir in the shrimp and marinate for 10 minutes.

Wash the spinach thoroughly. Drain and mince.

Heat the oil in a wok, add the spinach and stir-fry for 3 minutes. Stir in the seasoning and then immediately add the soup stock and flour mixture.

Cook until boiling, then stir in the shrimp and milk. Lower the heat and simmer for a further minute.

Sprinkle with white pepper just before serving.

油爆蝦

Sautéed Shrimp

(SERVES 6)
INGREDIENTS

4 cups green jumbo shrimp
¼ cup corn oil

SEASONING
1 tablespoon light soy sauce
½ teaspoon white pepper
1 tablespoon minced scallion
1 tablespoon grated fresh
   gingerroot
2 teaspoons rice wine or dry
   sherry
1 teaspoon salt

Remove the feelers and intestinal cords or spine on the shrimp with a pair of scissors (see Step 1, p. 59). Dry thoroughly on paper towels.

Mix the seasoning ingredients, add the shrimp and marinate for 30 minutes.

Heat the oil in a wok and add the shrimp. Stir-fry over a high heat for 2 minutes.

Remove the shrimp with a slotted spoon and serve immediately.

NOTE
The shrimp can be served with or without their shells. If serving with their shells, provide napkins and finger bowls for your guests.

奶油焗蚌

Baked Creamy Clams

(SERVES 6-8)
INGREDIENTS

2 lb. chowder clams
½ cup all-purpose flour
¼ cup light cream
3 scallions, minced
1 small carrot, grated
1 celery stalk, minced
2 tablespoons clear soup
   stock (see p. 261)
2 tablespoons Parmesan
   cheese
baby corn cobs and red
   cherries, for garnish

SEASONING
2 garlic cloves, minced
½ teaspoon salt
1 teaspoon white pepper
1 teaspoon sugar

Clean and rinse the clams in cold water and then place in a large pan and cover with boiling water. Leave for 3-4 minutes, shaking the pan occasionally, until the clams have opened. Drain thoroughly, discarding any that have not opened.

Discard one half of the shell and gently loosen the flesh in the other half with a sharp knife. Remove any grit or loose seaweed and arrange the clams on their half shells in a roasting pan.

Mix the flour with the cream and place in a pan with the scallions, carrot, celery, and stock. Add the seasoning and slowly heat, stirring, until the mixture is thick and creamy.

Spoon the mixture into the shells and sprinkle the cheese over the top.

Bake in a preheated hot oven (450°F) for 10 minutes.

Arrange the clams on a large plate and garnish with baby corn cobs and cherries.

Deep-Fried Squid Balls

(SERVES 4)
INGREDIENTS

20 squid balls (see NOTES)
1 teaspoon black sesame
   seeds (see NOTES)
¾ cup all-purpose flour
2 cups soft bread crumbs
2 egg yolks, beaten
corn oil, for deep frying
2 tomatoes, sliced, for
   garnish

Wash the squid balls in cold water and pat dry on paper towels.

Dry-fry the sesame seeds in a hot pan for a few seconds and set aside.

Mix the flour with a little water to make a thick paste and spread the bread crumbs over a sheet of waxed paper.

Roll the squid balls, first in the egg yolks, then in the flour paste and finally in the bread crumbs.

Heat the oil and deep fry the fish balls for about a minute or until they are golden brown, turning them occasionally.

Remove the balls with a slotted spoon and drain on paper towels. Roll in the toasted sesame seeds and serve, garnished with slices of tomato.

NOTES

Black sesame seeds have a nutty flavor. They are available from Oriental markets, or alternatively use white sesame seeds, which can be bought from most supermarkets.

Squid balls are usually available in Oriental markets, sold in sealed plastic packages from the cool chests. Should they be unobtainable, use fish balls instead.

Squid and fish balls are delicious served with a dipping sauce: Make one by mixing 3 tablespoons Worcestershire, 1 tablespoon vinegar, 1 tablespoon sugar, 1 tablespoon corn oil and 1-2 teaspoons sesame oil. Heat until just boiling.

Seafood Kebab

(SERVES 4)
INGREDIENTS

½ lb. fresh squid
1 green pepper
2 carrots
10 green jumbo shrimp,
   shelled and de-veined (see
   page 55)
10 fish balls

SEASONING

2-3 sheets laver, sliced (see
   NOTE p. 85)
2 scallions, minced
3 slices of fresh gingerroot
1 tablespoon sugar

Place the seasoning ingredients in a saucepan, bring to a boil, lower the heat and simmer gently for 5 minutes.

Meanwhile, pull away the head and entrails from the squid. Feel inside the body and remove the transparent cartilage. Peel off and discard the mottled skin from the body and rinse the squid under running water. Cut in large pieces.

Cut the pepper in large chunks, discarding any seeds and core and cut the carrots in small rectangles.

Thread the squid, pepper, carrots, shrimp and fish balls onto 10-12 bamboo skewers. Arrange on a broiler pan.

Brush the kebabs with a little of the sauce and then set under a medium-hot broiler for 5-6 minutes, brushing and turning the kebabs every two minutes.

NOTE
Seafood kebabs can be served with a sweet chili sauce.

Steamed Crab

(SERVES 6)
INGREDIENTS

2 large cooked crabs
Maraschino cherries, for
  garnish

SEASONING A
4½ tablespoons ginger juice
  (see NOTE 3, p. 39)
2 scallions, cut in large
  sections
1 tablespoon dry sherry

SEASONING B
3 tablespoons vinegar
1 teaspoon rice wine or dry
  sherry
1 tablespoon finely grated
  fresh gingerroot

Clean the crabs (see NOTE). Cut the bodies in half, and crack the claws with a mallet.

Put the crab shells, body and claws in a heatproof dish. Mix seasoning **A** in a bowl and pour over.

Place the dish in a steamer. Pour 2 inches water into a large saucepan and bring to a boil. Set the steamer over the saucepan, cover with a tight-fitting lid and steam over a high heat for 5 minutes.

Remove any pieces of scallion, and put the crab bodies back in the shells. Garnish with Maraschino cherries.

Mix seasoning **B** in a bowl and serve with the crab as a dipping sauce, using skewers to pick out the crab meat at the table.

NOTE
To clean the crab, lay each one on its back with the tail flap toward you and remove the tail flap. Prise the body away from the shell, using a long sharp knife and set aside. Remove the gills (dead men's fingers) and the stomach and discard. The remaining contents of the crab, and the body itself are edible.

簡易海鮮鍋餅

Seafood Pancakes

(SERVES 2-4)
INGREDIENTS

3 small dried scallops (see
   NOTE)
½ cup dried baby shrimp
3 Chinese mushrooms
⅔ cup cooked shelled shrimp
1 cup all-purpose flour
½ teaspoon salt
½ teaspoon white pepper
2 eggs
2 tablespoons milk
3 tablespoons corn oil

SEASONING
¼ cup ketchup
½ teaspoon salt
1 teaspoon sugar
1 tablespoon water

Place the dried scallops and shrimp in two bowls, cover with warm water and soak for 1 hour and 30 minutes respectively. Soak the Chinese mushrooms in warm water for 30 minutes. Shred the scallops and mince the shrimp. Remove and discard the stems from the mushrooms and mince the caps. Roughly chop the shrimp.

Sift the flour, salt and pepper into a bowl, add the eggs and then gradually beat in the milk and enough water to make a loose batter. Add the scallops, baby shrimp, mushrooms and shelled shrimp and stir.

Heat a little of the oil in a small pancake pan, add 2-3 tablespoons of batter and cook for 30-60 seconds until golden. Flip over and cook the other side. Cook the remainder of the batter in the same way.

Place the seasoning in a small pan with the water, heat gently and serve with the pancakes.

NOTE
Dried scallops are a great delicacy in China. Round and golden, they add a delicious sweet flavor to a dish. They can be found in most Oriental markets.

沙拉蝦片

Shrimp Salad

(SERVES 6)

INGREDIENTS

4 cups green jumbo shrimp
4 celery stalks

DRESSING
⅔ cup mayonnaise
3 tablespoons plain yogurt
½ small onion, grated
1 teaspoon sugar
½ teaspoon salt

Scald the shrimp in boiling water for 5 minutes. Drain well and soak in ice water for 2 minutes. Drain again. Remove the shells and de-vein (see Step 1, p. 55) and place in the refrigerator for 1 hour.

Wash the celery and cut in pieces. Soak in cold water for 5 minutes.

Blend the mayonnaise with the yogurt. Add the remaining dressing ingredients and beat for 1 minute.

Stir the celery into the shrimp, spoon onto a serving platter and pipe the dressing over or pass separately.

NOTE
If liked, cooked jumbo shrimp could be used in this recipe. If so, it is not necessary to scald, or cook them, but do remove the shells and de-vein.

Soup of Egg

(SERVES 2)
INGREDIENTS

2 eggs
4 scallions, minced
2½ cups water

SEASONING
½ teaspoon salt
½ teaspoon white pepper
4-5 drops of sesame oil

Beat the eggs thoroughly. Add the seasoning. Bring the water to a boil and remove from heat. Pour in the eggs and stir with chopsticks or a fork. Add the scallions and serve at once.

NOTE
This simple soup makes a light, delicate accompaniment to a spicy fish dish. Double all ingredients to serve four.

Baby Squid with Ginger Sauce

(SERVES 4)
INGREDIENTS

¾ lb. small squid
3 tablespoons corn oil
1 tablespoon grated fresh
  gingerroot
shreds of fresh gingerroot, for
  garnish

SEASONING
1 tablespoon light soy sauce
1 tablespoon rice wine or dry
  sherry
½ tablespoon sugar
½ teaspoon white pepper

Cut open the squid with a cleaver or sharp knife and remove the entrails and cartilage. Rinse thoroughly in cold water.

Heat the oil in a skillet or wok, add the grated ginger and stir-fry for 1 minute. Add the squid and stir-fry for 3 minutes.

Stir in the seasoning and cook, stirring for 5 minutes until the pan is almost dry.

Garnish with the gingerroot shreds and serve.

宫保双鱿

Stir-Fried Spicy Squid

(SERVES 6)
INGREDIENTS

¼ lb. dried squid
¾ lb. fresh squid
3-4 tablespoons corn oil
10 dried chili peppers
½ tablespoon grated fresh
   gingerroot
green chili pepper, for garnish

SEASONING

1 teaspoon salt
1 tablespoon light soy sauce
2 teaspoons cornstarch
2 teaspoons sesame oil
1 tablespoon rice wine or dry
   sherry
½ teaspoon sugar

Soak the dried squid in cold water for 24 hours. Drain, remove spine and cut in 1 inch pieces.

Pull away the head and entrails from the fresh squid. Feel inside the body and remove the transparent cartilage. Peel off and discard the mottled skin from the body and rinse the squid under running water. Cut in large pieces, scoring criss-cross patterns on one side.

Heat the oil in the wok and when hot, add the chili peppers. Stir-fry for 5 seconds and then add the ginger and stir-fry for 2 seconds.

Stir in the dried squid, stir-fry for 5 seconds until they curl up and then add the fresh squid and the seasoning ingredients. Cook, stirring, for 1 minute and then spoon onto a serving platter

Garnish with chili curls and serve.

簡易盐焗蝦

Salted Shrimp

(SERVES 4)
INGREDIENTS

1 lb. green jumbo shrimp
3 teaspoons cornstarch
corn oil, for deep frying
lettuce leaves, for garnish

SEASONING
½ tablespoon minced garlic
1 teaspoon salt
1 teaspoon white pepper

Trim the shrimp feelers with a pair of scissors and remove intestinal vein (see Step 1, p. 59). Wash the shrimp in cold water, pat dry with paper towels and dust with cornstarch.

Heat the oil and when hot, deep-fry the shrimp for 1 minute. Remove with a slotted spoon.

Heat an extra 1 tablespoon of the oil in a wok or skillet, add the cooked shrimp and the seasoning ingredients and stir-fry for a further minute.

Drain on paper towels and serve on a bed of lettuce.

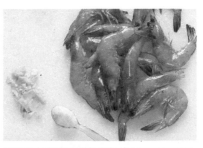

糖醋魚排
Sweet and Sour Fish

(SERVES 4)
INGREDIENTS

1½ lb. cod or halibut cutlets
3 tablespoons all-purpose
   flour
⅔ cup corn oil
2 tablespoons chopped onion
   or scallion
3 tablespoons white vinegar
2 teaspoons cornstarch
shredded Nappa cabbage,
   for garnish

SEASONING

3 tablespoons sugar
1 teaspoon salt
1 tablespoon ginger wine
   (see Glossary)
2 tablespoons water

Lightly coat the fish with the flour.

Heat ¼ cup of the oil in a wok or skillet. When the oil is very hot, add the fish and cook until both sides are browned. Remove.

Add the remaining oil to the pan and stir-fry the chopped onion over medium heat for 10 seconds.

Add the seasoning ingredients along with the water, and bring to a boil. Return the fish to the pan. Stir gently.

Mix the vinegar and cornstarch together and stir into the pan. Heat until just boiling, stirring all the time, then garnish with shredded Nappa cabbage leaves and serve.

Stewed Fish with Brown Sauce

(SERVES 4)
INGREDIENTS

1 large or 2 small red
  snappers or gray mullets,
  (total weight about 1½ lb.)
2 tablespoons all-purpose
  flour
4 scallions
2 red chili peppers
3 inch piece fresh gingerroot
9 tablespoons corn oil

SEASONING A
4 tablespoons ginger wine
  (see Glossary)
4 teaspoons salt

SEASONING B
3 tablespoons light soy sauce
1 tablespoon rice wine or dry
  sherry
1 tablespoon sugar
1 teaspoon salt
½ teaspoon white pepper

Clean and scale the fish. Wash in cold water and pat dry with paper towels. Score the fish deeply on both sides.

Mix seasoning **A** and spread over the fish. Leave to marinate for 10 minutes, then dust evenly with the flour.

Cut the scallions and chili peppers in lengthwise strips and shred the ginger.

Heat 4 tablespoons of the oil in a wok, add the fish and cook for 4 minutes, turning once.

In a separate pan, heat the remaining oil and sauté the chili peppers and ginger for 5 seconds. Add the scallions and seasoning **B**. Stir thoroughly.

Add the fish, cover and cook for 5 minutes. Drain and serve.

Sautéed Fish Slices

(SERVES 4)
INGREDIENTS

2 cups wood ear mushrooms
  (see NOTES)
1½ lb. cod or haddock steaks
3 scallions
⅓ cup corn oil
1 inch piece fresh gingerroot,
  thinly sliced
1 tablespoon light soy sauce
fresh parsley sprig, for
  garnish

SEASONING A
1 tablespoon ginger wine
  (see Glossary)
½ teaspoon white pepper
1 teaspoon sugar
2 teaspoons sesame oil
1½ tablespoons cornstarch

SEASONING B
2 teaspoons rice wine or dry
  sherry
1 teaspoon salt

Soak the mushrooms for 30 minutes in warm water. Drain, remove the stems and cut the caps in 1 inch pieces.

Cut the fish steaks in half, skin and then cut in 2 × 1 inch slices.

Mix seasoning **A** to a smooth paste and marinate the fish slices for 20 minutes.

Cut the scallions in large pieces.

Heat the oil in the wok, add the scallions and stir-fry for 30 seconds. Remove with a slotted spoon and discard the scallions. Add the ginger, stir-fry for 30 seconds and then remove and discard as well (see NOTES).

Add the mushrooms, stir-fry for 20 seconds and stir in the fish slices. Add seasoning **B** and stir well. Cook for 1-2 minutes, turning the fish once. Sprinkle with the soy sauce.

Spoon onto a serving platter and garnish with parsley.

NOTES
Wood ear mushrooms are commonly used in Chinese cooking. They are available from any Oriental market but must be soaked before using.

The scallions and ginger are there to give flavor to the oil and thus the fish. Discard them after cooking.

Stir-Fried Clams with Black Beans

(SERVES 4)
INGREDIENTS

1½ pints shucked clams
1 tablespoon salt
⅓ cup corn oil
2 scallions

SEASONING A
4 tablespoons dried black
    beans (scc NOTE)
3 garlic cloves, crushed
1 tablespoon finely grated
    fresh gingerroot
1 red chili, thinly sliced
1 tablespoon light soy sauce
½ tablespoon sugar
1 teaspoon salt

SEASONING B
1 tablespoon rice wine or dry
    sherry
½ teaspoon white pepper
2 teaspoons sesame oil

Place the clams in cold water with the salt and soak for 10 minutes. Drain.

Rinse the clams in boiling water and then soak again for 3 minutes. Drain thoroughly and pat dry with paper towels.

Heat the oil in the wok, add seasoning **A** and stir-fry for 30 seconds.

Stir in the clams and continue to cook for 3 minutes.

Slice the scallions diagonally and add to wok with seasoning **B**. Cook, stirring for 30 seconds and then serve.

NOTE
There are two kinds of black beans available, the canned fermented black beans which come in a sauce, and the dried beans. Dried black beans can be kept for 6 months if kept in a dry place. They should be soaked for 2-3 hours before using. If dried beans are unavailable, use canned ones, but rinse thoroughly before use.

Golden Fried Clams

(SERVES 4)
INGREDIENTS

1½ pints shucked clams
1 tablespoon salt
1 cup plus 3 tablespoons
    sweet potato flour (see
    NOTE)
corn oil, for deep frying
fresh parsley or fennel sprigs,
    for garnish

SEASONING
1 teaspoon salt
1 small egg white
½ teaspoon sugar
1 teaspoon light soy sauce

Place the clams in cold water with the salt and soak for 10 minutes. Drain.

Rinse the clams in boiling water and then soak again for 3 minutes. Drain thoroughly and pat dry on paper towels. Place in a bowl and add the seasoning ingredients, the potato flour and a little extra salt, making sure to coat each clam thoroughly.

Heat the oil in a deep-fat fryer and cook the clams until golden.

Remove with slotted spoon and serve garnished with fennel sprigs or parsley.

NOTE
Sweet potato flour is available in some Oriental markets, however, regular potato flour can be used instead.

Celery with Mustard Paste

(SERVES 4)
INGREDIENTS

1 large head of celery
5 cups of water

SEASONING
1 tablespoon prepared
   English mustard
½ teaspoon salt
1 tablespoon soy sauce

Separate the celery in individual stalks, and wash thoroughly. Cut the stalks in sticks about 4 inches long.

Blanch the celery sticks in the boiling water for 30 seconds. Remove with a slotted spoon. Soak the celery in a bowl of ice water until cool, then remove with a slotted spoon. Wrap in a clean dish towel or double thickness of unbleached muslin and place in the refrigerator for 1 hour.

Mix the seasoning ingredients together, and serve as a dipping sauce with the celery sticks.

NOTE
This is a very light, pleasant salad which goes well with "Steamed Cod" or any delicately-flavored fish dish.

Steamed Cod

(SERVES 4)
INGREDIENTS

1½ lb. cod cutlets
3 tablespoons corn oil
2 tablespoons finely grated
   fresh gingerroot
2 scallions, finely sliced

SEASONING
3 tablespoons soy sauce
2 tablespoons rice wine or
   dry sherry
2 tablespoons water

Place the cod cutlets on a plate and set in a steamer. Pour 2 inches water into a large pan and bring to a boil. Set the steamer over the pan, cover with a tight-fitting lid and steam for 4 minutes. Remove from the heat and set aside for a further 5 minutes before removing the lid. Pour off the liquid.

Heat the oil in a wok or skillet and add the ginger, scallions, and seasoning ingredients with the water. Bring to a boil and cook for 5 minutes.

Arrange the cod on a serving dish, top with the sauce and serve.

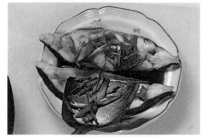

開洋蒸白菜

Steamed Cabbage with Dried Shrimp

(SERVES 4)
INGREDIENTS

3 tablespoons dried shelled
   shrimp
1 white cabbage
2½ cups clear soup stock
   (see p. 261)

SEASONING
1 teaspoon salt
1 teaspoon sugar
1 teaspoon white pepper
1 tablespoon sesame oil

Soak the dried shrimp in warm water for 30 minutes. Drain. Cut the cabbage in even-size wedges and arrange in a large deep bowl.

Mix the shrimp with the seasoning ingredients and place in the dish with the cabbage. Add the soup stock.

Place the bowl in a steamer and steam, covered, over a high heat for 30 minutes or until the soup is very hot. Check occasionally to make sure the saucepan does not boil dry.

Serve immediately.

玉蓮素捲

Stuffed Cabbage Rolls

(SERVES 4)
INGREDIENTS

8 Chinese black mushrooms
1 large carrot
4 inch piece bamboo shoot
1 white cabbage
3 inch square piece spiced
   bean curd
1 tablespoon malt vinegar
1 tablespoon light soy sauce

SEASONING
1 tablespoon sesame oil
2 tablespoons light soy sauce
1 teaspoon salt
½ teaspoon white pepper

Remove the stems from the Chinese mushrooms, place in a bowl and cover with warm water. Soak for 20 minutes, drain and roughly chop. Place in a steamer, cover and steam for 10 minutes.

Blanch the carrot and bamboo shoot in boiling water for 2 minutes and then cut in small cubes.

Make 4 deep cuts around the cabbage root with a cleaver or sharp knife, then boil the cabbage for 5 minutes.

Gently separate 12 outer leaves. (You may have to return the cabbage to the boiling water to loosen the inner leaves.)

Cube the bean curd and mix with the mushrooms, carrot and bamboo shoot. Stir in the vinegar and soy sauce.

Place a spoonful of mixture at the bottom of each cabbage leaf. Fold in the sides and roll up. Arrange in one or two layers of a steamer. Steam for 10 minutes.

Mix together all the seasoning ingredients and serve with the cabbage rolls.

NOTE
This makes a delicious vegetable accompaniment to a fish course. Shelled shrimp could also be added to the mushroom mixture if liked.

Deep-Fried Shrimp Rolls

(SERVES 4)
INGREDIENTS

20 green jumbo shrimp
1 cup cornstarch
10 salted duck egg yolks,
  optional (see NOTE)
5 tablespoons ground pork
  fat
1 egg, beaten
1½ cups dry golden bread
  crumbs
corn oil, for deep frying
fresh parsley sprigs, for
  garnish

SEASONING
1 tablespoon sesame oil
1 teaspoon salt
½ teaspoon white pepper

Shell and de-vein the shrimp (see Step 1, p. 55). Split each one open, but do not separate. Dust in the cornstarch and then flatten them slightly by patting with a rolling pin.

Divide each of the duck egg yolks, if using, in half and flatten slightly with the back of a knife.

Mix the pork fat with the seasoning ingredients and spread a little of the mixture over the inside of the shrimp. Place a portion of yolk on top and roll up.

Dip the shrimp in the beaten egg and then roll in the bread crumbs.

Heat the oil in a deep-fat fryer and cook the shrimp for about 4 minutes or until golden. Remove with a slotted spoon, drain on paper towels and serve, garnished with a little parsley.

NOTE
Salted duck eggs can be bought from Oriental markets.

Quick Fried Shrimp with Asparagus

(SERVES 4)
INGREDIENTS

20 green jumbo shrimp
¼ cup corn oil
1 can (12 oz) asparagus,
  drained

SEASONING A
2 teaspoons cornstarch
½ egg white, lightly beaten
1 tablespoon rice wine or dry
  sherry
1 teaspoon salt

SEASONING B
2 tablespoons finely grated
  fresh gingerroot
1 tablespoon light soy sauce
2 teaspoons rice wine or dry
  sherry
1 tablespoon white vinegar

Shell the shrimp and remove the thin "vein" or intestinal cord that runs down the spine (see Step 1, p. 55).

Butterfly the shrimp by cutting each one down the center, but do not separate them. Flatten slightly with the back of a knife.

Blend seasoning **A** in a bowl and add the shrimp. Stir gently and leave to marinate for 20 minutes.

Heat 3 tablespoons of the oil in a wok, add the shrimp and stir-fry for 2 minutes. Remove with a slotted spoon.

Heat the remaining oil. Add the asparagus and stir-fry for 30 seconds. Push the asparagus to one side of the wok and place the shrimp in the center. Stir-fry for 5 seconds and then add seasoning **B**. Stir to mix and serve.

蠔油吊片

Squid in Oyster Sauce

(SERVES 4)
INGREDIENTS

3 large dried squid (see
  NOTES)
2 tablespoons corn oil
2 inch piece fresh gingerroot,
  grated
1 teaspoon rice wine or dry
  sherry
½ cucumber, shredded
6 slices abalone, optional
  (see NOTES)

SEASONING

3 tablespoons oyster sauce
½ teaspoon salt
½ teaspoon sugar
1 teaspoon ginger juice (see
  NOTES)
3 tablespoons clear soup
  stock (see p. 261)
½ teaspoon white pepper

Rinse the squid thoroughly. Cut in half lengthwise and then, using a sharp knife, slice in thin strips.

Place squid strips in a bowl, cover with boiling water and scald for 1 minute. Drain and plunge in ice water for a few seconds. Drain and dry on paper towels.

Heat the oil in a wok and add the ginger and rice wine. Stir-fry for a few seconds and then add the squid. Stir-fry for 1 minute.

Mix all seasoning ingredients and stir into squid mixture. Stir well.

Spoon onto a serving platter and garnish with the shredded cucumber and abalone.

NOTES

Dried squid needs to be soaked for 24 hours before use. Place in a bowl of cold water, add 1 tablespoon salt and leave in a cool place.

Abalone should be scalded in boiling water for 5 minutes before use.

Ginger juice is simply the juice from fresh gingerroot ginger. Either press a little sliced fresh ginger through a garlic press, or use finely grated ginger instead.

纸包鱼

Paper-Wrapped Fish

(SERVES 4)
INGREDIENTS

1½ lb. flounder or silver hake
    fillets
¼ cup butter
1 tablespoon cornstarch
corn oil, for deep frying

SEASONING
1 teaspoon salt
½ teaspoon minced fresh
    gingerroot
3 teaspoons cornstarch

Rinse the fish in cold water. Remove the skin.
    Cut each of the fillets in 1 inch diagonal slices.
Place in a bowl and toss with the seasoning
ingredients. Let stand for 20 minutes.
    Cut out some 3½ inch square cellophane pieces,
sufficient to wrap each of the fish slices.
    Place a fish slice at the corner of each square, dot
the fish with the butter and roll up, tucking the sides
in as you go. Mix the cornstarch with a little water,
and use to seal the final edges.
    Heat the oil and deep-fry the fish packages for 6-8
minutes. Remove and serve in their paper wrappers.

煎味噌鱼

Pan-Fried Tuna

(SERVES 2)
INGREDIENTS

2 tuna steaks
¼ cup corn oil
lemon juice, to serve

SEASONING
4 tablespoons yellow bean
    sauce (see NOTE)
3 tablespoons sugar
½ teaspoon white pepper
1 tablespoon finely grated
    fresh gingerroot

Rinse the fish and pat dry on paper towels.
    Mix all the seasoning ingredients and spread
evenly over both sides of the fish. Place in the
refrigerator and marinate for 24 hours.
    The next day, rinse off the marinade and pat dry.
Heat the oil in a large pan and cook the fish until
golden brown.
    Serve at once with a little lemon juice.

NOTE
Yellow bean sauce is a slightly sweet paste made from
fermented soy beans. It is available in cans or jars from
any Chinese market.

炸鮑魚排

Deep-Fried Fish Steaks

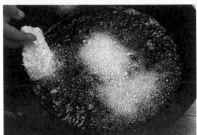

(SERVES 4)
INGREDIENTS

1½ lb. flounder or silver hake
   fillets
2 cups soft white bread
   crumbs
1 egg, beaten
corn oil, for deep frying
sweet chili sauce, to serve

SEASONING
1 teaspoon salt
1 tablespoon ginger wine
   (see Glossary)
½ teaspoon white pepper

Rinse the fish in cold water and pat dry with paper towels. Cut the fillets in four pieces.

Mix the seasoning ingredients in a bowl, stir in the fish and set aside for 30 minutes.

Place the bread crumbs on a piece of waxed paper and then dip the fish slices in the beaten egg and coat evenly with the bread crumbs.

Heat the oil in a deep-fat fryer and carefully add the fish slices. Deep fry the fish for 2-3 minutes until golden brown.

Remove with a slotted spoon and drain on paper towels. Serve with sweet chili sauce.

清炒金瓜

Stir-Fried Pumpkin

(SERVES 4)
INGREDIENTS

½ small pumpkin
¼ cup corn oil

SEASONING
1 teaspoon salt
½ teaspoon white pepper
2 tablespoons water

Remove the pumpkin seeds, but do not peel. Cut in ½ × 1 inch pieces.

Heat the oil in a wok. Add the pumpkin and the seasoning and stir-fry over a medium heat for 3 minutes. Reduce the heat slightly and cover. Simmer for a further 4-5 minutes until the pumpkin is tender, stirring occasionally.

NOTE
This is a tasty dish and goes well with the Deep-Fried Fish Steaks. It's a good choice in late fall, when pumpkins are abundant.

海鮮焗飯

Steamed Rice with Seafood

(SERVES 6)
INGREDIENTS

10 oz. collard greens
10 sea scallops
6 crab claws
3 tablespoons Chinese
  mushrooms, soaked (see
  NOTES)
2 tablespoons dried baby
  shrimp, soaked (see
  NOTES)
1½ cups long-grain rice
5 cups clear soup stock (see
  p. 261)

SEASONING
1 teaspoon salt
½ teaspoon white pepper
2 tablespoons corn oil
½ tablespoon rice wine or
  dry sherry
2 teaspoons sugar

Wash and trim the collard greens and cut in small pieces.

Slice 5 of the sea scallops thinly, leaving the others whole. Chop the crab claws in pieces.

Mix all the ingredients and seasoning ingredients in a large heatproof bowl. Place the bowl in a steamer, cover and steam over boiling water for about 30 minutes, or until the rice is tender. Serve.

NOTES
Soak the Chinese black mushrooms in warm water for 30 minutes before use, then remove and discard the stems and slice finely.

Soak the dried shrimp in warm water for 30 minutes before use.

海鮮粥

Seafood Congee

(SERVES 4-6)
INGREDIENTS

¼ lb. cod fillet
3 dried scallops, soaked (see
  NOTES)
1 piece of bean curd sheet,
  soaked (see NOTES)
½ cup short-grain rice
6¼ cups water
2 hard-cooked eggs,
  chopped
1 teaspoon salt
⅓ cup cooked shelled shrimp
⅓ cup crab meat
2 clams, shucked and diced
1 egg
2 sticks of twisted doughnuts
  or Yiu-tiao, thinly sliced
  (see NOTE on p. 301)
1 tablespoon chopped fresh
  parsley
parsley sprigs, for garnish

SEASONING
½ teaspoon white pepper
1 tablespoon sesame oil
1 tablespoon rice wine or dry
  sherry

Cut the fish in bite-size pieces, finely slice the soaked scallops and dice the soaked bean curd.

Place the rice, cod, scallops and bean curd in a large pan. Add the water and bring to a boil. Lower the heat, cover and simmer gently for 30 minutes.

Add the hard-cooked eggs and salt, and simmer for a further 5 minutes.

Mix the shrimp, crab meat and clams with the seasoning ingredients and stir into the soup. Cook for a further 10 minutes.

Place the egg, doughnuts and parsley in a bowl. Pour the cooked broth over the top, beat lightly and serve, garnished with parsley sprigs.

NOTES
Congee is a porridge made principally from boiled rice, which is often eaten for breakfast in China.

To soak the dried scallops, cover with boiling water and soak for 1 hour, then drain.

To soak the dried bean curd sheet, place it in cold water for about 10 minutes, till soft. Drain, and wrap in a dish towel.

Sweet and Sour Squid

(SERVES 4)
INGREDIENTS

1 lb. squid
2 red chili peppers
1 green pepper
⅓ cup corn oil
1 tablespoon grated fresh
   gingerroot
2 tablespoons cornstarch
2 teaspoons sesame oil

SEASONING

1 tablespoon ginger wine
   (see Glossary)
1 teaspoon salt
3 tablespoons sugar
¼ cup white vinegar
¼ cup clear soup stock (see
   p. 261)

Pull away the head and entrails from the squid. Feel inside the body and remove the transparent cartilage. Peel off and discard the mottled skin from the body and rinse the squid under running water.

Cut the squid in thin 2 inch square pieces. Make tiny slits along each edge, approximately ¼ inch long. Place in a bowl, cover with boiling water and set aside for 2 minutes. Drain.

Cut the chili peppers diagonally and remove the seeds (see NOTE). Cut the pepper in cubes, discarding the seeds and core.

Heat the oil in the wok, add the ginger and chili peppers and stir-fry for 10 seconds. Add the green pepper, squid and seasoning ingredients. Cook, stirring for 5 minutes.

Mix the cornstarch with a little water and stir into the squid with the sesame oil. Bring back to a boil, cook for 30 seconds and serve.

NOTE
Chili peppers can be very hot. Take care preparing them; wear rubber gloves if liked and take care not to rub your eyes. The chilis' seeds are especially hot. Unless you enjoy very hot food, it's probably advisable to remove them.

Five-Willow Fish

(SERVES 2)
INGREDIENTS

1 whole flounder or fluke
3 red chili peppers
3 tablespoons corn oil
2 tablespoons grated fresh
  gingerroot
¾ cup clear soup stock (see
  p. 261)
2 tablespoons cornstarch
1 tablespoon malt vinegar

SEASONING A
1 tablespoon ginger wine
  (see Glossary)
½ teaspoon white pepper

SEASONING B
½ tablespoon pork fat
1 tablespoon sliced Chinese
  mushrooms (see NOTE)
3 tablespoons white vinegar
1 garlic clove, crushed
1 teaspoon salt
2 teaspoons sugar

Clean the fish if not already gutted. Trim the tail
and cut away the fins. Rinse under cold water and pat
dry with paper towels.
Mix together seasoning **A** and spread evenly over
the fish. Set aside for 20 minutes.
Thinly slice the chili peppers, removing the seeds.
Heat the oil in the wok and stir-fry the chilis and
grated ginger for 5 seconds. Add the soup stock and
seasoning **B** and bring to a boil.
Gently lower the fish into the wok, cover and
simmer for 5 minutes, turning over midway through
cooking.
Mix the cornstarch with the malt vinegar and add
to the wok. Stir gently, taking care not to disturb the
fish and cook for 2-3 minutes.
Remove the fish and place on a serving platter.
Pour the sauce over and serve at once.

NOTE
Chinese mushrooms are only available dried and
should be soaked for 30 minutes before use. Remove
stems and slice caps after soaking.

Fish Mold

(SERVES 4-6)
INGREDIENTS

1 Chinese mushroom
  (see NOTE above)
1¼ lb. cod cutlets
1 carrot
1 cup clear soup stock (see
  p. 261)
1 tablespoon dried agar-agar
2 tablespoons canned whole
  kernel corn
fresh parsley sprigs, for
  garnish

SEASONING
1 teaspoon salt
1 teaspoon rice wine or dry
  sherry
1 teaspoon ginger wine (see
  Glossary)
½ teaspoon white pepper

Soak the Chinese mushroom in warm water for 30
minutes. Remove and discard the stem.
Bone and skin the fish cutlets and cut in thin
pieces, about 1 × 2 inches. Place in a steamer and
steam over a high heat for 8-10 minutes until cooked.
Peel the carrot. Use aspic cutters to cut in pretty
shapes.
Place the soup stock in a saucepan and bring to a
boil. Add the carrot, lower the heat and simmer for 10
minutes.
Remove the carrot with a slotted spoon and set
aside. Add the agar-agar, bring to a boil, lower the
heat and simmer for 10 minutes. Strain the soup
through fine unbleached muslin and mix with the
seasoning ingredients.
Place the mushroom in the center of a rectangular
mold. Arrange the carrot pieces around the outside
and scatter the corn on top. Arrange the fish over the
corn and then carefully pour on the soup stock.
Cool, and then refrigerate for 24 hours. To unmold,
place the mold up to the rim in a bowl of boiling water.
Leave for 5-10 seconds, then invert onto a serving
platter and the molded fish should come away. If not,
repeat this process. Serve, garnished with parsley.

49

作 脆 皮 蝦 球

Crispy Fried Shrimp Balls

(SERVES 6)

INGREDIENTS

2 lb. cooked shrimp
2 cups soft white bread
   crumbs
1 tablespoon cornstarch
1 egg yolk, beaten
corn oil, for deep frying
scallions and tomatoes, for
   garnish

SEASONING

1 tablespoon ginger wine
   (see Glossary)
3 tablespoons cornstarch
½ teaspoon white pepper
1 teaspoon sugar
2 teaspoons sesame oil
1 egg white
1 teaspoon salt

Mince the shrimp and then crush with a cleaver or heavy knife until they resemble a paste. Mix thoroughly with all the seasoning ingredients.

Place the bread crumbs and cornstarch on separate sheets of waxed paper.

Take a small handful (about 1 rounded tablespoon) of the shrimp mixture and roll into a ball between your hands. Dip the ball into the beaten egg and then roll first in the cornstarch and then in the bread crumbs, coating firmly and evenly. Continue until all the mixture has been used up.

Heat the oil in a deep-fat fryer and cook the shrimp balls, a few at a time, until golden brown. Remove with a slotted spoon and drain on paper towels. Serve, garnished with scallions and tomatoes.

海鲜末粉

Shrimp and Clam Rice Noodles

(SERVES 4-6)
INGREDIENTS

2 tablespoons dried baby
   shrimp, optional
1 cup thinly sliced cooked
   chicken
½ lb. thin dried rice noodles
2 cups green jumbo shrimp
1 cup littleneck clams
¼ cup corn oil
1 scallion, minced
5 pints clear soup stock (see
   p. 261)
2½ cups bean sprouts
2 shredded mushrooms (see
   NOTE p. 45)
1 teaspoon salt
2 or 3 lettuce leaves
1 teaspoon white pepper

SEASONING
1 teaspoon cornstarch
2 teaspoons ginger wine (see
   Glossary)

Place the dried baby shrimp in a bowl, cover with warm water and soak for 30 minutes, if using. Drain.

Mix the seasoning ingredients in a bowl, add the chicken and marinate for 10 minutes. Drain.

Place the noodles in a bowl, cover with boiling water and soak for 10 minutes until soft. Drain.

Shell the shrimp and remove the thin "vein" or intestinal cord that runs down the spine (see Step 1, p. 55).

Rinse the clams in cold water and then place in a large pan and cover with boiling water. Cook rapidly for 2-3 minutes, shaking the pan occasionally, until the clams have opened. Drain thoroughly, discarding any that have not opened. Gently loosen the flesh from each shell with a sharp knife. Remove any grit or loose seaweed.

Heat the oil in a wok or skillet. When hot, add the minced scallion and dried baby shrimp if using. Stir-fry for 2 minutes.

Add the soup stock, shrimp, clams, marinated chicken, bean sprouts, shredded black mushrooms and salt. Bring to a boil, lower the heat and simmer for 5 minutes. Add the noodles and boil for a further 1 minute.

Mix together the lettuce and pepper, and serve over the noodle mixture.

鱼皮大滷麵

Noodles with Fish and Pork

(SERVES 6)
INGREDIENTS

¼ lb. pork tenderloin, sliced
3 Chinese mushrooms
½ lb. cod steak
6-8 tablespoons cornstarch
1½ lb. rice noodles
⅓ cup oil
2 scallions, chopped
5 cups clear soup stock (see
   p. 261)
2 teaspoons salt
1 teaspoon rice wine
½ cup water
⅔ cup cooked shelled shrimp
2 eggs, beaten

SEASONING A
½ tablespoon soy sauce
1 teaspoon ginger juice

SEASONING B
3 tablespoons cornstarch
1 teaspoon white pepper
1 tablespoon sesame oil

Combine seasoning **A** ingredients in a bowl and add the pork tenderloin. Marinate for 1 hour.

Rinse the mushrooms and soak in warm water for 30 minutes until softened. Remove the stalks and cut into shreds.

Cut the fish in large pieces, and coat each piece generously with the cornstarch. Pat the pieces flat with a rolling pin.

Place the noodles in a bowl and cover with boiling water. Soak for 3-5 minutes, then drain. Plunge in a bowl of cold water, and stir to separate the strands.

Heat the oil in a large wok or skillet. Add the scallions and stir-fry for a few seconds. Add the stock, salt, wine, mushrooms, and pork tenderloin. Bring to a boil.

Mix seasoning **B** in a bowl with the water. Add the pieces of fish to the wok, then stir in the seasoning.

Drain the noodles and add to the wok along with the shrimp. Bring back to a boil, stirring all the time, then remove from the heat. Leave for 5 minutes to cool slightly before adding the beaten eggs. Serve immediately. Garnish with cucumber slices.

Red Snapper with Black Bean Sauce

(SERVES 4)
INGREDIENTS

4 small red snappers
⅓ cup corn oil
2 red chili peppers, seeded and finely sliced
2 tablespoons fermented black beans, mashed (see NOTES)
6 garlic cloves, crushed
3 tablespoons water
parsley sprigs, for garnish

SEASONING
2 tablespoons light soy sauce
½ tablespoon rice wine or dry sherry
1 teaspoon salt
2 teaspoons sugar

Clean and draw the fish and trim the tail and gills. Pat dry with paper towels.

Heat the oil in a large skillet or wok and carefully add the fish. Cook for 2 minutes, turn the fish over and cook the other side for 1 minute. Remove.

Add the chili peppers, black beans, garlic and seasoning ingredients and bring to a boil, stirring. Return the fish to the pan, add the water and cover. Simmer for 3 minutes and spoon onto a serving platter. Garnish with a little parsley and serve at once.

NOTES
The silver-gray fish pictured are commonly available in China, but are not obtainable fresh in this country. Small red snappers, however, are of a similar size and work very well in this recipe.

Fermented black beans are commonly used in fish recipes. Since they are very salty, they should be thoroughly rinsed before use.

蝦 仁 炒 蛋

Shrimp Omelet

(SERVES 4)
INGREDIENTS

1 lb. green jumbo shrimp (see
   NOTE)
2 teaspoons all-purpose flour
6 eggs
⅓ cup corn oil
scissored chives and
   shredded carrots, for
   garnish

SEASONING A
½ tablespoon ginger wine
   (see Glossary)
1 tablespoon cornstarch
large pinch of white pepper

SEASONING B
1 teaspoon rice wine or dry
   sherry
2 teaspoons salt

Shell the shrimp and remove the thin "vein" or
intestinal cord that runs down the spine (see small
picture 1, right).

Mix seasoning **A** in a bowl, add the shrimp and
marinate for 15 minutes.

Scald the shrimp with boiling water and let stand
for 5 minutes. Drain and dust with the all-purpose
flour.

Beat the eggs, add seasoning **B** and stir in the
shrimp.

Heat the oil in a large wok or skillet or pancake
pan, pour in the egg mixture and cook over a medium
heat until the egg sets.

Slide onto a serving platter and garnish with
chives and carrot shreds.

NOTE
Cooked shrimp could also be used for this recipe,
either shelled or unshelled. Follow method, but do not
scald with boiling water, simply dust with all-purpose
flour after marinating.

坮菊花大蝦

Deep-Fried Shrimp with Black Sesame Seeds

(SERVES 4)
INGREDIENTS

12 green jumbo shrimp
1 teaspoon cornstarch
4 eggs
2-3 tablespoons rice flour
½ cup corn oil plus 1
    tablespoon
1 tablespoon black sesame
    seeds

SEASONING A

½ teaspoon salt
1 tablespoon ginger wine
    (see Glossary)

SEASONING B

1 teaspoon ground cinnamon
½ teaspoon salt
1 teaspoon white pepper

Remove the heads and shells of the shrimp but leave their tails intact. Remove the intestinal cord (see Step 1, p. 55). Cut each one in half.

Mix seasoning **A** with the cornstarch in a bowl and add the shrimp. Stir well to mix.

Beat the eggs and add enough rice flour to make a smooth batter.

Heat the ½ cup oil in a saucepan. Dip the shrimp in the batter and then carefully drop into the hot oil. Deep-fry for 2 minutes. Remove with a slotted spoon.

Heat the remaining 1 tablespoon of the oil in a separate pan. When hot, re-fry the shrimp with the black sesame seeds for 1 minute. Add seasoning **B**. Mix well and serve.

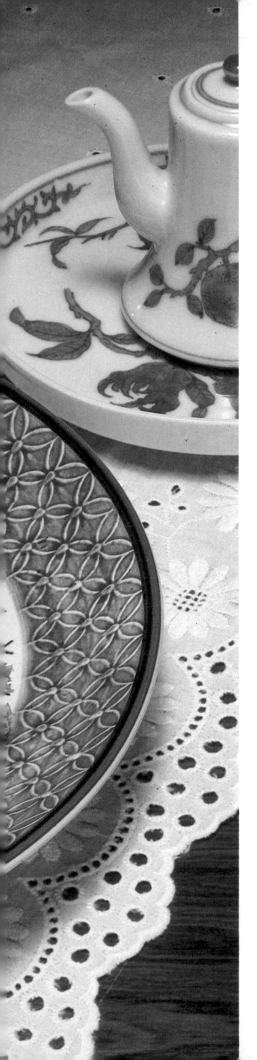

Drunken Shrimp

(SERVES 4)
INGREDIENTS

12 green jumbo shrimp
2 thin slices fresh gingerroot
1¼ cups rice wine or dry
　sherry

SEASONING
1 teaspoon salt
1 teaspoon white pepper

Trim the feelers and legs of the shrimp and remove the thin "vein" or intestinal cord that runs down the spine with a pair of scissors (see small picture, above).

Bruise the ginger slices with a cleaver or heavy rolling pin (see NOTE) and place in a large pan with the shrimp.

Add the rice wine and slowly bring to a boil.

Lower the heat and simmer the shrimp for 1 minute or until they turn pink.

Remove the shrimp with a slotted spoon and arrange on a platter. Sprinkle with the seasoning and serve.

NOTE
Bruising the ginger (crushing it slightly with a heavy object) helps to release its juices and flavor.

串烤鮮魷

Roast Squid

(SERVES 4)
INGREDIENTS

3 squid, (total weight about
   1½ lb.)
2 garlic cloves, crushed
1 large carrot
3 scallions
1 tablespoon corn oil

SEASONING
½ teaspoon salt
½ teaspoon white pepper
2 teaspoons rice wine or dry
   sherry

Pull away the head and entrails from the squid. Feel inside the body and remove the transparent cartilage. Peel off and discard the mottled skin from the body and rinse the squid under running water. Pat dry with paper towels.

Mix the seasoning ingredients in a bowl and add the squid. Marinate for 20 minutes.

Remove the squid from the marinade and rub the inside of the bodies with the crushed garlic.

Cut the carrot lengthwise in 6 long thin strips. Cut off the roots and tops of the scallions, peel away any discolored leaves.

Insert two carrot strips and a scallion into the body cavity of the squid. Arrange on a roasting pan and brush with the oil. Bake in a preheated moderately hot oven (375°F) for 20 minutes.

Cut in sections, arrange on a serving platter and serve.

糟香炸鰻

Eel with Red Bean Sauce

(SERVES 4)
INGREDIENTS

14 oz. eel
3 tablespoons red bean sauce
   (see NOTE)
2 tablespoons water
⅔ cup potato flour
½ cup corn oil
salt and pepper to serve

SEASONING
1½ tablespoons sugar
½ tablespoon grated fresh
   gingerroot
½ teaspoon white pepper

Rinse the eel in cold water and pat dry with paper towels. Cut in half, remove the central bone and cut in lengthwise pieces.

Mix the red bean sauce, the seasoning ingredients and the water in a large bowl. Add the eel pieces and marinate for 2 hours.

Remove the eel, scrape off any excess marinade and coat each piece evenly with the potato flour.

Heat the oil in a wok, add the eel and stir-fry for 6-8 minutes, turning the pieces over occasionally.

Remove with a slotted spoon and drain on paper towels. Serve hot with plenty of salt and pepper.

NOTE
Red bean sauce or sweet bean sauce can be bought from most Oriental markets. When not available, use Hoisin sauce.

Fish Fluff with Lettuce

(SERVES 4)
INGREDIENTS

1 wood ear mushroom
½ head iceberg lettuce
1 lb. white fish steak e.g.
  lingcod, white sea bass
1 tablespoon rice flour
1 egg
corn oil, for deep frying
1 piece (about 2 oz.) bamboo
  shoot
½ cup ground pork
1 cooked potato, diced
½ cup salted peanuts,
  chopped

SEASONING A
½ teaspoon salt
1 tablespoon finely grated
  fresh gingerroot
½ teaspoon ground
  cinnamon

SEASONING B
1 tablespoon light soy sauce
½ teaspoon salt
½ teaspoon white pepper
1 teaspoon sesame oil

Soak the mushroom in warm water for 30 minutes. Drain, remove the stem and roughly chop the cap.

Separate the lettuce leaves, rinse them in cold water and shake dry. Arrange in a salad bowl.

Skin and bone the fish and cut in small cubes. Mix seasoning **A** in a bowl, add the fish and stir to blend thoroughly. Set aside for 30 minutes.

Beat together the rice flour and egg and stir into the marinated fish.

Heat the oil in deep-fat fryer, add spoonfuls of the fish mixture and deep-fry for 4-5 minutes until well browned. Remove with a slotted spoon and drain on paper towels.

Chop the bamboo shoots and add to the chopped mushroom and pork. Heat 3 tablespoons of oil in a wok and stir-fry the mixture for 1 minute. Add the potato and seasoning **B** and stir to mix.

Stir in the fish mixture and cook until heated through.

Spoon onto one half of a large serving platter, with the chopped peanuts on the other side. Serve immediately.

NOTE
The way to eat this tasty dish, is to take a leaf of lettuce, place a spoonful of Fish Fluff in the center and add a sprinkling of chopped peanuts. Roll up and eat with your fingers.

Squid Broth

(SERVES 4)

INGREDIENTS

1 large dried squid
¾ lb. fish paste (see NOTE)
2 Chinese mushrooms
4 cups clear soup stock (see p. 261)
2 slices lean cooked pork, cut in fine strips
1 small piece (about 1 oz) bamboo shoot, sliced
1 carrot, grated
¼ cup cornstarch
¼ cup water

SEASONING A

½ teaspoon salt
½ tablespoon ginger wine (see Glossary)
2 tablespoons chopped celery
1 teaspoon soy sauce
1 teaspoon sugar

SEASONING B

1 teaspoon salt
1 tablespoon light soy sauce

SEASONING C

3 teaspoons sesame oil
2 tablespoons malt vinegar

Soak the dried squid in cold water overnight. Soak the dried Chinese mushrooms in warm water for 30 minutes.

Drain squid and cut in pieces. Pat dry on paper towels. Mix the fish paste with seasoning **A** and add squid. Mix together thoroughly.

Bring a large saucepan of water to a boil. Drop the fish paste-coated squid into it, a few pieces at a time, and cook until they float and the coating is firm. Remove with a slotted spoon and set aside.

Drain the mushrooms and shred finely. Bring the stock to a boil and add seasoning **B**. Boil for 3 minutes and add the pork, bamboo shoot and carrot, together with the cooked squid. Bring to a boil again, then lower the heat and simmer for 3 minutes.

Mix the cornstarch with the water and stir into the soup. Bring to a boil and cook until thickened, then stir in seasoning **C** and serve at once.

NOTE

To make the fish paste, put ¾ lb. raw cod or flounder into a food processor and grind. Add ½ an egg white, 1 tablespoon cornstarch and ½ teaspoon chili powder and process again until everything is well mixed.

Deep-Fried Shellfish Patties

(SERVES 4)

INGREDIENTS

¾ pint shucked clams
½ tablespoon cornstarch
1 bunch scallions
¾ cup finely shredded white cabbage
⅔ cup lean ground pork
3½ cups all-purpose flour
1 teaspoon salt
½–⅔ cup water
corn oil, for deep frying

SEASONING A

½ teaspoon salt
1 teaspoon white pepper

SEASONING B

3 garlic cloves, minced
3 tablespoons light soy sauce
1 tablespoon sweet chili sauce

Wash and drain the clams thoroughly. Toss with the cornstarch.

Trim and chop the scallions and add the cabbage. Mix these vegetables with the pork, clams and seasoning **A**. Set aside.

Sift flour and salt into a large bowl and add sufficient water to make a fairly thick, coating batter.

Heat the oil in a deep-fat fryer. Place about 1 tablespoon of the batter in a ladle and cover with 3 tablespoons shellfish mixture. Cover with another 1 tablespoon of the batter, then lower ladle into oil. Cook until golden brown, then remove and drain on paper towels. Keep warm while cooking remaining patties in the same way.

Mix seasoning **B** and serve with the patties.

Hot Salmon Steaks

(SERVES 2)

INGREDIENTS

2 salmon steaks
2 tablespoons cornstarch
¼ cup corn oil
2 red chili peppers, seeded
   and finely sliced

SEASONING

1 clove garlic, crushed
2 tablespoons dark soy sauce
1 tablespoon rice wine or dry
   sherry
½ teaspoon sugar
1 teaspoon white pepper
3 tablespoons water

Wipe the fish dry and dust with the cornstarch.

Heat the oil in a skillet and add the fish steaks. Cook for 2 minutes, turn them over and cook for a further 2 minutes until just tender.

Drain all the surplus oil from the skillet into a small skillet or wok. Add the chili peppers and seasoning ingredients along with the water. Bring to a boil, stirring.

Pour the chili seasoning over the fish and cook over a low heat for 5 minutes.

Serve immediately, with the sauce spooned over the fish.

涸 肫 肝

Fish Steaks with Red Sauce

(SERVES 4)
INGREDIENTS

2 cod or halibut steaks
¼ cup corn oil

SEASONING
1 tablespoon red bean sauce
    (see NOTE)
1 tablespoon water
½ tablespoon sugar

Mix the seasoning ingredients thoroughly in a bowl. Add the fish, turning to coat both sides thoroughly. Marinate for 1-2 hours and then drain.

Heat the oil in a wok or skillet, add the fish slices, and cook over medium heat until both sides are browned slightly. Serve.

NOTE
Red bean sauce adds a distinct and delicious piquancy to this dish. If it is unavailable, use Hoisin sauce.

醬 瓜 肉

Steamed Dried Fish

(SERVES 4)
INGREDIENTS

1 dried fish
1 tablespoon rice wine or dry
    sherry
2 tablespoons finely grated
    fresh gingerroot
3 tablespoons white vinegar

Trim off the tail and gills of the fish and soak in water for 1 hour.

Rinse the fish, and pat dry with paper towels. Rub thoroughly with the wine.

Spread the grated ginger over the fish and place in a steamer. Pour 2 inches water into a large saucepan and bring to a boil. Set the steamer over the saucepan, cover with a tight-fitting lid and steam over a high heat for 40 minutes. Remove from heat.

Cut the fish in bite-size pieces and serve the vinegar as a dipping sauce.

NOTE
Dried fish are commonly available in Chinese supermarkets. Buy garoupa or sea-eel, if available.

MEAT AND POULTRY

Although meat does not feature as prominently in Chinese cuisine as it does in the West, there are still hundreds of exciting and authentic meat and poultry dishes to choose from and it would be a shame not to include at least one of these in a Chinese meal.

The cooking methods employed for meat cooking are gentle and quick. Steaming is very common and even whole chickens and ducks can be steamed. Stir-frying, where the meat has been chopped or sliced in advance and is then cooked with a variety of vegetables, is popular as well, since it is quick and economical. Look out also for twice-cooked dishes. Here meat is first lightly cooked (either by boiling, steaming or stir-frying) to seal in flavor, and then cooked again, normally by deep-frying or stir-frying, when extra and stronger seasoning is added. The result is a rich, distinctive flavor and a delicious crispy texture.

Apart from poultry, the most popular meat in Chinese cuisine is undoubtedly pork. This extremely versatile meat appears in all sorts of Chinese dishes – cooked by itself as an impressive centerpiece, stir-fried with vegetables or simmered with noodles. Beef is also popular in parts of China and lamb dishes can also be found in Peking and North China.

Although the cuts of meat that would be sold in a typical Chinese market would be very different from our own, American cuts are perfectly acceptable. Seek out tender cuts for stir-frying – rump or sirloin steak for beef dishes and pork tenderloin or scallops for pork ones. Boneless chicken breasts, now widely available in supermarkets, are convenient when sliced chicken meat is required. However, you could always bone a whole chicken, in which case use the carcass for Chicken Stock (see p. 149).

辣味牛肉

Hot Beef

(SERVES 4)
INGREDIENTS

¾ lb. rump steak
3 tablespoons water
¼ cup corn oil
2 or 3 chili peppers, seeded
    and minced
1 teaspoon chopped dried
    orange peel (see NOTE)

SEASONING
3 garlic cloves, sliced
1 teaspoon salt
1 tablespoon soy sauce
½ tablespoon rice wine or
    dry sherry
2 teaspoons cornstarch
1½ tablespoons corn oil

Slice the beef in thin slices, cutting against the grain.

Mix the seasoning ingredients with the water in a bowl and add the slices of beef. Marinate for 30 minutes. Drain.

Heat the oil in a wok or skillet. Add the chili peppers and dried orange peel and cook over a medium heat for a few seconds. Add the beef and stir-fry over a high heat for 2 minutes. Serve.

NOTE
Dried orange peel is available from Oriental markets. (You can use fresh peel instead, but the flavor is less concentrated.) To prepare, soak the dried peel in warm water till soft, then chop.

京醬牛柳

Beef Slices in Sauce

(SERVES 4)
INGREDIENTS

¾ lb. rump steak
⅓ cup corn oil
broccoli stems, for garnish

SEASONING A
1 tablespoon soy sauce
½ tablespoon chopped garlic
½ tablespoon rice wine or
    dry sherry
½ teaspoon salt
1 teaspoon black bean sauce
1 tablespoon cornstarch
3 tablespoons water

SEASONING B
1 tablespoon cornstarch
1 teaspoon sesame oil
1 tablespoon soy sauce
1 tablespoon water

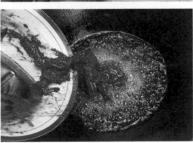

Slice the beef against the grain in thick slices.

Mix seasoning **A** in a bowl, add the slices of beef and marinate for 30 minutes. Drain.

Mix seasoning **B** ingredients in another bowl.

Heat the oil in a wok or skillet. Add the beef and stir-fry over a high heat for 3-4 minutes. Off heat, pour in seasoning **B** and bring to a boil, stirring all the time. Garnish with slices of cooked broccoli stems and serve.

Beef and Tomato Soup

(SERVES 6)
INGREDIENTS

1¼ lb. stew beef
2 large tomatoes
5 cups water
½ × 1 inch piece fresh
    gingerroot
⅔ can (16 oz. size) bean
    sprouts, rinsed and
    drained
2 teaspoons rice wine or dry
    sherry

SEASONING
1-2 teaspoons salt
2 teaspoons light soy sauce

Cut the beef in 1½ inch cubes and cut the tomatoes in wedges.

Bring the water to a boil and add the ginger and beef. Lower the heat and simmer for 1 hour or until the meat is just tender. Add the tomatoes and cook for a further 15 minutes.

Stir in the bean sprouts and rice wine and simmer for a further 5 minutes. Add the seasoning and stir.

Remove the slice of ginger and serve piping hot.

雞 絲 燴 豌 豆

Shredded Chicken and Pea Broth

(SERVES 4)
INGREDIENTS

½ lb. boneless chicken
  breasts, skinned
2 tablespoons cornstarch
2 tablespoons light soy sauce
1 cup garden peas (see
  NOTE)
2 tablespoons vegetable oil
1 teaspoon salt
1½ cups water
½ teaspoon white pepper
½ teaspoon sugar

Slice the chicken in thin ¼ × 1 inch shreds.

Mix 1 teaspoon of the cornstarch with the soy sauce in a bowl. Stir in the chicken and set aside for 20 minutes.

Place the peas in a bowl, cover with boiling water and scald for 3 minutes. Drain.

Heat the oil in a large Dutch oven. Stir in the peas, the salt and 1 cup water. Set over a high heat and bring to a boil.

Add the shredded chicken and bring back to a boil, stirring constantly to keep the chicken shreds separated.

Lower the heat, cover and simmer very gently for 15 minutes.

Mix the remaining cornstarch with the rest of the water to make a smooth paste and stir into the Dutch oven with the pepper and sugar. Cook until the soup thickens and then serve piping hot.

NOTE
Thawed frozen peas can be used if fresh garden peas are not available. You will require ½ package (10 oz. size). They do not need scalding.

雞球菜心

Chicken Balls with Lettuce

(SERVES 4)
INGREDIENTS

2 boneless chicken breasts, skinned
1 cup minced pork tenderloin
½ teaspoon salt
½ teaspoon sugar
1½ teaspoons rice wine or dry sherry
4 tablespoons cornstarch
1 Romaine or Boston lettuce
4 cups chicken stock (see p. 149)
corn oil, for deep frying

Mince the chicken. Place in a bowl with the pork and add the salt, sugar and rice wine. Form into walnut-size balls and roll in the cornstarch.

Break the lettuce in separate leaves and rinse in cold water. Bring the stock to a boil and drop the lettuce leaves in. Bring back to a boil. As soon as the water begins to boil again, remove the lettuce and arrange on a serving platter, reserving the stock.

Heat the oil in a deep-fat fryer and cook the chicken balls until they are golden. Remove with a slotted spoon, and drain on paper towels. Place on top of the lettuce. Season the soup with a little salt and pour over chicken balls.

五香雞塊

Five-Spice Chicken Pieces

(SERVES 6)
INGREDIENTS

1 broiler-fryer (about 2½ lb.
   in weight)
2 teaspoons salt
¼ cup corn oil
cucumber slices and carrot
   flowers, for garnish

SEASONING
2 tablespoons rice wine or
   dry sherry
2 tablespoons soy sauce
1 scallion, minced
½ star anise
½ teaspoon Szechuan
   peppercorns (see NOTE)
½ cup water

Using a cleaver or meat ax, cut the chicken in
large pieces. Sprinkle with the salt.

Mix the seasoning ingredients in a bowl.

Heat the oil in a wok or skillet, add the chicken
pieces and cook until golden. Pour the seasoning over
the chicken, bring to a boil, then lower the heat. Cook
uncovered over a low heat for about 20 minutes, or
until the chicken is cooked.

Arrange the chicken in a serving dish. Garnish
with cucumber slices and carrot flowers, and serve.

NOTE
Szechuan peppercorns are available from Oriental
groceries. They are not really peppercorns at all, but
dried berries from a citrus shrub, with a pungent
aroma and spicy flavor.

Chinese-Style Steak

(SERVES 6)
INGREDIENTS

4 slices rump or sirloin steak,
　　(total weight about 1¾ lb.)
¼ cup butter

SEASONING
3 tablespoons soy sauce
1 tablespoon chopped garlic
½ teaspoon salt
1½ teaspoons black pepper
2 teaspoons sugar
1 tablespoon ginger wine
　　(see Glossary)
2 tablespoons corn oil
1 teaspoon cornstarch
⅓ cup water

　　Tenderize the beef by beating it with a meat mallet or heavy rolling pin.
　　Mix the seasoning ingredients with the water in a large bowl. Add the beef and marinate for 1 hour.
　　Melt the butter in a skillet, add the steak and cook over a medium-high heat until both sides are browned. Serve.

麻辣手撕雞

Hand-Torn Chicken with Spicy Sauce

(SERVES 6)
INGREDIENTS

1 large broiler-fryer, about
    (3¼ lb. in weight)
2 tomatoes and fresh parsley
    sprigs, for garnish

SEASONING
2 tablespoons sesame paste
    (see NOTE)
2-3 cloves garlic, crushed
1 tablespoon sugar
½ teaspoon salt

Rinse the chicken and pat dry with paper towels.
    Place the chicken in a large steamer. Pour 2 inches
water into a large saucepan and bring to a boil.
    Set the steamer containing the chicken over the
saucepan. Cover with a tight fitting lid and steam
the chicken over a medium heat for 45-60 minutes,
adding more water to the pan if necessary. The
chicken is cooked when the flesh is no longer pink and
the meat juices run clear when pierced with a knife. If
these are still pink, continue steaming for a further
15-20 minutes.
    Remove the chicken and pour the remaining
steaming liquid into a measuring cup. Make up to ½
cup liquid with a little water if necessary.
    When the chicken is cool enough to handle, use
your hands to tear the flesh from the bones. Arrange
on a large serving platter.
    Mix the seasoning ingredients with the reserved
steaming liquid, heat gently and pour over the chicken
pieces.
    Garnish with slices of tomato and sprigs of parsley
and serve with mustard or a sweet chili sauce.

NOTE
Sesame seed or tahini paste is available from most
health food stores as well as gourmet food stores.
Stir thoroughly before using.

雞茸粟米

Chicken and Corn Chowder

(SERVES 4)
INGREDIENTS

¼ lb. boneless chicken
    breast, skinned
2 egg whites
½ teaspoon salt
4 cups chicken stock (see
    p. 149)
1 can (16 oz.) vacuum-
    packed whole kernel corn
2 tablespoons cornstarch
3 tablespoons water

SEASONING
2 teaspoons light soy sauce
pinch of sugar

Mince the chicken and place in a bowl. Add
the seasoning ingredients and stir to mix.
    Lightly beat the egg whites until frothy. Add the
salt and stir into the chicken mixture.
    Bring the chicken stock to a boil and add the corn.
Cook for 5 minutes and then lower the heat and add
the chicken. Simmer gently for 15 minutes or until the
chicken is cooked, stirring occasionally.
    Mix the cornstarch with the water to make a
smooth paste. Stir into the soup and cook for a few
minutes until the soup thickens.
    Garnish with parsley and serve.

軟兜猪排

Pork Chops in Spicy Sauce

(SERVES 6)
INGREDIENTS

6 pork loin chops (total
   weight about 1¾ lb.)
corn oil, for deep frying
scallion flowers, for garnish
   (see NOTE)

SEASONING
1 garlic clove, crushed
2 tablespoons soy sauce
1 tablespoon ginger wine
   (see Glossary)
1 teaspoon cornstarch
1 tablespoon sesame oil
¼ teaspoon salt
½ teaspoon white pepper
1 teaspoon sugar

Tenderize the pork chops by beating them with a
meat mallet or heavy rolling pin. Score them slightly
using a sharp knife.

Mix the seasoning ingredients in a bowl. Add the
pork chops and marinate for 30 minutes. Drain.

Heat the oil in a deep-fat fryer and deep fry the
pork chops for 5-7 minutes. Remove with a slotted
spoon and serve garnished with scallion flowers.

NOTE
To make scallion flowers or curls, cut out 2½-inch
lengths of spring onion. Make star-shaped cuts, about
1-inch deep, in both ends. Drop the scallions in ice
water. They will curl within 30 minutes-1 hour.

炸 八 塊

Deep-Fried Eight Pieces

(SERVES 6)
INGREDIENTS

1 broiler-fryer (about 2½ lb.
   in weight)
corn oil, for deep frying
1 teaspoon sesame oil
red cabbage leaves, for
   garnish

SEASONING A
1 scallion, cut in 3 pieces
3 slices fresh gingerroot
1 star anise, crushed
¼ cup soy sauce
1 tablespoon rice wine or dry
   sherry
1 egg white
1 tablespoon cornstarch

SEASONING B
2 teaspoons salt
2 teaspoons Szechuan
   peppercorns (see NOTE)

Using a cleaver or meat ax, cut the chicken in
eight pieces.

Mix seasoning **A** ingredients in a bowl and add the
chicken pieces. Marinate for about 1 hour. Drain.

Heat a wok or skillet over a low heat and add
seasoning **B** ingredients. Stir-fry until the salt turns
slightly brown. Place in a mortar and pestle or coffee
grinder and crush to a fine powder.

Heat the corn oil in a deep-fat fryer, and deep-fry
the chicken pieces for 3 minutes. Remove with a
slotted spoon, sprinkle with the sesame oil and
garnish with the cabbage leaves. Serve with
seasoning **B**.

NOTE
This mixture of dry-roasted salt and Szechuan
peppercorns (which are not true peppercorns but
dried berries) is served all over China as a dip for
deep-fried foods.

83

青辰蛤肉湯

Pork, Clam and Fuzzy Melon Soup

(SERVES 4)
INGREDIENTS

1 large fuzzy melon (see NOTES)
2 oz pork tenderloin
2 cups littleneck clams
1 tablespoon minced gingerroot
4 cups water
½ piece laver (see NOTES)
1 teaspoon sesame oil

SEASONING
1 teaspoon rice wine or dry sherry
1 teaspoon salt
1 teaspoon white pepper

Peel the fuzzy melon and remove the stem. Cut lengthwise in eight pieces and cut away the seeds, then slice the melon diagonally in ½ inch pieces.

Cut the pork tenderloin in thin pieces and scrub the clams thoroughly.

Place the pork, ginger and water in a large saucepan and bring to a boil. Add the clams, bring back to a boil and add the fuzzy melon. Lower the heat and simmer for 10 minutes.

Tear the laver into small pieces and add to the soup. Add the seasoning ingredients and stir to mix.

Sprinkle the sesame oil on top and serve at once.

NOTES
Fuzzy melon is a very popular Chinese summer vegetable. It is sometimes available in Chinese markets, but if not, use a large cucumber instead.

Laver is dried pressed seaweed, in wafer-thin sheets. It's available from most Oriental markets.

笋火魚乾湯

Pork and Dried Fish Clear Soup

(SERVES 4)
INGREDIENTS

1 piece (about 2 oz.) bamboo shoot
¼ lb. pork tenderloin
10 oz. dried salt fish (see NOTES)
2 inch piece fresh gingerroot, finely shredded
2½ cups boiling water
2 teaspoons rice wine or dry sherry

SEASONING
½ teaspoon white pepper
1 teaspoon sugar

Cut the bamboo shoots into small pieces and slice the pork tenderloin thinly. Place in a bowl, cover with boiling water and set aside for 5 minutes. Drain.

Rinse the salt fish in cold water. Cut in 1 inch pieces.

Arrange the bamboo shoots, pork, fish and ginger in large bowl. Add the boiling water. Place over a pan of boiling water, cover and steam for 40 minutes. Stir in the rice wine.

Sprinkle with the seasoning ingredients just before serving.

NOTES
Dried salt fish is regularly available at Oriental markets. The most common variety is dried yellow fish.

This soup can be boiled rather than steamed. However, it will become opaque, not transparent as shown here.

貢丸湯
Meat Ball Soup

(SERVES 4)
INGREDIENTS

12 Chinese meat balls (see NOTE)
2 celery stalks
4 cups chicken stock (see p. 149)
1 teaspoon salt
½ teaspoon white pepper

Wash the meat balls. Using a sharp knife, score a criss-cross pattern on each one.

Wash and trim the celery, and cut in small cubes.

Place the stock and the meat balls in a saucepan, bring to a boil and boil for 3 minutes. Remove from the heat.

Add the diced celery, salt and pepper, and serve immediately.

NOTE
Buy the Chinese meat balls from any Chinese grocery. They can be bought fresh, but are more commonly available in sealed packages.

清蒸豬排
Steamed Ham Steaks

(SERVES 4)
INGREDIENTS

4 uncooked ham steaks (total weight about 1¼ lb.)

SEASONING
1 tablespoon ginger wine (see Glossary)
1 tablespoon salt
½ teaspoon white pepper
1 tablespoon cornstarch
2 teaspoons sesame oil
3 tablespoons water

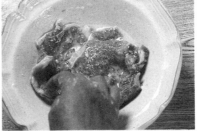

Tenderize the meat by beating it lightly with a meat mallet or heavy rolling pin. Using a sharp knife, score slightly.

Mix the seasoning ingredients in a bowl. Add the ham steaks, turning to ensure they are evenly coated. Marinate for 30 minutes.

Place the steaks on a heatproof plate in a large steamer. Pour 2 inches boiling water into a large saucepan. Set the steamer containing the ham steaks over the saucepan. Cover with a tight-fitting lid and steam the ham steaks over high heat for 12 minutes or until they are cooked.
Remove from the heat.

Arrange on a serving dish and serve.

鮑魚鷄翅

Chicken Wings with Abalone

(SERVES 6)

INGREDIENTS

1 small can abalone
(see NOTE)
12 chicken wings
3 dried scallops, soaked in
cold water for 2 hours
2 canned asparagus spears,
for garnish, optional

SEASONING

1 tablespoon finely grated
fresh gingerroot
1 teaspoon white pepper
1 teaspoon salt
1 teaspoon sugar

Drain the canned abalone and reserve the juice. Cut 2 of the abalone in 6 slices each and set aside (the remaining canned abalone will not be required).

Place the chicken wings in a bowl, cover with boiling water and scald for 10 minutes. Drain.

Cut the soaked scallops in thin slices.

Place the abalone slices, the chicken wings and the scallops in a deep bowl. Mix the reserved abalone juice with the seasoning ingredients and pour over the abalone and chicken. Place in a large steamer and set over a pan of boiling water. Cover and steam for 30 minutes.

Serve, garnished with asparagus spears, if liked.

NOTE

Abalone are a popular delicacy in China. These molluscs with a delicate fishy taste and a similar texture to scallops are occasionally available on the West Coast, but are more often sold (as frozen steaks) in gourmet food stores. Canned abalone are available from Chinese markets.

原汁玉米雞

Chicken with Corn

(SERVES 4)

INGREDIENTS

14 oz. boneless chicken
   breasts, skinned
½ lb. broccoli
1½ tablespoons corn oil
1 can (7 oz.) vacuum-packed
   whole kernel corn
1 egg white, lightly beaten
1½ tablespoons cornstarch
2 tablespoons water
radish slices, for garnish

SEASONING

1 tablespoon rice wine or dry
   sherry
2 teaspoons salt
½ teaspoon white pepper
½ teaspoon sugar
½ cup water

Cut the chicken breasts in small cubes and place in a bowl. Add the seasoning ingredients including the water and stir thoroughly.

Place the bowl in a steamer over a pan of boiling water. Cover and steam over a high heat for 10 minutes or until the chicken is cooked, stirring occasionally.

Meanwhile, break the broccoli in flowerets and place in a large bowl. Cover with boiling water and blanch for 3 minutes. Drain and keep warm.

Drain the chicken and keep warm. Reserve the liquid from the bowl.

Heat the oil in a wok. Add the corn and the reserved chicken liquid. Bring to a boil and beat in the egg white. Stir constantly for 30 seconds.

Mix the cornstarch with 2 tablespoons cold water to form a paste. Stir into the corn mixture and cook for a few minutes, stirring, until the sauce thickens.

Arrange the broccoli around the outside of a plater and pile the chicken in the center. Pour the corn sauce over the top and garnish with radish slices.

Chicken with Sesame Oil and Honey

(SERVES 6)
INGREDIENTS

1 broiler-fryer (about 3½ lb.
    in weight)
4 Chinese dried mushrooms,
    optional
2 tablespoons vegetable oil
½ cup water
2 tablespoons sesame oil
lettuce and tomatoes, for
    garnish

SEASONING
¼ cup light soy sauce
3 tablespoons clear honey
1 tablespoon rice wine or dry
    sherry
½ teaspoon ground ginger
1 teaspoon salt

Using a cleaver or meat ax, cut the chicken in bite-size pieces.

Mix the seasoning ingredients in a bowl and add the chicken. Marinate for 1 hour.

Soak the mushrooms, if using, in warm water for 30 minutes.

Drain the chicken, reserving the marinade. Heat the vegetable oil in a wok and add the chicken pieces.

Stir-fry over a high heat until chicken begins to brown. Add the water and bring to a boil.

Stir in the reserved marinade and the sesame oil lower the heat and simmer gently for 40 minutes.

Meanwhile drain the mushrooms, remove the stems and steam the caps, over a pan of boiling water for 20 minutes.

Serve the chicken with the steamed mushrooms, garnished with lettuce and tomatoes.

Velvet Chicken

(SERVES 4)

INGREDIENTS

6 oz. boneless chicken
    breast, skinned
4 egg whites
⅓ cup water
3 teaspoons cornstarch
2 cups corn oil
2 slices cooked ham
½ cucumber, quartered and
    sliced
8 straw mushrooms
3 tablespoons chicken stock
    (see p. 149)
1 teaspoon salt

SEASONING

½ teaspoon salt
1½ teaspoons rice wine or
    dry sherry

Slice the chicken thinly and place in a bowl. Beat 1 egg white with 1 tablespoon water and the seasoning ingredients and stir into the chicken. Set aside for 15 minutes.

Beat the remaining egg whites with 1 tablespoon water and beat into the chicken mixture. Continue beating for 5 minutes.

Blend 2 teaspoons of the cornstarch with 1 tablespoon water and stir into the chicken mixture. Mix thoroughly.

Heat the oil in a large wok. Add the coated chicken pieces and cook for 5 minutes. Remove the chicken with a slotted spoon and drain.

Drain off all but 2 tablespoons of the oil and re-heat. Add the ham, cucumber and mushrooms and stir-fry for 2 minutes. Mix the remaining 1 teaspoon of cornstarch with 1 tablespoon water and stir into the mixture with the chicken stock and salt. Cook for 1 minute until thick and bubbly, then return the chicken to the pan and cook for a further minute.

Sprinkle in the remaining water, stir and serve.

Chinese-Style Hot Pot

(SERVES 6)
INGREDIENTS

2 lb. stew lamb
1 section of peeled sugar
   cane (see NOTES)
½ lb. water chestnuts (see
   NOTES)
1 star anise
½ tablespoon rice wine or
   dry sherry
5 cups water

SEASONING
1½ teapoons salt
2 teaspoons sugar

Trim the lamb and cut in 2 inch thick strips. Scald in boiling water for 1 minute. Drain and rinse in cold water.

Cut the sugar cane in 1 inch sections. Peel the water chestnuts, if fresh, or drain canned ones.

Place the meat, sugar cane, water chestnuts, star anise and rice wine in a large Dutch oven. Add the water and bring to a boil. Cover, lower the heat and simmer for 1½-2 hours or until the meat is tender.

Add seasoning and serve.

NOTES
Sugar cane is available from Chinese, Indian and West Indian markets.

Fresh water chestnuts are occasionally available from Oriental markets. If you cannot get hold of them, use canned ones instead which are widely available from most supermarkets.

Shredded Chicken with Bean Sprouts

(SERVES 4)
INGREDIENTS

½ lb. boneless chicken
  breasts, skinned
1 egg white
2 teaspoons cornstarch
2 cups bean sprouts
⅓ cup corn oil
raspberries and celery tops,
  for garnish

SEASONING

1½ teaspoons salt
½ teaspoon white pepper

Shred the chicken in thin pieces and place in a bowl. Lightly beat the egg white, add the cornstarch and stir into the chicken.

Rinse the bean sprouts in cold water and drain.

Heat the oil in the wok. Add the chicken and stir-fry over a high heat for 45-60 seconds. Remove with a slotted spoon and set aside.

Drain all but 2 tablespoons of the oil. Reheat the wok, add the bean sprouts and stir-fry for a few seconds. Add the seasoning ingredients and stir well.

Return the chicken and cook, stirring for 15 seconds. Serve garnished with celery tops and raspberries.

Crystal Paper-wrapped Chicken

(SERVES 4-6)
INGREDIENTS

1¼ lb. boneless chicken
  breasts, skinned
1 egg white
corn oil, for deep frying
lemon slices, for garnish

SEASONING

3 tablespoons light soy sauce
½ teaspoon rice wine or dry
  sherry
1 tablespoon finely grated
  fresh gingerroot
½ teaspoon sugar

Cut the chicken in rectangles about ¾ × 1½ inches.

Mix the seasoning ingredients with the egg white and stir into the chicken pieces. Marinate for 3 hours in a cool place, stirring occasionally.

Cut a sheet of cellophane in about 12 (6 inch) squares. Place a spoonful of the chicken mixture at the corner of each square and wrap up, twisting the ends to seal.

Heat the oil in a deep-fat fryer and deep-fry the packages for 3 minutes.

Serve the chicken in the wrappers, garnished with slices of lemon.

Boiled Chicken with Scallions

(SERVES 4)
INGREDIENTS

2 chicken legs
1 bunch scallions
2 inch piece fresh gingerroot
¼ cup corn oil

SEASONING
1 teaspoon salt
½ teaspoon white pepper

Place the chicken legs in a saucepan or Dutch oven. Add sufficient water to cover the chicken and bring to a boil. Lower the heat and simmer for 15 minutes. Off heat, set the pan aside, covered, for 20 minutes.

Remove the chicken pieces from the stock, skin and strip away the flesh from the bones. Arrange the meat on a serving platter.

Trim the scallions and cut lengthwise in 3 inch pieces. Peel the ginger and cut in fine shreds. Place both in a bowl and mix with the seasoning ingredients.

Heat the oil in a wok, add the scallions and ginger and stir-fry for 30 seconds. Pour the contents of the wok over the shredded chicken and serve.

NOTE
The chicken stock will make a good soup base. Place in a rigid container, seal, and refrigerate for up to 3 days or freeze for up to 3 months.

Chicken with Wood Ear Mushrooms

(SERVES 4-6)
INGREDIENTS

1 tablespoon wood ear
 mushrooms
4 chicken pieces
¼ cup dark soy sauce
corn oil, for deep frying
2 scallions, thinly sliced
1 inch piece fresh gingerroot,
 cut in 3 slices
2 cups chicken stock (see
 p. 149)
2 tablespoons cornstarch
fresh parsley sprigs and baby
 corn cobs, for garnish

SEASONING
1 tablespoon rice wine or dry
 sherry
2 tablespoons light soy sauce
1 teaspoon dark soy sauce
1 teaspoon sugar
1 teaspoon salt

Soak the wood ear mushrooms in warm water for 30 minutes. Drain and thinly slice.

Rub the chicken pieces evenly with the dark soy sauce and marinate for 30 minutes.

Heat the oil in a large wok or deep-fat fryer and deep-fry the chicken pieces, two at a time, until well browned. Remove the chicken and set aside; drain the oil from the wok and reserve.

Heat 1 tablespoon of the reserved oil in the wok and stir-fry the scallions, wood ear mushrooms and ginger slices for 30 seconds.

Remove the ginger and discard. Add the chicken, the chicken stock and the seasoning ingredients. Stir thoroughly, cover and simmer over a low heat for 25 minutes.

Remove the chicken and cool slightly. When cool enough to handle, pull away the meat from the bones and arrange on a serving platter.

Remove the wood mushrooms from the wok with a slotted spoon and scatter over the chicken.

Mix the cornstarch with a little water and stir into the wok. Bring to a boil, stirring, and cook for a few minutes until the sauce thickens slightly.

Pour the sauce over the chicken and garnish with the parsley and baby corn cobs. Serve.

Spicy Braised Chicken

(SERVES 6)
INGREDIENTS

1 broiler-fryer (about 3 lb. in
 weight)
¼ cup corn oil
2½ cups water
½ tablespoon sesame oil
2 teaspoons salt
lettuce leaves and sliced
 radishes for garnish

SEASONING A
10 garlic cloves
5 red chili peppers, seeded
 and minced (see NOTE)
1 inch fresh gingerroot,
 sliced
1 scallion, minced

SEASONING B
3 tablespoons light soy sauce
1 tablespoon rice wine or dry
 sherry

Using a heavy cleaver or meat ax, cut the chicken in bite-size pieces.

Using a coffee grinder or mortar and pestle, grind seasoning **A** to form a paste.

Heat the corn oil in a wok and stir-fry the paste for 1 minute. Add the chicken pieces and cook over a medium-high heat until golden brown. Drain excess oil.

Add the water and seasoning **B** to the chicken, stir thoroughly and bring to a boil. Lower the heat and simmer gently for about 1 hour.

Spoon chicken out onto a serving platter and sprinkle with the sesame oil and salt. Garnish with lettuce and sliced radishes and serve.

NOTE
This is quite a hot dish, perhaps too spicy for those who prefer milder flavors. If you prefer to play it safe, use only 2 or 3 chili peppers.

簡易义烧
Quick and Easy Roast Pork

(SERVES 4)
INGREDIENTS

1¼ lb. pork tenderloin
¼ cup corn oil
sesame oil, to serve

SEASONING
1 tablespoon soy sauce
2 tablespoons chili sauce
    (see NOTES)
1 scallion, minced
½ inch piece fresh gingerroot,
    chopped
¼ teaspoon five-spice
    powder
¼ cup sugar
½ cup water
1 tablespoon rice wine or dry
    sherry

Using a sharp knife, score the pork on both sides in several placcs.

Place the seasoning ingredients in a bowl and mix thoroughly. Add the pork, turning to ensure it is evenly coated. Marinate for at least 4 hours. Drain.

Heat the oil in a wok or skillet until medium-hot. Add the pork, and cook for about 5 minutes, turning to brown all sides. Remove from the heat and drain.

Place the pork in a roasting pan in a preheated hot oven (450°F) and bake for 15 minutes. Remove from the oven and let cool.

When the meat is cold, sprinkle with the sesame oil, slice thinly and serve.

NOTES
This dish is perfect for summer meals and picnics. In northern China, cold platters are often served at banquets.

Chili sauce is available from many supermarkets and from gourmet food stores.

醃味白肉
Marinated Pork

(SERVES 4)
INGREDIENTS

1¼ lb. pork tenderloin
2 tablespoons rice wine or
    dry sherry
1½ tablespoons salt

SEASONING
3 garlic cloves, minced
6 teaspoons sesame oil

Rub the rice wine over the pork tenderloin and then rub with the salt until it is all absorbed. Place in a non-metal bowl and leave to marinate in the refrigerator for 24 hours.

Rinse the pork lightly, and place in a large steamer. Place 2 inches boiling water in a large saucepan, set the steamer over the saucepan and cover with a tight-fitting lid. Steam for 20-25 minutes or until pork is tender and cooked through.

Slice the pork thinly. Mix the seasoning ingredients and serve as a dipping sauce.

White Cooked Chicken

(SERVES 6)
INGREDIENTS

5½ pints water
4 slices fresh gingerroot
1 broiler-fryer (about 3 lb.
  in weight)
fresh cilantro, for garnish
  (see NOTE)

DIP
1 tablespoon finely grated
  fresh gingerroot
2 scallions, minced
1 tablespoon corn oil
1 teaspoon salt

Place the water in a large saucepan. Add the ginger and bring to a boil. Add the chicken, bring back to the boil and cook rapidly for 10 minutes. Lower the heat, cover and simmer for 20 minutes. Off heat, set the pan aside, covered, until the chicken is cool.

Drain the chicken and using a meat cleaver or heavy knife, chop the chicken in large pieces. Arrange on a serving platter and garnish with the cilantro.

Make the dip by mixing all the ingredients in a bowl. Serve with the chicken.

NOTE
Cilantro is sometimes known as coriander and is widely available. If unavailable, substitute regular parsley.

Braised Duck

(SERVES 4-6)
INGREDIENTS

1 whole duck (about
  3 lb. in weight)
2 tablespoons dark soy sauce
¼ cup corn oil
3 scallions, sliced
2-3 red chili peppers, seeded
  and sliced
2 zucchini, roughly chopped
2 tablespoons cornstarch

SEASONING
2 tablespoons light soy sauce
4 slices fresh gingerroot
2 star anise
2 teaspoons rice wine or dry
  sherry

Rub the duck with the dark soy sauce and then chop in bite-size pieces.

Heat the oil in a wok or skillet, add the duck and cook for 2-3 minutes until golden brown on all sides. Remove with a slotted spoon and place in a large saucepan with the scallions, chili peppers and seasoning ingredients.

Add sufficient water to cover, bring to a boil and then lower the heat and simmer, covered, for 1¼ hours. Add the zucchini and continue cooking for 20-30 minutes or until the duck is tender.

Mix the cornstarch with a little water and stir into the pan. Cook until the sauce has thickened and then serve at once.

Barbecued Chicken with Sweet Bean Sauce

(SERVES 6)
INGREDIENTS

¼ cup rice wine or dry sherry
1 broiler-fryer (about 3 lb. in weight)
1 tablespoon corn oil
about ½ cup sweet or red bean sauce, to serve

SEASONING A
¼ cup sweet or red bean sauce
1 teaspoon salt
1½ teaspoons sugar
1 teaspoon chopped fresh gingerroot

SEASONING B
4 tablespoons soy sauce
4 tablespoons sugar

Pour the rice wine slowly over the chicken, rubbing it in with your fingers.

Mix seasoning **A** ingredients and rub the cavity of the chicken with this mixture. Close the cavity with a skewer.

Place the chicken in a steamer and steam, covered, over boiling water for 40 minutes, turning the chicken once midway through cooking.

Remove the chicken from the steamer, and rub with the oil.

Mix seasoning **B** ingredients together in a saucepan, and heat gently. Keep hot.

Place the chicken on a spit, brush with a little of seasoning **B** and charcoal grill or cook in a preheated very hot oven (425°F) for 30-45 minutes, basting frequently with the seasoning.

Using a cleaver or meat ax, cut the chicken in pieces, and arrange on a serving dish. Pour some sweet bean sauce on top and serve.

一品雞排

Chicken Cutlets

(SERVES 6)
INGREDIENTS

6 boneless chicken breasts,
 skinned
3 eggs
½ cup lean ground pork
2 teaspoons cornstarch
2 cups coating bread crumbs
corn oil, for deep frying
2 large tomatoes, for garnish

SEASONING A
4 tablespoons rice wine or
 dry sherry
2 teaspoons salt

SEASONING B
2 garlic cloves, crushed
1 teaspoon ground ginger
1 teaspoon salt
½ teaspoon sesame oil

Beat the chicken breasts out lightly with a meat mallet or heavy rolling pin. Mix seasoning **A** in a bowl and add the chicken, turning to coat each piece evenly. Marinate for 20 minutes.

Beat one of the eggs and mix with the ground pork, the cornstarch and seasoning **B**. Spread the mixture over the chicken pieces.

Beat the other two eggs and place the bread crumbs on a sheet of waxed paper. Dip each coated chicken cutlet in the beaten egg and then in the bread crumbs.

Heat the oil in a deep-fat fryer and deep-fry the chicken for 5-10 minutes or until golden brown and cooked through. Drain on paper towels and then arrange on a serving platter. Garnish with tomato slices and serve with a homemade tomato sauce, if liked.

果汁牛肉

Beef in Fruit Juice

(SERVES 4)
INGREDIENTS

1 lb. sirloin or rump steak
1 tablespoon dried orange
   peel (see NOTE p. 73)
⅓ cup corn oil
1 cup cubed fresh pineapple
1 tablespoon cornstarch
3 tablespoons water
strawberries and a scallion
   curl, for garnish (see NOTE
   p. 82)

SEASONING

2 garlic cloves, crushed
3 tablespoons fresh orange
   juice
1 tablespoon dark soy sauce
½ tablespoon rice wine or
   dry sherry
1½ tablespoons sugar
1 teaspoon salt

Cut the steak, against the grain, in long thin strips.
Finely chop the dried orange peel.
   Mix the seasoning ingredients in a small bowl.
Heat the oil in a wok, add the seasoning and stir-fry
for 1 minute.
   Add the steak and stir-fry vigorously over a high
heat for 2 minutes.
   Stir in the pineapple and cook for 30 seconds.
   Mix the cornstarch with the water and stir into the
beef mixture. Cook for a few minutes until the sauce
thickens and then spoon onto a serving platter.
   Garnish with strawberry halves and a scallion curl.
Serve at once.

麻辣蘆筍雞

Spicy-Hot Chicken with Asparagus

(SERVES 4)
INGREDIENTS

¾ lb. boneless chicken
  breasts, skinned
1 lb. fresh asparagus

SEASONING
4 garlic cloves, minced
2 tablespoons sesame oil
2 tablespoons light soy sauce
2 tablespoons hot chili oil
1 tablespoon sugar
2 teaspoons white vinegar
pinch of salt

Cut the chicken in 1 × 2 inch strips. Remove the woody stems from the asparagus and cut in 2 inch lengths.

Place the chicken and asparagus in a saucepan, just cover with boiling water and simmer for 5-10 minutes or until the chicken is cooked and the asparagus is tender.

Drain and arrange the chicken and asparagus on a serving plate.

Mix the seasoning ingredients together in a serving bowl. Spoon a little over the chicken and asparagus and serve the remainder separately, as a dipping sauce.

豌豆燉雞

Chicken and Pea Casserole

(SERVES 6)
INGREDIENTS

1¼ lb. boneless chicken
  breast, skinned
3 tablespoons butter
1 small onion, thinly sliced
1 can (16 oz.) chopped
  tomatoes
2 ½ cups chicken stock
  (see p. 149)
1 cup frozen peas
1 tablespoon cornstarch

SEASONING
1 teaspoon rice wine or dry
  sherry
½ teaspoon white pepper
1½ teaspoons salt
1 teaspoon sugar

Cut the chicken in ½ × 2 inch pieces and place in
a small pan. Cover with boiling water and leave for 1
minute. Drain.

Melt the butter in a large Dutch oven. Add the
onion and sauté for 2-3 minutes until lightly brown.

Add the chicken, chopped tomatoes and chicken
stock. Bring to a boil and add the seasoning
ingredients. Lower the heat, cover and simmer for
1 hour.

Add the peas and cook for a further 10 minutes.
Mix the cornstarch with a little cold water and stir into
the Dutch oven. Cook for 2-3 minutes until the sauce
thickens and serve.

Chicken with Cucumber

(SERVES 4)
INGREDIENTS

1 cucumber
2 teaspoons salt
2 teaspoons sesame oil
1 lb. boneless chicken breast, skinned
1 package of pea-starch noodles (see NOTE)

SEASONING

1½ teaspoons chopped fresh gingerroot
1½ teaspoons chopped garlic
1 tablespoon chili oil
1 tablespoon sesame oil
3 tablespoons soy sauce
1 tablespoon vinegar
2 teaspoons sugar
2 tablespoons sesame paste
1 teaspoon salt

Slice the cucumber thinly then cut the slices in half. Sprinkle with the salt and marinate for 10 minutes. Rinse off the salt, pat dry and mix with the sesame oil. Arrange on a platter.

Place the chicken breasts in a saucepan, add boiling water to cover, lower the heat a little and cook for 15 minutes. Drain and cool. When cool, use your fingers to shred in small pieces.

Place the pea-starch noodles in cold water and bring to a boil. Off heat, let stand for 30 minutes. Drain and chop roughly. Arrange on top of the cucumber slices, and place the shredded chicken on top.

Mix the seasoning ingredients together and sprinkle over the chicken.

NOTE

Pea-starch noodles, also known as mung bean threads or transparent vermicelli, are available from Chinese groceries. Made not from a grain but from ground mung beans, they are always served as part of another dish, never on their own.

Broiled Chicken Pieces

(SERVES 4)
INGREDIENTS

1¼ lb. boneless chicken
    breasts, skinned
1 egg, beaten
6 tablespoons cornstarch
¼ cup corn oil
½ cup chicken stock (see
    p. 149)

SEASONING A
1 tablespoon rice wine or dry
    sherry
1 tablespoon light soy sauce
1 teaspoon white salt
½ teaspoon pepper

SEASONING B
¼ cup ketchup
1 teaspoon sugar
1 teaspoon Worcestershire
    sauce
1 teaspoon sesame oil

Cut the chicken ino 1 × 2 inch pieces and beat out
slightly with a meat mallet or heavy rolling pin.

Mix seasoning **A** in a bowl, add the chicken and
marinate for 30 minutes.

Drain the chicken and dip first in the beaten egg
and then in the cornstarch.

Brush lightly with the oil and broil under a low
heat for 10-15 minutes. Turn the pieces over and broil
for a further 5 minutes or until the chicken is very
tender.

Place the chicken stock and any meat juices from
the broiler pan in a saucepan. Add the seasoning **B**
ingredients and bring to a boil.

Pour the sauce over the chicken and serve. Garnish
with lemon slices and lettuce leaves, if liked.

111

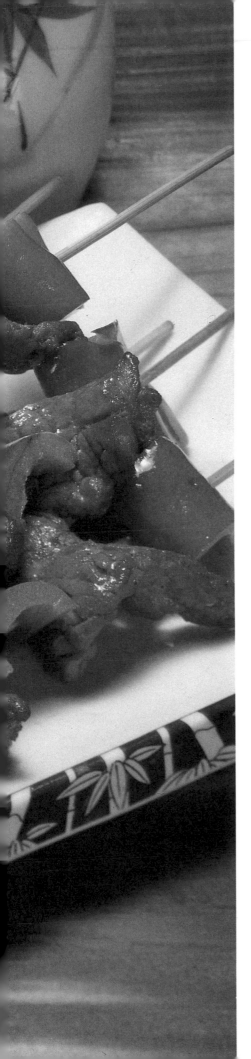

Barbecued Beef

(SERVES 6)
INGREDIENTS

1¼ lb. rump steak
2 green peppers
½ cup clear soup stock (see
   p. 261)

SEASONING A
1 tablespoon Hoisin or
   barbecue sauce
1 tablespoon light soy sauce
½ tablespoon ginger wine
   (see Glossary)
1 teaspoon cornstarch
2 teaspoons sugar
½ teaspoon black pepper

SEASONING B
3½ tablespoons smooth
   peanut butter
1 tablespoon Hoisin or
   barbecue sauce
2 garlic cloves, crushed
1 teaspoon salt
2 tablespoons minced
   parsley
½ teaspoon black pepper

Cut the steak across the grain in thin 2 inch long slices.

Mix seasoning **A** in a bowl. Add the steak and set aside for 20 minutes.

Cut the peppers in half, remove the seeds and then cut in small chunks. Place in a saucepan of boiling water and boil for 2 minutes. Drain.

Drain the meat and then thread alternate pieces of pepper and steak onto 6 large or 12 small bamboo sticks.

Broil or barbecue the kebabs for 5 minutes, turning the sticks occasionally.

Mix together seasoning **B** and the stock in a saucepan and bring to a boil. Lower the heat and simmer for 1 minute and then transfer to a serving bowl.

Serve as a dipping sauce with the meat and pepper kebabs.

Chicken in the Pot

(SERVES 6)
INGREDIENTS

1 roasting chicken (about 4
  lb. in weight)
5 star anise
2 cups water

SEASONING
1 cup dark soy sauce
1 cup rice wine or dry sherry
⅔ cup rock sugar
 (see NOTE)

Using a cleaver or meat ax, chop the chicken in
bite-size pieces and place in a bowl.

Mix the seasoning ingredients to make a rich
marinade and pour ⅓ cup over the chicken. Marinate
for 1 hour.

Place the chicken in its marinade in a large Dutch
oven with the star anise, water and the remaining
marinade. Bring to a boil, lower the heat, cover and
simmer gently for 45-60 minutes or until chicken is
tender.

NOTE
Rock sugar or sugar crystals are pale yellow or amber
and aren't quite as sweet as regular sugar. If it can't
be found at a Chinese market, use ½ cup packed
turbinado sugar instead.

Pork Spareribs with Dried Squid

(SERVES 4)

INGREDIENTS

2 large dried squid, soaked
    (see NOTE)
1 lb. pork spareribs
1 inch piece fresh gingerroot
2 scallions
white pepper
fresh parsley, for garnish

SEASONING

3 tablespoons light soy sauce
1 tablespoon rice wine or dry
    sherry
1 tablespoon sugar
1 teaspoon salt

Peel away the skin from the soaked squid and
discard the head and tentacles. Cut in 1 × 2 inch
pieces.

Chop the spareribs in 1 inch pieces. Bruise the
ginger by patting firmly with a heavy cleaver or rolling
pin. Slice the scallions.

Place the squid, spareribs, ginger and scallions
along with the seasoning ingredients, in a large
saucepan or Dutch oven. Cover with water and bring
to a boil. Lower the heat and simmer for about 1 hour
or until the stock has reduced by half.

Stir in a little pepper and garnish with parsley.
Serve piping hot.

NOTE

Dried squid is available from Oriental markets all year.
It should be kept in a dry place and used within a few
months of purchase. Dried squid needs to be soaked
for 24 hours in cold water before use in a recipe.

115

Stewed Duck with Taros

(SERVES 4)
INGREDIENTS

½ large duck, (about 1¼ lb.
  in weight)
1 lb. taros (dasheens)
  (see NOTES here and on
  p. 255)
corn oil, for deep frying
3 scallions, sliced
2½ cups clear soup stock
  (see p. 261)
2 teaspoons sesame oil

SEASONING A
4 tablespoons light soy sauce
2 tablespoon ginger wine
  (see Glossary)
2 teaspoons sugar

SEASONING B
2 tablespoons light soy sauce
1 teaspoon sugar
½ teaspoon salt
½ teaspoon white pepper

Rinse the duck and dry on paper towels. Cut in bite-size pieces, using a cleaver or meat ax.

Mix together seasoning **A** in a large bowl, add the duck and marinate for 30 minutes. Drain, reserving the marinade.

Soak the taros in boiling water for 10 minutes and then peel. Cut into large chunks.

Heat the oil in a deep fat fryer and deep-fry the taros for 5 minutes. Remove with a slotted spoon.

Heat 2 tablespoons oil in a wok and stir-fry the duck for 3 minutes. Remove. Add ¼ cup more oil to the wok and stir-fry the scallions for a few seconds.

Add the duck pieces, the reserved marinade, the taros, the seasoning **B** ingredients and the soup stock. Bring to a boil and then lower the heat and simmer for 30 minutes.

Sprinkle with sesame oil just before serving.

NOTE
Sweet potatoes can be used in place of taros.

Spicy Chicken

(SERVES 4)
INGREDIENTS

1¼ lb. boneless chicken
   breasts, skinned
3 tablespoons sesame oil
1 red chili pepper, seeded
   and minced
2 scallions, chopped
2 tablespoons corn oil
cherry tomatoes and baby
   corn cobs, for garnish

SEASONING A
1 garlic clove, minced
1 teaspoon grated fresh
   gingerroot
½ teaspoon white pepper

SEASONING B
2 tablespoons light soy sauce
2 teaspoons white vinegar
1 teaspoon sugar
1 teaspoon salt

Place the chicken in a pan. Add boiling water to
cover and cook for 5 minutes. Drain and thickly slice.

Heat the sesame oil in a wok, add the chili pepper
and scallions and gently stir-fry for a few seconds.
Remove and set aside.

Heat the corn oil in the wok and add the chicken
and seasoning **A**. Stir-fry for 1 minute and then stir in
seasoning **B**. Cook for a further 2 minutes, stirring all
the time.

Arrange the chicken on a serving platter and
sprinkle the chili pepper and scallions over the top.
Garnish with cherry tomatoes and baby corn cobs and
spoon the cooking sauce over.

簡易家常焗鶏

Easy Roast Chicken

(SERVES 4-6)
INGREDIENTS

1 broiler-fryer (about 3 lb. in weight)

SEASONING
4 scallions, minced
2 slices fresh gingerroot
3 star anise
1½ tablespoons salt
1 tablespoon rice wine or dry sherry
2 tablespoons chopped peppermint leaves (see NOTE)

Mix the seasoning ingredients together in a bowl, and stuff in the body cavity of the chicken.

Wrap the chicken in aluminum foil, place in a roasting pan and bake in a preheated moderately hot oven (400°F) for 1½ hours. Remove foil and serve.

NOTE
If peppermint leaves are not available, use any type of garden mint, preferably fresh, although dried could be used if necessary.

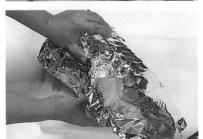

119

炸鶏腿

Deep-Fried Drumsticks

(SERVES 4)
INGREDIENTS

4 chicken drumsticks
1 cup all-purpose flour
corn oil, for deep frying

SEASONING A
2 tablespoons ginger wine
  (see Glossary)
2 teaspoons five-spice
  powder
2 tablespoons light soy sauce
1 teaspoon sugar
1 teaspoon salt
½ teaspoon white pepper

SEASONING B
3 tablespoons
  Worcestershire sauce
½ teaspoon salt
½ teaspoon white pepper

Mix seasoning **A** in a bowl and add the chicken drumsticks. Marinate for 1 hour, turning occasionally.

Drain the chicken and coat lightly with the flour.

Heat the oil in a deep-fat fryer and deep-fry the chicken drumsticks for 4-5 minutes until cooked and golden brown. The chicken is cooked when meat juices run clear when the flesh is pierced with a knife.

Mix seasoning **B** to make a dipping sauce and spoon into a serving bowl.

Wrap a little foil around the joint end of the chicken drumsticks and serve with the dipping sauce.

檸檬雞片

Lemon Chicken

(SERVES 4)
INGREDIENTS

10 oz. boneless chicken
   breasts, skinned
1 egg yolk
7 tablespoons cornstarch
3 tablespoons all-purpose
   flour
corn oil, for deep frying
2 tablespoons water
3 tablespoons chicken stock
   (see p. 149)

SEASONING A
½ tablespoon rice wine
1½ tablespoons soy sauce
pinch of white pepper
1 teaspoon cornstarch

SEASONING B
3 tablespoons lemon juice
3 tablespoons sugar
1 teaspoon sesame oil

Cut the chicken breasts in 1 × 2 inch strips.
   Mix seasoning **A** and stir in the chicken strips.
Marinate for 1 hour. Drain.
   Mix 6 tablespoons of the cornstarch with the
all-purpose flour and coat the chicken strips evenly.
   Heat the oil in a deep-fat fryer and deep-fry the
chicken strips for 30 seconds. Remove with a slotted
spoon and set aside.
   Mix the remaining cornstarch with the water. Heat
1 teaspoon of oil in a skillet, add the cornstarch
mixture along with the chicken stock and seasoning
B. Cook over a medium heat until slightly thickened.
   Reheat the oil in the deep-fat fryer and cook the
chicken strips for about 10-20 seconds. Remove and
arrange on a serving platter and pour the lemon sauce
over.

Chicken with Ham

(SERVES 6)
INGREDIENTS

1 large broiler-fryer about
   3½ lb. in weight
4 cups water
1 small onion, minced
1 teaspoon minced fresh
   gingerroot
4 smoked ham slices, halved
2 tablespoons corn oil
1 teaspoon cornstarch

SEASONING
1 teaspoon salt
1½ teaspoons rice wine or
   dry sherry

Place the chicken in a large saucepan or casserole,
add the water and the onion and ginger. Bring to a
boil, cover, lower the heat and simmer for 40 minutes
or until the chicken is cooked.

Drain, reserving ½ cup of the liquid. Let the
chicken cool and then slice.

Arrange alternate slices of chicken and ham on a
platter and place in a steamer to keep warm.

Heat the oil in a small pan and add the reserved
chicken liquid. Bring to a boil and add the seasoning
ingredients.

Mix the cornstarch with a little water and add to
the chicken stock. Cook for a few minutes until the
mixture thickens, and then pour over the chicken and
ham and serve.

NOTE
Keep any remaining stock from the chicken for soups
or casseroles.

滷牛肝

Spiced Beef Liver

(SERVES 4)
INGREDIENTS

1 pack of spices (see NOTE)
1 inch piece fresh gingerroot, sliced
2½ cups water
10 oz. beef or pork liver
1 tablespoon sesame oil

SEASONING

3 tablespoons light soy sauce
2 tablespoons rice wine or dry sherry
1 tablespoon rock sugar (see NOTE p. 114)
1 teaspoon salt
½ teaspoon white pepper

Wrap the spices and the sliced ginger in a piece of unbleached muslin, knotting the end.

Place the water in a saucepan, bring to a boil, add the spice pack and boil for 30 minutes.

Add the liver along with all the seasoning ingredients. Bring to a boil and then lower the heat, cover and simmer gently for 40 minutes. Off heat, let stand, covered, for 10 minutes.

Remove the liver and brush with the sesame oil. Let cool and then slice thinly. Serve with a salad.

NOTE

A pack of spices is a common provision at Oriental markets. It contains licorice, five-spice powder, star anise, dried orange peel, fennel and cinnamon.

滷牛腱

Spiced Brisket

(SERVES 6)
INGREDIENTS

1 lb. boneless beef brisket
1 pack of spices (see NOTE above)
5 cups water

SEASONING

¼ cup dark soy sauce
1 tablespoon rock sugar (see NOTE p. 114)
3 tablespoons rice wine or dry sherry
pinch of salt
pinch of white pepper

Rinse the piece of meat and then scald in boiling water for 2 minutes.

Wrap the pack of spices in a piece of unbleached muslin, knotting the end. Bring the water to a boil in a large saucepan. Add the spice package and boil for 30 minutes.

Add the meat to the liquid and bring back to a boil. Lower the heat, cover and simmer for 1½ hours. Off heat, set the pan aside, covered, for 20 minutes.

Remove the meat, reserving the cooking liquid, and slice thinly. Discard the spice package.

Place the seasoning ingredients in a large skillet. Add ½ cup of the reserved liquid and bring to a boil. Add the slices of brisket and simmer until the liquid has evaporated and the pan is almost dry. Serve.

素釀青椒

Stuffed Green Peppers

(SERVES 4)
INGREDIENTS

4 small green peppers
1 tablespoon cornstarch
⅓ cup corn oil
¾ cup clear soup stock (see p. 261)

STUFFING
1 cup ground pork
1 egg white, lightly beaten
2 teaspoons sesame oil
2 tablespoons cornstarch
3 tablespoons minced water chestnuts
1 tablespoon shredded carrot
1 scallion, chopped

SEASONING
½ teaspoon salt
2 tablespoons soy sauce
1 tablespoon sugar

Wash the green peppers and pat dry with paper towels. Cut in half lengthwise, and remove the seeds and core. Sprinkle the inner surface of the peppers with the cornstarch.

Mix the stuffing ingredients thoroughly.

Stuff the pork mixture in each pepper as tightly as possible.

Heat a wok or skillet with the oil, and cook the peppers, stuffing side down, for 2 minutes. Turn the peppers over and cook for a further 1 minute.

Mix the seasoning ingredients and add to the pan, shaking the pan carefully to ensure the seasoning is evenly distributed. Continue cooking for 1 more minute.

Pour in the soup stock, cover and simmer for 5-8 minutes.

Arrange on a serving dish and serve. Pineapple cubes may be used as a garnish, if wished.

Quick Fried Chicken and Pork

(SERVES 4)

INGREDIENTS

12 Chinese dried
    mushrooms, optional
¼ lb. boneless chicken
    breasts, skinned
¼ lb. lean pork
1 egg white
2 teaspoons cornstarch
¼ cup corn oil
3 tablespoons chicken stock
    (see p. 149)
carrot and bamboo shoot
    slices, for garnish

SEASONING

2 garlic cloves, crushed
1½ teaspoons rice wine or
    dry sherry
1 tablespoon light soy sauce
½ teaspoon sugar
1 teaspoon salt

Place the mushrooms in a bowl, cover with warm water and let soak for 30 minutes. Drain; remove stems and squeeze out excess liquid.

Cut the chicken and pork into bite-size pieces. Place in 2 bowls. Beat the egg white with 1 teaspoon cornstarch, add to chicken and pork.

Heat 2 tablespoons of oil in a wok and add the chicken. Stir-fry vigorously for 4 minutes and remove. To the oil remaining in the wok, add the mushrooms. Stir-fry for 2 minutes and reserve for garnish.

Add another 1 tablespoon oil to the wok, heat and add the pork. Stir-fry for 7-8 minutes or until cooked through. Push the pork up the sides of the wok, add the remaining oil to the center. Add the chicken and cook for 30 seconds, and then stir in with the pork.

Blend the remaining cornstarch with a little cold water, stir in the chicken stock and the seasoning ingredients. Stir into the chicken and pork and bring to a boil, stirring. Cook until slightly thickened and then spoon onto a serving platter. Garnish with the mushrooms, sliced carrots and bamboo shoots.

胡蘿蔔燜牛肉

Stewed Beef with Carrots

(SERVES 4)
INGREDIENTS

1½ lb. beef chuck
2-3 carrots
1 piece of dried orange peel,
   soaked (see NOTE)
1 scallion, chopped
1 tablespoon grated fresh
   gingerroot
2 star anise
2 cups water

SEASONING

3 tablespoons soy sauce
¼ teaspoon salt
1 tablespoon rice wine or
   dry sherry

Cut the beef in 2 inch cubes. Place in boiling water and scald for 1 minute, then remove with a slotted spoon and rinse again.

Peel the carrots and cut them in chunks. Drain and rinse the dried orange peel.

Place all the ingredients, including the seasoning ingredients, in a saucepan with the water, cover and bring to a boil. Lower the heat and simmer for 1-1½ hours or until the meat is tender. Add more water, if necessary, while the meat is cooking. Serve at once.

NOTE
The orange peel should be soaked in warm water for 20 minutes before using.

羅漢果燉牛肉丸湯

Stewed Beef Balls

(SERVES 4)
INGREDIENTS

1¼ lb. lean ground beef
1 onion, quartered
5 cups clear soup stock (see
   p. 261)
2 teaspoons sugar

SEASONING A
½ teaspoon white pepper
1 teaspoon chopped scallion
½ teaspoon dried orange
   peel, soaked (see NOTE
   above)
¼ teaspoon salt
1 tablespoon ginger wine
   (see Glossary)
2 tablespoons cornstarch
½ teaspoon five-spice
   powder

SEASONING B
¾ teaspoon salt
½ teaspoon rice wine or dry
   sherry

Mix the beef with seasoning **A** and marinate for 30 minutes. Form into balls about 1½ inches in diameter.

Place the meat balls, onion, soup stock, sugar and seasoning **B** in a saucepan or wok. Cover and bring to a boil. Lower the heat and simmer for 1½ hours, adding more water if necessary during cooking. Serve immediately.

鶏肝串烤

Roasted Pork and Chicken Liver Rolls

(SERVES 4)
INGREDIENTS

½ lb. chicken livers
¾ lb. pork tenderloin
¼ cup corn oil

SEASONING A
1 tablespoon plum sauce
pinch of salt

SEASONING B
1 tablespoon Hoisin or
   barbecue sauce
1 tablespoon light soy sauce
1 tablespoon ginger wine
   (see Glossary)
2 teaspoons sugar
½ teaspoon salt
½ teaspoon white pepper

Rinse and trim the chicken livers. Pat dry and cut in thin slices. Mix seasoning **A** in a bowl, add the chicken livers and marinate for 30 minutes.

Slice the pork in strips about ½ × 3 inches. Mix seasoning **B**, add the pork and marinate for 30 minutes.

Place slices of chicken liver inside the slices of pork. Roll up and secure with a wooden cocktail pick.

Heat half the oil in a wok. Add the pork and chicken liver rolls and cook gently, for 4 minutes. Turn the rolls over, add the remaining oil and cook for a further 4 minutes.

Remove and serve immediately.

洋葱十錦

Assorted Shreds

(SERVES 4)
INGREDIENTS

¼ cup corn oil
¼ lb. lean pork, cut in thin
   strips
1 carrot, cut in thin strips
2 inch piece dried bean curd,
   cut in thin strips
½ sweet red pepper, seeded
   and cut in thin strips
½ green pepper, seeded and
   cut in thin strips
1 onion, cut in thin rings

SEASONING
1 teaspoon salt
½ teaspoon white pepper
1 teaspoon sugar

Heat the oil in a wok. Stir-fry the pork strips for 5 minutes, add the carrot, bean curd and sweet red and green pepper and stir-fry for 2 minutes.

Add the onion and seasoning ingredients and cook for a further 3-4 minutes or until the vegetables are tender but still crisp. Serve at once.

Bird's Nest Chicken

(SERVES 4)
INGREDIENTS

¾ lb. boneless chicken
   breasts, skinned
2 large potatoes
1 cup cornstarch
½ teaspoon salt
corn oil, for deep-fat frying
2 scallions, chopped
1 tablespoon finely grated
   fresh gingerroot
10 straw mushrooms
   (see NOTE)
1 small green pepper, seeded
   and chopped
¼ cup chopped water
   chestnuts,
1 carrot, diced

SEASONING A
1 egg white
1½ tablespoons cornstarch
1 tablespoon light soy sauce

SEASONING B
2 tablespoons light soy sauce
1 tablespoon rice wine or
   dry sherry
1½ teaspoons cornstarch
pinch of salt
pinch of sugar
½ teaspoon sesame oil

Dice the chicken and marinate in seasoning **A** for 30 minutes.

Cut the potatoes into very, very fine strips (alternatively grate the potatoes coarsely). Rinse in cold water and pat dry thoroughly.

Mix the potato with the cornstarch and salt and spread this mixture around the inside of a large colander or wire net basket. Place a slightly smaller colander inside, so that the potato mixture is pressed between the two wire frames.

Take a large deep-fat fryer, large enough to take the "potato" basket, and add sufficient oil to come about halfway up the fryer. Do not overfill as the oil will bubble up.

Heat the oil, and when hot, lower the "potato" basket into the oil and deep fry until the potato turns golden-brown. Drain thoroughly and gently ease the baskets apart, so that you are left with a potato nest.

Heat 3 tablespoons of oil in a wok and add the mushrooms and the prepared vegetables. Stir-fry for 3 minutes and add the marinated chicken and seasoning **B.**

Cook for a few minutes until the mixture thickens and is hot and bubbly and then pour into the potato nest. Serve at once.

NOTE
Straw mushrooms are available in 10 oz. cans and are sold at most Oriental markets. Button mushrooms can be substituted if liked.

Deep-Fried Chicken with Straw Mushrooms

(SERVES 4-6)
INGREDIENTS

1 broiler-fryer (about 3 lb.)
3 tablespoons all-purpose
　flour
¼ cup cornstarch
corn oil, for deep frying
2 cans (16-oz size) straw
　mushrooms (see NOTE on
　p. 133)
2 tablespoons corn oil
1 teaspoon salt
¼ cup water
shrimp crackers, for garnish

SEASONING
4 tablespoons soy sauce
2 tablespoons rice wine or dry
　sherry
2 teaspoons sugar

Cut the chicken in 1 inch cubes. Mix the
seasoning ingredients in a bowl. Add the chicken
pieces and marinate for 3 hours. Drain.

Mix the all-purpose flour and 2 tablespoons of the
cornstarch in a large bowl. Add the chicken pieces
and toss to coat lightly.

Heat the oil in a deep-fat fryer and deep-fry the
chicken pieces for 5 minutes. Remove the chicken and
drain. Arrange on a serving dish.

Drain the straw mushrooms, rinse in cold water
and pat dry with paper towels.

Heat 2 tablespoons oil in a wok or skillet, add the
straw mushrooms and stir-fry for 1 minute. Add the
salt.

Mix the remaining 2 tablespoons cornstarch with
the water, and add to the straw mushrooms. Heat
until slightly thickened, stirring all the time, then pour
over the chicken.

Garnish with the shrimp crackers.

Braised Chicken with Chestnuts

(SERVES 4)
INGREDIENTS

½ lb. boneless chicken
   breasts, skinned
2 tablespoons corn oil
½ inch piece fresh
   gingerroot, sliced
½ cup chicken stock (see
   p. 149)
⅔ cup dried chestnuts,
   soaked (see NOTE)

SEASONING A
2 tablespoons light soy sauce
1 teaspoon sugar

SEASONING B
3 tablespoons dark soy sauce
1 teaspoon rice wine or dry
   sherry
½ teaspoon salt
1 teaspoon sugar

Cut the chicken in large bite-size pieces and
marinate in seasoning **A** for 30 minutes.
   Heat the oil in a wok, add the ginger and stir-fry for
20 seconds.
   Add the marinated chicken and stir-fry for 10
seconds. Stir in seasoning **B** along with the chicken
stock. Cover and simmer over a low heat for 10
minutes.
   Add the soaked chestnuts and continue to simmer
for 30 minutes. Spoon onto a serving platter and serve
at once.

NOTE
Dried chestnuts should be soaked in cold water for 24
hours before using.

醤豬排

Saucy Pork Chops

(SERVES 4)
INGREDIENTS

1¼ lb. pork loin chops
¼ cup corn oil
1 scallion, minced

SEASONING
3 tablespoons black bean
 sauce
1 tablespoon sugar
1¼ teaspoons salt
3 tablespoons soy sauce
½ tablespoon rock sugar (see
 NOTE)
1 tablespoon ginger wine
 (see Glossary)
1 cup water

Tenderize the pork chops by beating them with a meat pounder or heavy rolling pin.

Heat the oil in a wok or skillet, add the scallion and stir-fry for 2 minutes. Add the seasoning ingredients with the water, and bring to a boil. Boil for 1 minute.

Place the pork chops in the wok or skillet, and bring back to a boil over a medium-low heat. Lower the heat slightly and simmer for 3 minutes, then lower the heat to a low simmer, cover and cook for a further 20-25 minutes or until the pork is tender. Serve at once.

NOTE
Rock sugar is available from Chinese delicatessens, but amber coffee sugar crystals or turbinado sugar could be substituted.

糟香豬排

Red-Spiced Spareribs

(SERVES 4)
INGREDIENTS

1¾ lb. pork spareribs (see
 NOTE)
¼ cup corn oil
3 garlic cloves, crushed
1 scallion flower, for garnish
 (see p. 82)

SEASONING
2 tablespoons red bean sauce
 (see NOTE p. 61)
1 tablespoon sugar
1 tablespoon rice wine or dry
 sherry
3 tablespoons water

Cut the spareribs in 1 inch pieces using a meat cleaver or heavy knife.

Mix the seasoning ingredients in a bowl with the water, add the pork pieces and marinate for 30 minutes. Drain.

Heat the oil in a wok or skillet. Add the chopped garlic, and stir-fry over high heat for a few seconds. Add the spareribs, and stir-fry for 2-3 minutes until lightly browned. Reduce the heat, cover and simmer for 6 minutes. Remove the lid, increase the heat slightly and stir-fry for 3 minutes. Garnish with a scallion flower, and serve.

NOTE
Be sure to ask your butcher for Chinese-style spareribs, rather than the American country-style ribs which are a slightly different cut.

Cold Spicy Diced Chicken

(SERVES 4)
INGREDIENTS

2 boneless chicken breasts,
  skinned
6 dried bean curd sheets
¾ cup roasted cashews
⅔ cup broccoli flowerets
carrot flowers, for garnish

SEASONING
1 tablespoon soy sauce
1 teaspoon sugar
1 tablespoon hot chili oil
½ teaspoon Szechuan
  peppercorns, crushed
1 teaspoon sesame paste
1 teaspoon sesame oil
¼ teaspoon salt

Place the chicken breasts in a shallow pan, cover with boiling water, and poach gently for about 10 minutes or until they are cooked. Drain and cool thoroughly. Cut in small cubes.

Soak the dried bean curd sheets in cold water for 30 minutes until soft. Drain and then pat dry. Cut in small pieces and mix with the diced chicken. Stir in the cashews.

Mix the seasoning ingredients in a bowl, and add to the chicken mixture, stirring thoroughly.

Place the broccoli flowerets in a large bowl. Cover with boiling water and blanch for 3 minutes. Drain.

Arrange the broccoli around the outside of a serving dish, and pile the chicken mixture in the center.

Garnish with carrot flowers and serve.

Shredded Cold Chicken with Hot Sauce

(SERVES 4)
INGREDIENTS

¾ lb. boneless chicken
  breast, skinned
lettuce leaves, orange slices,
  cherry tomatoes and
  parsley sprigs, for garnish

SEASONING
1½ teaspoons sugar
1 tablespoon salt
2 tablespoons sesame paste
2 tablespoons hot prepared
  mustard
4 cloves garlic, crushed

Place the chicken in a steamer or large colander.
Put 2 inches boiling water in a large saucepan. Set the
chicken over the saucepan, cover and steam for 30
minutes. Remove the chicken from the steamer and
let cool.

When it is cool enough to handle, shred in long,
thin pieces, and arrange on a serving dish.

Mix the seasoning ingredients in a bowl, adding a
little water or chicken stock to thin, if necessary. Pour
over the chicken, or serve as a dipping sauce along
with the chicken. Serve with lettuce, orange slices,
parsley sprigs and cherry tomatoes.

煎牛肉碎餅

Chinese-Style Beef Patties

(SERVES 4)
INGREDIENTS

1¼ lb. lean beef, roughly
   chopped
1 piece (about 2 oz.) pork fat
1 small carrot, roughly
   chopped
1 celery stalk, chopped
½ small onion, chopped
1½ teaspoons chopped dried
   orange peel, soaked (see
   NOTE)
¼ cup corn oil

SEASONING
½ teaspoon salt
½ teaspoon black pepper
1 tablespoon ginger wine
   (see Glossary)
1½ teaspoons sugar
1 tablespoon oil
1 tablespoon cornstarch

Place the beef, pork fat, carrot, celery, onion,
orange peel and the seasoning ingredients in a food
processor and grind to make a smooth paste.

Divide the mixture equally in eight balls, and form
into patties, compressing them with your hands.

Heat the oil in a wok or skillet and cook the patties
over a medium heat until both sides are well browned.

NOTE
Soak the dried orange peel in warm water for 20
minutes before using.

咖哩牛腩

Chinese Curried Beef

(SERVES 4)
INGREDIENTS

1¼ lb. beef fore shank
1 scallion plus 1 tablespoon
   chopped scallion bulb
1 tablespoon grated fresh
   gingerroot
2 star anise
¼ cup corn oil
½ onion, sliced
2-3 teaspoons Chinese curry
   powder (see NOTE)
½ tablespoon chopped
   sweet red pepper
1½ teaspoons salt
1 tablespoon rice wine or dry
   sherry
1 tablespoon sugar
⅞ cup milk
2 tablespoons cornstarch
2 tablespoons water

Cut the beef in large pieces.

Immerse the beef in boiling water for 1 minute,
drain and pat dry with paper towels.

Put the beef, whole scallion, grated ginger and star
anise in a pan and just cover with water. Bring to a
boil, lower the heat and simmer very gently
uncovered, for 2-2½ hours, or until the meat is tender.
(The juice remaining in the pan when the cooking is
completed should be no more than ½ cup.)

Heat a wok or skillet with the oil. Add the chopped
scallion bulb and stir-fry for 1 minute. Add the onion,
curry powder and chopped sweet red pepper, and
stir-fry for 2 minutes.

Add the beef with the juice from the pan, along
with the salt, rice wine, sugar and milk. Simmer for
1 minute. Remove from the heat. Mix the cornstarch
with the water and add to the meat mixture. Return to
the heat and bring back to a boil, stirring constantly.
Serve.

NOTE
Be sure to use Chinese curry powder – not an Indian
one. Chinese curry powder can be bought from
Oriental markets.

滷鷄腿
Spiced Chicken Legs

(SERVES 4)
INGREDIENTS

5 cups water
6 scallions, cut in ½ inch
    sections
4 chicken legs
Maraschino cherries and
    parsley sprigs, for garnish

SEASONING
½ inch piece of fresh
    gingerroot, cut in thin
    slices
1 pack of spices containing
    star anise, chili pepper,
    fennel and cinnamon
⅓ cup soy sauce
1 teaspoon salt
1½ tablespoons rock sugar

Place the water in a saucepan. Add the scallions and the seasoning ingredients and bring to a boil. Boil for 30 minutes.

Rinse the chicken legs, and add to the saucepan. Cook over a medium heat for 10 minutes, and then remove the pan from the heat.

Leave the chicken in the liquid for 5 minutes and then arrange on a serving dish. Garnish with parsley sprigs and Maraschino cherries and serve.

蔴醬鷄絲
Chicken Shreds with Sesame Paste

(SERVES 4)
INGREDIENTS

2 cooked chicken legs or 2
    cooked chicken breasts
2 inch piece agar-agar (about
    ¾ oz. in weight) (see
    NOTE)
½ cup water
1 small cucumber, cut in thin
    strips
Maraschino cherry, for
    garnish

SEASONING
2 tablespoons sesame paste
    (see NOTE on p. 81)
1 tablespoon chili oil
1 tablespoon soy sauce
¾ teaspoon salt
2 tablespoons sesame oil

Using your fingers, tear the chicken meat in shreds.

Soak the agar-agar in warm water for 5 minutes, and then tear in pieces with your fingers and squeeze dry.

Mix the seasoning ingredients together in a bowl with the water.

Arrange the cucumber strips on a serving dish, and place the shredded agar-agar and chicken on top. Pour the seasoning over the top, garnish with a Maraschino cherry and serve.

NOTE
If fresh agar-agar is unobtainable it might be possible to buy the dried variety which comes in strips. If this too is unavailable, it's still possible to follow this recipe, but without the agar-agar garnish.

143

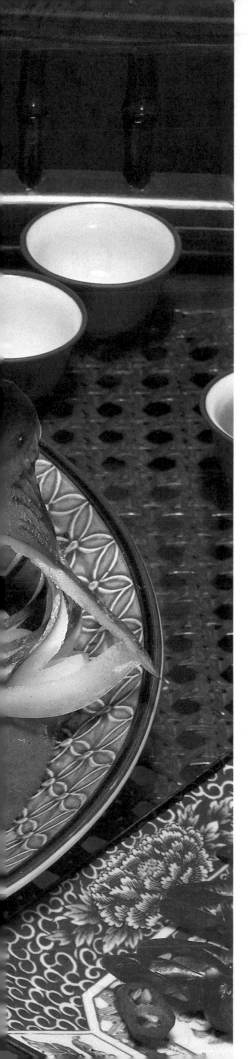

Chinese Curried Chicken

(SERVES 4)
INGREDIENTS

2 large chicken legs
¼ cup corn oil plus oil for
   deep frying
1 tablespoon chopped
   scallion bulb
½ tablespoon grated fresh
   gingerroot
1 garlic clove, chopped
2 chili peppers, seeded and
   minced or 1 tablespoon
   cayenne
1 small onion, cut in wedges
3-5 tablespoons Chinese
   curry powder (see NOTE)
1 large carrot, cut in large
   cubes
1 large potato, cut in large
   cubes
1 cup milk
1 cup water

SEASONING

1½ teaspoons salt
1 tablespoon sugar
1 tablespoon rice wine or
   sherry

Using a cleaver or meat ax, cut the chicken in bite-size pieces.

Heat the ¼ cup of oil in a wok or skillet. Add the chopped scallion, ginger, garlic and chili peppers or cayenne and cook for a few seconds.

Add the onion and stir-fry for 3 minutes. Add the curry powder and stir well.

Add the chicken pieces, and stir-fry over a medium-high heat for 3 minutes. Lower the heat, cover and simmer gently for 10 minutes, turning the chicken pieces over occasionally.

Heat the oil in a deep-fat fryer. When the oil is very hot, add the cubed carrot and potato. Deep-fry for about 3 minutes, or until they are browned. Remove with a slotted spoon and drain.

Add the carrots and potatoes to the pan with the chicken and continue simmering for a further 5-10 minutes, until almost dry.

Add the milk, water and all the seasoning ingredients. Bring to a boil, lower the heat and simmer, uncovered for 3-5 minutes, turning the chicken pieces occasionally.

NOTE
Use Chinese curry powder for this recipe – available from most Oriental markets.

糟 味 鶏 塊

Chicken with Red Fermented Sauce

(SERVES 4)
INGREDIENTS

6 chicken wings
¼ cup corn oil
½ tablespoon grated fresh
   gingerroot
celery tops, for garnish
1½ cups water

SEASONING
1 tablespoon red bean sauce
1 tablespoon rice wine or dry
   sherry
1 tablespoon sugar

Using a cleaver or meat ax, cut the chicken wings in large pieces.
   Mix the seasoning ingredients in a bowl with 1 cup of the water. Add the chicken and marinate for 30 minutes. Drain.
   Heat the oil in a wok or skillet, add the ginger and stir-fry over a high heat for 10 seconds.
   Add the chicken, and stir-fry for 1 minute. Add remaining water. Lower the heat to medium-low, cover and simmer for 5 minutes, stirring occasionally. Garnish with celery tops, and serve.

豉 汁 鶏 球

Steamed Chicken with Black Beans

(SERVES 4)
INGREDIENTS

2 small boneless chicken
   breasts

SEASONING
1 tablespoon fermented
   black beans (see NOTE)
2 teaspoons cornstarch
1 tablespoon water
½ tablespoon chopped garlic
1 teaspoon sugar
1 teaspoon salt
1 tablespoon sesame oil
1 tablespoon rice wine or dry
   sherry

Using a cleaver or meat ax, cut the chicken in large pieces.
   Rinse the black beans, and crush them lightly with the back of a heavy knife.
   Mix the cornstarch with the water then stir in the remaining seasoning ingredients. Add the crushed beans and mix well. Add the chicken, stirring thoroughly, and marinate for 20 minutes.
   Place the chicken on a heatproof plate, and set inside a steamer or large colander. Place 2 inches boiling water in a large saucepan. Set the steamer over the saucepan, cover with a tight-fitting lid and steam for 5 minutes over a high heat. Serve.

NOTE
Fermented black beans, also called salted beans, are available from Oriental groceries. They are fermented with salt and spices in order to preserve them, and are very salty. They should be soaked or rinsed in cold water before use.

Simmered Cornish Hens

(SERVES 4)
INGREDIENTS

2 Rock Cornish game hens
2 tablespoons soy sauce
½ lb. spinach
⅔ cup sesame oil
1 slice fresh gingerroot
2 scallions, halved
½ teaspoon Szechuan
   pepper
1 tablespoon sugar
¾ teaspoon salt
2 cups boiling water
3 tablespoons corn oil

Place the Cornish hens in a large bowl, pour the soy sauce over the top and marinate for 30 minutes. Drain, reserving the soy sauce.

Wash and drain the spinach.

Heat the oil in a wok or skillet and sauté the Cornish hens, browning them on all sides. Remove and place in a Dutch oven.

Add the reserved soy sauce, ginger, scallions, Szechuan pepper, sugar, ½ teaspoon salt and boiling water to the Cornish hens. Bring to a boil. Simmer, covered, over a very low heat for 2 hours.

Heat a wok or skillet with the corn oil, and sprinkle in the remaining ¼ teaspoon salt. Add the spinach, and stir fry for 1-2 minutes. Remove from the pan and arrange around the Cornish hens. Serve.

Chicken Stock

INGREDIENTS

1¼ lb. uncooked chicken
  bones, eg legs, wings,
  carcass etc.
  (see NOTE) .
5 cups cold water
6 slices fresh gingerroot
4 scallions, trimmed but left
  whole

Place the chicken bones in a large pan, add boiling water to cover and boil for 5 minutes. Drain off the water.

Add the cold water along with the ginger and scallions. Bring to a boil slowly then lower the heat and simmer over a low heat for 1 hour.

Press the stock through a fine strainer. Use right away or keep refrigerated for up to 3 days. The stock can also be frozen for up to 6 months.

NOTE

Cooked chicken bones also make a fine stock. Place in a pan, then follow the above recipe from Step 2. Alternatively, use 1 chicken bouillon cube to every cup of liquid.

Chopping Meat

Where large pieces of chicken are required, cut in ½ × 2 inch strips.

Use a chopper or heavy knife to cut chicken in small ½ inch cubes.

For cutlets, beat the meat firmly with the back of a meat mallet or heavy rolling pin.

For ultra-quick stir-frying, finely shred chicken in thin strips.

To grind chicken coarsely, cut in fine strips and then roughly chop.

To grind chicken finely, chop as for coarsely ground chicken, but re-chop several more times.

VEGETABLES AND SALADS

A large percentage of Chinese people are vegetarian – some through necessity, because meat and fish are scarce and thus expensive, some through choice, because of their religion, Buddhism. The Chinese vegetarian diet is in fact extremely healthy, since a huge range of vegetables is grown in China and protein is provided through the popular Chinese ingredient, bean curd.

The vegetables of China are the key to the exotic tastes and textures that make Chinese meals so unique and delicious. Taros (dasheens), fresh bamboo shoots, water chestnuts and the huge variety of Chinese cabbages and greens are just some of the exciting vegetables used frequently in Chinese cooking. Mushrooms and fungi, which add not only a delicate flavor, but more important still, a distinct texture to a meal, are also extremely important in Chinese cooking, as are the various seaweeds, like black moss and laver, which add a slightly glutinous texture and a faint "sea" flavor to a dish.

Flexibility is one of the marks of Chinese cookery and Chinese cooks will always use fresh ingredients to hand. Consequently, when a recipe calls for a fresh vegetable that is unavailable, the cook will not hesitate to replace the specified vegetable with another fresh ingredient, in order to retain the essential freshness of the dish. This attitude is helpful for the Western cook, since many common vegetables can be substituted for the rarer Chinese varieties. For instance, sweet potatoes can be used instead of taros (dasheens), while collard greens can be used in place of Chinese broccoli. When it comes to cooking Chinese vegetables, a little ingenuity in the true Chinese tradition, will give you greater scope and much more variety.

素釀大黃瓜
Stuffed Cucumber

(SERVES 4)
INGREDIENTS

6 Chinese mushrooms
1 large cucumber
1 tablespoon cornstarch
⅓ cup water chestnuts
1 small carrot
½ a salted cabbage root
1 bean curd
⅓ cup corn oil
1½ teaspoons sesame oil
5 cups clear soup stock (see p. 261)

SEASONING A
⅔ teaspoon salt
½ teaspoon dry mustard
1 tablespoon cornstarch
1 egg white

SEASONING B
1 teaspoon salt
½ teaspoon white pepper

Soak the Chinese mushrooms in boiling water for 20 minutes. Drain. Cut off and discard the stems.

Cut off and discard the end parts of the cucumber. Peel and chop in 1-inch rounds. Scoop out the seeds. Wash the cucumber rings and wipe dry on paper towels. Dust the inside with the cornstarch.

Peel the water chestnuts and carrot. Remove outer pieces of cabbage root. Wash all these ingredients then mince them, along with the Chinese mushrooms.

Blanch the bean curd in boiling water for 3 minutes. Mash it and drain off the water. Mix with the chopped ingredients, together with seasoning **A**. Combine everything thoroughly.

Heat the oil in a wok and stir-fry the mixture for 2 minutes. Pack into the cucumber rings.

Tip the oil from the wok into a skillet and sauté the stuffed cucumber rings over medium heat until lightly browned. Pour the soup stock over them and bring to a boil. Lower the heat and simmer very gently for 20 minutes. Add seasoning **B** and the sesame oil. Transfer to a serving dish and serve.

釀金錢
Stuffed Chinese Mushrooms

(SERVES 4)
INGREDIENTS

16-20 large Chinese mushrooms
1 tablespoon cornstarch
1 bean curd
2 tablespoons water chestnuts
1 small carrot
¼ a salted vegetable
½ cup corn oil
16-20 green beans

SEASONING A
½ teaspoon white pepper
½ teaspoon salt
1 teaspoon sugar
1 tablespoon cornstarch

SEASONING B
1½ tablespoons light soy sauce
1 teaspoon sugar
3 tablespoons clear soup stock (see p. 261)
⅓ teaspoon salt

Soak the Chinese mushrooms in boiling water for 20 minutes. Drain. Cut off and discard the stems, then coat the inner sides with the cornstarch.

Wash the bean curd, water chestnuts, carrot and salted vegetable. Peel the water chestnuts and the carrot, then mince all the vegetables and mix them together with seasoning **A**.

Heat ¼ cup of the oil in a wok and stir-fry the chopped ingredients for 1½ minutes. Remove from the oil with a slotted spoon.

Divide the stuffing among the mushrooms, pressing them firmly. Wash the beans and cook in boiling water for 2-3 minutes. Press one into the top of each stuffed mushroom.

Pour the oil from the wok into a large skillet. Put the mushrooms into the pan, stuffing side down in a single layer. Cook for a few minutes, then turn over carefully. Add seasoning **B**, bring to the simmering point and simmer, covered, for 1 minute. Serve.

菇香菜糗

Broth of Mushrooms and Cabbage

(SERVES 4)
INGREDIENTS

5-6 Chinese mushrooms
1 small cabbage
2 bunches (about ¼ lb.) long-
  stem mushrooms
1 tablespoon shredded
  preserved vegetable
¼ cup corn oil
1 tablespoon minced scallion
4 cups clear soup stock (see
  p. 261)
2 tablespoons cornstarch
  mixed with 2½
  tablespoons water

SEASONING

1⅓ teaspoons salt
1 teaspoon sugar
⅔ teaspoon white pepper

Soak the Chinese mushrooms in boiling water for
20 minutes. Drain. Cut off and discard the stems and
shred the caps.

Cut off and discard the root and any withered
leaves from the cabbage. Shred the remainder and
wash. Cut off and discard the muddy roots from the
long-stem mushrooms and wash clean. Wash the
shredded preserved vegetables.

Heat the oil in a wok and stir-fry the Chinese
mushroom and the scallion for 2 minutes. Add the
shredded cabbage and the seasoning and stir for 1
minute. Add the stock, bring to a boil, lower the heat
and simmer, covered until the cabbage is tender –
about 10 minutes. Add the long-stem mushrooms and
cook, stirring, for 1 minute more.

Stir in the cornstarch mixture and cook until the
mixture thickens. Wash the shredded preserved
vegetables and sprinkle this over the surface of the
broth. Serve.

永结同心

Black Moss with Vegetables and Dried Bean Curd Knots

(SERVES 4)
INGREDIENTS

1 tablespoon black moss
1 carrot
¼ cup corn oil
1 tablespoon minced scallion
¼ lb. dried bean curd knots
  (see NOTES)
¼ teaspoon baking soda
⅔ cup clear soup stock (see
  p. 261)
10 straw mushrooms
1 tablespoon cornstarch
  mixed with 2 tablespoons
  water

SEASONING

1 teaspoon salt
1 teaspoon sugar
½ teaspoon white pepper

Soak the black moss in water for 10 minutes. Drain.
Peel the carrot and dice.

Heat the oil in a wok and stir-fry the scallion until
beginning to brown. Add the bean curd knots, baking
soda and the soup stock and bring to a boil. Boil for 3
minutes.

Add the seasoning, straw mushrooms, drained
black moss and diced carrot and cook for 2 minutes
more. Stir in the cornstarch mixture and cook until the
sauce thickens. Serve at once.

NOTES

To make bean curd knots, soak bean curd sheets in
cold water until soft. Pat dry in a clean cloth and cut in
4 × 1-inch strips. Tie in knots and drop back into cold
water for 5 minutes more, (see small picture 3, right).

Add 1 sliced, large white turnip to make the dish
more substantial.

圍園春濃

Cream of Green Peas

(SERVES 4)
INGREDIENTS

1 can (16 oz) green sweet
   peas, drained
1 tomato
8 button mushrooms
6 tablespoons whole kernel
   corn
1 cup clear soup stock (see p.
   261)
1 cup milk
2½ tablespoons cornstarch
1½ tablespoons light cream
2-3 grains orange comfit

SEASONING
1½ teaspoons salt
⅓ teaspoon white pepper

Purée the drained peas. Wash the tomato and chop. Wash the button mushrooms and dice. Wash the kernel corn.

Mix these ingredients with the drained green peas and the soup stock in a saucepan. Bring to a boil over a medium heat, lower the heat and simmer for a few minutes, stirring. Stir in the milk and the seasoning.

Mix the cornstarch with the cream and stir into the pea mixture. Simmer for 3 minutes, stirring all the time to keep the mixture thick and creamy.

Chop the orange comfit and sprinkle it over the soup.

NOTE
Substitute ¼ cup chopped almonds for the orange comfit.

鳳 梨 盡

Pineapple Cup

(SERVES 4)
INGREDIENTS

1 large fresh pineapple
¼ lb gluten puff
10 baby corn cobs
¼ cup water chestnuts
⅓ cup green beans
1 piece (about 3 oz) taro
   (dasheen)
1 tablespoon corn oil
2½ cups clear soup stock
   (see p. 261)

(see p. 261)

SEASONING
1½ teaspoons salt
½ tablespoon sugar
½ teaspoon white pepper

Scrub the pineapple and cut off the tuft to make a lid. Scoop out the pulp, taking care not to pierce through the skin. Place the pineapple container in a large pan of water and bring to a boil, lower the heat and simmer for 3 minutes, then remove the pineapple and rinse it under cold water.

Soak the gluten puff in cold water for 20 minutes. Chop roughly.

Wash the baby corn cobs and chop in half. Peel the water chestnuts and wash them along with the green beans. Chop taro in pieces and stir-fry in the oil for 3-4 minutes.

Put the gluten puff, corn, water chestnuts, green beans, fried taro, soup stock and seasoning into the pineapple cup. Place in a dish and put this into a steamer. Steam over boiling water for 30 minutes. Serve at once with pineapple tuft as lid.

鉄板豆腐

Bean Curds with Onions

(SERVES 4)
INGREDIENTS

3 cakes bean curds
1 onion
3 red chili peppers
4 garlic cloves, crushed
2 tablespoons Hoisin sauce
¼ cup corn oil
1 tablespoon cornstarch
    mixed with 2 tablespoons
    water
3 scallions

SEASONING A
1½ teaspoons salt
1 tablespoon soy sauce
½ tablespoon sugar
3 tablespoons clear soup
    stock (see p. 261)

SEASONING B
½ tablespoon dry sherry
½ tablespoon vinegar
1 teaspoon black pepper

Put the bean curds into a saucepan and cover with water. Bring to a boil over a medium heat for 3-5 minutes. Then drain and cut in 1-inch cubes.

Peel the onion and cut off the ends. Slice thinly. Wash the chili peppers and mince them.

Blend seasoning **A** with the chopped chilis, crushed garlic and Hoisin sauce. Heat the oil in a wok and stir-fry this mixture for a few seconds, then add the bean curd cubes. Stir over a medium heat until they are well coated with the sauce, then lower the heat and simmer, covered, for 5-10 minutes.

Remove the lid and add the sliced onion and seasoning **B**. Increase the heat and cook, stirring, for 1½ minutes.

Stir in the cornstarch mixture to thicken and serve sprinkled with the scallion cut in diagonal slices.

NOTE
If you have an iron plate, heat it until it is very hot and serve this dish on it. The ingredients should "hiss" as you spoon them onto the iron plate.

Congee of Green Beans

(SERVES 4)
INGREDIENTS

1 cup green beans
3 tablespoons millet
4 cups water

SEASONING
1 teapoon salt
¼ cup sugar

Wash the green beans and millet. Drain well.
Bring the water to a boil and add the beans and millet. Lower the heat and simmer until the mixture has thickened – about 1 hour. Stir in the seasoning and serve at once.

NOTE
Green beans can be used to make a drink which is said to relieve hypertension. Wash a good handful and put into a thermos pitcher. Pour in boiing water, screw on the lid and leave for 15 minutes. Strain and drink the liquid.

Soup of Lily Petals with Lotus Seeds

(SERVES 4)
INGREDIENTS

1 cup dried lily (or about ¼ lb. fresh)
2 cups dried lotus seeds (or ½ lb. fresh)
4 cups water
¼ cup powdered rock sugar (see NOTE p. 114)

Soak dried lily overnight, then wash under cold running water. (If using fresh, just wash.)
Soak dried lotus seeds in cold water for 4 hours, then wash under cold running water. (If using fresh, just wash.)
Pour the water into a saucepan. Add the drained lily and lotus seeds and the rock sugar powder. Bring to a boil, then lower the heat and simmer for 40 minutes. Serve at once.

NOTE
Lily and lotus seeds both make cooling tonics that provide particularly refreshing summer drinks.

鮮魚麵湯

Soup of Dough Slices

(SERVES 4)
INGREDIENTS

3 large Chinese mushrooms
1¼-2 cups all-purpose flour
½ teaspoon salt
1 egg
2 cups (about 2 oz.) fungus
1 carrot
¼ lb. Chinese greens
4 cups clear soup stock (see
   p. 261)

Soak the Chinese mushrooms in boiling water for 20 minutes. Drain. Cut off and discard the stems and slice the caps.

Mix the flour with the salt, then beat in the egg and sufficient water to make a very thick batter. Let it stand for 20 minutes, then beat again thoroughly.

Wash the fungus and slice it. Peel and slice the carrot, and wash and shred the Chinese greens, using only the green parts.

Put all the vegetables in a large pan with the soup stock. Bring to a boil, then add spoonfuls of the batter, keeping the soup boiling all the time. When you have added all the batter to the pan, lower the heat and simmer for 5 minutes, then serve.

NOTE
A few cooked, shelled shrimp can be added to the soup, if liked.

玉米湯

Cream of Corn Soup

(SERVES 4)
INGREDIENTS

4 cups clear soup stock (see
   p. 261)
½ cup all-purpose flour
2½ cups whole kernel corn
1 carrot
⅓ cup green peas
1½ teaspoons salt
2 tablespoons sugar
1 teaspoon black pepper
2 tablespoons light cream
1 slice bread, toasted

Put about a third of the soup stock into a saucepan and stir in the flour, keeping the mixture smooth.

Purée the kernel corn in a blender or food processor with the rest of the soup stock and gradually stir this into the mixture in the pan, keeping it smooth and free from lumps.

Peel the carrot and chop in cubes. Add to the soup with the peas, salt and sugar and simmer for 5 minutes. Just before serving, stir in the pepper and cream and sprinkle the toast, cut in cubes, over the surface.

鳳尾生雲

Clear Soup of Bamboo Shoots

(SERVES 4)
INGREDIENTS

5 oz. pickled bamboo shoots
4 cups clear soup stock (see
. p. 261)

SEASONING
1½ teaspoons salt
½ teaspoon white pepper

Wash the pickled bamboo shoots and chop off the ends. Tear the remainder of the shoots into long shreds.

Bring the soup stock to a boil, add the bamboo shoots and seasoning, bring back to a boil, lower the heat and simmer for 3 minutes.

NOTE
Use tender bamboo shoots for this dish. It is a particularly refreshing soup for a summer evening. The torn shreds of bamboo shoots resemble birds' tails, which is how it gets its more romantic name of Cloudbuilt Phoenix Tails.

菇香呈祥

Golden Mushrooms in Ginger Juice

(SERVES 4)
INGREDIENTS

1 lb. button mushrooms
salt
½ cup plus 2 extra
    tablespoons corn oil
2 tablespoons soy sauce
½ tablespoon ginger juice
    (see NOTE p. 39)
½ tablespoon cornstarch
    mixed with 1 tablespoon
    water

SEASONING
⅔ teaspoon salt
1 tablespoon sugar
⅓ teaspoon white pepper

Wash the button mushrooms in water mixed with a little salt. Dry on paper towels and make slanting cuts around the caps.

Heat the ½ cup of oil in a wok and stir-fry the mushrooms until they have turned golden. Remove with a slotted spoon and soak in the soy sauce for 20 minutes.

Heat the remaining 2 tablespoons oil in a clean pan and stir-fry the ginger juice for ½ minute. Add the mushrooms and the seasoning and stir-fry for a few minutes. Add the cornstarch paste, let the sauce thicken and serve.

Vegetarian Shark's Fins

(SERVES 4)
INGREDIENTS

1 cup (about 1 oz) fungus
1 bundle transparent vermicelli
4 Chinese mushrooms
2 green-stemmed flat cabbages
2 tablespoons shredded bamboo shoot
2 tablespoons shredded carrot
¼ cup corn oil
2 tablespoons water
4 cups clear soup stock (see p. 261)

SEASONING A
1½ teaspoons salt
1 tablespoon light soy sauce
½ teaspoon white pepper

SEASONING B
1 tablespoon cornstarch mixed with 2 tablespoons water and 1 teaspoon sesame oil

Soak the fungus in cold water for 1 hour.

Soak the vermicelli in boiling water for 20 minutes. Drain and cut in even sections using scissors.

Soak the Chinese mushrooms in boiling water for 20 minutes. Drain, cut off and discard the stems and shred the caps.

Cut away the root and withered outer leaves from the cabbages. Wash the leaves and chop in shreds.

Drain the fungus, then remove the stem and chop the remainder into shreds.

Heat the oil in a wok and stir-fry all the prepared ingredients together with the 2 tablespoons water. Add seasoning **A** and stir-fry for 2 minutes more.

Pour in the stock and bring to a boil. Stir in seasoning **B** and cook, stirring until the mixture thickens slightly. Serve at once.

NOTE

The cooked transparent vermicelli resembles shark's fins, which is why the recipe has its name.

You can substitute 4 cups bean sprouts (see small picture 3, right) for the fungus.

Long-Stem Mushrooms with Sesame Oil

(SERVES 4)
INGREDIENTS

1 lb. long-stem mushrooms
salt
⅓ tablespoon black sesame seeds
3 tablespoons corn oil
1 tablespoon ginger juice or 1½ tablespoons ginger wine (see Glossary)

SEASONING A
1 teaspoon salt
½ tablespoon sesame oil

SEASONING B
½ tablespoon cornstarch mixed with 3 tablespoons water

Pick out any hard stems from the mushrooms (if using fresh ones), then chop off the root ends. Wash the mushrooms with water mixed with a little salt, then drain and wash again under cold running water. Drain well.

Pick out and discard any impurities in the black sesame seeds. Stir-fry the remainder with 1 tablespoon oil over a gentle heat for 2 minutes. Tip onto a plate and rinse out the pan.

Put the oil and ginger juice or wine into the pan. Add the mushrooms and stir-fry for a minute or so. Add seasoning **A** and stir-fry for 2 minutes more.

Stir in seasoning **B**, and when the mixture has thickened, remove from the heat. Sprinkle with the black sesame seeds and serve.

洋葱濃湯

Onion Soup

(SERVES 4)
INGREDIENTS

2 small onions
1 slice bread
¼ cup corn oil
2½ cups water

SEASONING
1½ teaspoons salt
½ tablespoon sugar
½ teaspoon black pepper

Peel the onions and cut off ends. Shred the remainder finely.
Toast the bread lightly and cut in cubes.
Heat the oil in a pan and stir-fry the onions until well browned. Add the water and bring to a boil. Lower the heat and simmer for 30 minutes. Add the seasoning and serve with the croûtons sprinkled on the surface.

NOTE
If you want a creamy soup, use cream instead of oil to stir-fry the onions.

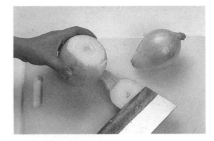

茄汁豆酥

Beans with Tomato Sauce

(SERVES 4)
INGREDIENTS

2 cups hulled fava beans
1 cup all-purpose flour
⅓ teaspoon salt
⅓ teaspoon white pepper
1 egg white
¼ cup corn oil
¼ cup water
1 pan of corn oil for deep frying
½ tablespoon crushed garlic
3 tablespoons tomato ketchup
¼ cup water

SEASONING
2 tablepoons sugar
1 tablespoon vinegar
1 teaspoon salt

Wash the beans and drain. Steam for 5 minutes.
Make a smooth batter with the flour, salt, pepper, egg white, 1 tablespoon oil and water. Add the beans to this and mix to coat them thoroughly.
Heat the oil for deep frying and drop in spoonfuls of the bean mixture, cooking them until they are golden brown. Remove and drain on paper towels. Keep warm.
Heat the remaining 3 tablespoons oil in a wok and stir-fry the garlic for 1 minute. Add the ketchup, water and seasoning and bring to a boil. Add the fried beans to this sauce, stirring to coat them evenly. Serve at once.

Hot and Sour Soup

(SERVES 4)
INGREDIENTS

4 Chinese mushrooms
1 tablespoon black moss
3-4 red chili peppers
¼ lb. long-stem mushrooms
2 cakes of square bean curds
1 carrot
¾ cup sour cabbage
⅓ cup corn oil
4 cups clear soup stock (see p. 261)
2 tablespoons cornstarch mixed with ¼ cup water
1 egg, beaten

SEASONING A
2 tablespoons dark soy sauce
1½ teaspoons salt
½ teaspoon white pepper

SEASONING B
¼ cup malt vinegar
1 tablespoon white vinegar
2 teaspoons sesame oil
1 tablespoon chopped fresh parsley

Soak the Chinese mushrooms in boiling water for 20 minutes. Drain. Cut off and discard the stems and shred the caps.

Soak the black moss for 20 minutes. Drain.

Wash the chili peppers and shred finely. Cut off and discard the roots from the long-stem mushrooms and wash.

Shred the bean curds. Peel the carrot and shred finely. Wash the sour cabbage and shred finely.

Heat the oil in a wok and stir-fry the Chinese mushrooms for 1 minute. Add all the other shredded ingredients and the long-stem mushrooms. Stir well, then add the soup stock and seasoning **A**. Bring to a boil, lower the heat and simmer for 2 minutes.

Stir in the cornstarch mixture and bring to a boil again, stirring until the soup thickens. Switch off the heat and leave for 1 minute, then stir in the beaten egg. Pour into a soup bowl and stir in seasoning **B**. Serve at once.

NOTE
If you cannot get long-stem mushrooms, use bean sprouts instead.

Bean Curds with Sesame Sauce

(SERVES 4)
INGREDIENTS

4 cakes of square bean curds
4 cups water
1 tablespoon minced scallion

SEASONING
1½ tablespoons sesame sauce
1 tablespoon sesame oil
1½ tablespoons soy sauce
½ teaspoon salt
¼ cup cold boiled water
1 teaspoon sugar

Put the bean curds into a large saucepan with the water and bring to a boil for 1 minute. Drain and place in a deep plate.

Blend the seasoning together and pour it over the bean curds. Sprinkle with the scallion and serve.

NOTE
For a different taste, add a small bunch of cedar shoots (see small picture 1 right) to the ingredients in this recipe. Rinse them in cold water, then drop into a pan of boiling water for 2 minutes and serve separately.

牡丹富貴

Stewed Cabbage with Mixed Vegetables

(SERVES 4)
INGREDIENTS

2-3 Chinese mushrooms
1 piece (about 2 oz.) bamboo
  shoot
1 medium Chinese cabbage
4 cups clear soup stock (see
  p. 261)
1½ tablespoons diced carrot
1½ tablespoons whole kernel
  corn
1½ tablespoons green beans
1½ tablespoons preserved
  vegetable

SEASONING

1½ teaspoons salt
½ teaspoon white pepper

Soak the Chinese mushrooms in boiling water for 20 minutes. Drain. Cut off and discard the stems. Shred the bamboo shoot and soak in cold water.

Cut off and discard any old or withered leaves and the root part from the cabbage. Wash the leaves and shred them.

Put the soup stock into a large saucepan with the cabbage. Sprinkle all the other vegetables on top. Add the seasoning, bring to the boiling point over a medium heat, then lower the heat and simmer very gently for 30 minutes. Serve at once.

NOTE

If you like you could sprinkle 2 minced scallion over the soup just before serving.

韭花銀芽

Chive Flowers with Bean Sprouts

(SERVES 4)
INGREDIENTS

1 bunch (about 2 oz.) chives
    with flowers (see NOTE)
4 cups bean sprouts
¼ cup corn oil

SEASONING
⅔ teaspoon salt
1 tablespoon light soy sauce
½ teaspoon white pepper

Wash the chives. Discard any old or withered stems and chop the remainder in 1-inch pieces.

Chop off the ends of the bean sprouts. Wash the remainder clean and dry in a clean cloth.

Heat the oil in a wok and stir-fry the chives and bean sprouts with the seasoning over a high heat for 1 minute. Serve at once.

NOTES

This is a fresh attractive-looking dish which is also very nutritious.

Although the chives shown here are rather broader-stemmed than those commonly grown in the U.S.A., regular chives would be perfectly suitable for this recipe and the one below. Pick them just as the flower buds have appeared.

炸韭菜结

Fried Chive Knots

(SERVES 4)
INGREDIENTS

1 cup all-purpose flour
⅓ teaspoon salt
2 tablespoons potato starch
2 eggs, beaten
approx ¾ cup water
4 bunches (about 4 oz.)
    chives (without flowers)
1 pan of corn oil for deep
    frying

SEASONING
3 tablespoons dark soy sauce
½ tablespoon chili sauce
½ tablespoon sugar
1 teaspoon garlic powder

Mix together the all-purpose flour, salt and potato starch in a large bowl. Make a well in the center and tip in the beaten eggs. Stir, adding the water gradually, to incorporate the flour, keeping the mixture smooth. Add sufficient water to make a batter the consistency of heavy cream.

Discard any old or withered leaves from the chives and wash the remainder. Scald a handful of chives in boiling water to soften them.

Divide the remainder of the chives into bundles of 3. Fold these in 3-inch long sections and bind them together with the softened chives.

Coat the bundles of chives in the batter, making sure they are evenly covered. Cook a few at a time in the hot oil until golden brown. Drain on paper towels while you cook the remainder.

Cut the knots in diagonal slices and serve with the seasoning mixed together in a small bowl.

盛世太平火鍋

Dish of the Flourishing

(SERVES 4)
INGREDIENTS

8 Chinese mushrooms
2 bundles vermicelli
½ a salted or preserved
    vegetable
¾ lb. spinach
1 bamboo shoot
¼ cup corn oil
2 tablespoons minced shallot
1 tablespoon light soy sauce
6¼ cups clear soup stock
    (see p. 261)
10 pieces triangular shaped
    fried bean curds
¼ lb. dried bean curds
1 cup fungus slices

SEASONING
2 teaspoons salt
1 teaspoon white pepper

Soak the Chinese mushrooms in boiling water for 20 minutes. Drain. Cut off and discard the stems. Soak the vermicelli in cold water for 20 minutes. Drain and cut in 1-inch sections.

Wash the salted or preserved vegetable. Discard outer skin, then cut in thin slices.

Discard any old or withered leaves from the spinach. Scrape off the dirt and rootlets from the spinach root, but do not chop off the root itself. Wash the spinach well and chop.

Wash the bamboo shoot and cut in slices.

Heat the oil in a wok and stir-fry the shallot until browned. Add the soy sauce, soup stock, fried bean curds, dried bean curd, the fungus, bamboo shoot and salted vegetable slices, the Chinese mushrooms and half of the seasoning. Bring to a boil.

Add the vermicelli and spinach with the rest of the seasoning and boil for 2 minutes more. Transfer to an earthenware pot and serve.

NOTE
This dish is so-called because very good weather conditions are necessary to produce all the vegetables at the same time.

興子旺孫暖鍋

Pot of Prosperity

(SERVES 4)
INGREDIENTS

12 Chinese mushrooms
3 ears of fresh corn
1½ cups green beans
½ cup snow peas
16 straw mushrooms
1½ cups button mushrooms
6 abalone mushrooms
2 bunches (about 6 oz.) long-
    stem mushrooms
1 large onion
¼-⅓ cup corn oil
¾ cup all-purpose flour
6¼ cups clear soup stock
    (see p. 261)

SEASONING
2 teaspoons salt
½ teaspoon white pepper
1 tablespoon sugar
½ teaspoon minced fresh
    gingerroot

Soak the Chinese mushrooms in boiling water for 20 minutes. Drain. Cut off and discard stems.

Cut off and discard the husks and silk from ears of corn. Wash the cobs and chop in 1-inch sections.

Wash the beans and snow peas. Rub off the membranes from the beans, and trim the snow peas.

Wash all the mushrooms, then cut off and discard the stems. Mince the onion.

Heat the oil in a wok and stir-fry the onion until lightly browned. Mix together the flour and soup, adding the liquid gradually to the flour to keep it smooth. Pour this into the pan with the onion and bring to a boil over medium heat, stirring all the time. Add the seasoning.

Add all the vegetable ingredients and boil for 2 minutes more. Transfer to an earthenware pot and serve.

NOTES
Substitute ½ cup shredded bamboo shoot for the long-stem mushrooms.

Substitute 1 cup fresh dark-gilled mushrooms for the abalone mushrooms.

红乳燴豆腐

Bean Curds in Red Fermented Sauce

(SERVES 4)
INGREDIENTS

2 bean curds
1 teaspoon salt
⅓ cup corn oil
1 red fermented bean curd
½ tablespoon red juice from the fermented bean curd
1½ tablespoons sugar

SEASONING
¼-⅓ cup water
½ teaspoon white pepper
2 teaspoons seasame oil

Blanch bean curds in boiling water with the salt for 3 minutes. Drain and dice.

Heat the oil in a wok. Mix the fermented bean curd with red juice and the sugar, add to the wok and stir-fry over a medium heat, mashing the bean curd as you stir. Add the diced bean curds and the seasoning and stir everything together. Put the lid on the wok, and simmer until most of the liquid has been absorbed. Stir occasionally.

NOTE
If you prefer, you can use cheese instead of the fermented bean curd. Any type of fermented bean curd can be used in this recipe; it does not have to be the red variety.

醬爆青菽

Stir-Fried Green Peppers with Bean Sauce

(SERVES 4)
INGREDIENTS

4 green peppers
¼ cup corn oil
1 tablespoon cornstarch mixed with 2 tablespoons water

SEASONING A
½ tablespoon minced scallion
½ tablespoon crushed garlic

SEASONING B
2 tablespoons hot bean sauce
1 teaspoon minced red chili
½ tablespoon sugar
1 tablespoon dark soy sauce
⅓ cup clear soup stock (see p. 261)

Wash the green peppers. Discard the stems and seeds, then chop in 1-inch sections.

Heat the oil in a wok and stir-fry seasoning **A** until lightly colored. Add seasoning **B** and stir-fry for 1-2 minutes.

Add the green peppers to the wok and stir-fry over a high heat for 1 minute. Pour in the cornstarch mixture and stir until the sauce thickens. Serve at once.

NOTE
Add other vegetables such as shredded fungus, bamboo shoots and spiced bean curds to add variety, but do not use too many ingredients or you will spoil the clear taste of the dish.

金鈎掛玉牌

Golden Hooks with Jade Plates

(SERVES 4)
INGREDIENTS

4 cups yellow bean sprouts
2 cakes bean curd
1 × 1½-inch slice fresh
   gingerroot, pared
2½ cups clear soup stock
   (see p. 261)

SEASONING
1½ teaspoons salt
½ teaspoon white pepper

Cut off and discard the end parts of the bean sprouts. Wash the remainder and the bean curd.

Crush the ginger slightly with the edge of the chopper; this makes it easier to pare and also releases the juices.

Put all the ingredients except for the seasoning into a pan and bring to a boil over medium heat. Lower the heat and simmer for 30 minutes. Remove the ginger, add the seasoning and serve.

NOTES

This is a delicately flavored dish that is particularly refreshing in the summertime.

The recipe is so-called because yellow bean sprouts look like golden hooks and the bean curds like jade plates – to the imaginative!

豉汁蒸白蔯

Steamed Water Chestnuts with Black Bean Sauce

(SERVES 4)
INGREDIENTS

2 cups water chestnuts
⅔ cup corn oil
2 tablespoons black
   fermented beans
½ tablespoon crushed garlic
3 tablespoons green beans

SEASONING
½ teaspoon salt
½ teaspoon sugar
1 teaspoon white pepper

Peel the water chestnuts and wash them. Stir-fry in hot oil for 2 minutes. Remove with a slotted spoon and drain off the oil, reserving 1 tablespoon in the pan.

Stir-fry the fermented beans and garlic until the garlic has browned. Wash the green beans and add them to the pan, stir-frying them for 1 minute.

Mix the stir-fried ingredients with the water chestnuts in a bowl. Place this in a steamer and steam over boiling water for 15-20 minutes. Add the seasoning and serve.

NOTE
Fermented beans have a salty taste, and water chestnuts are quite sweet. Season this dish carefully therefore, tasting it to make sure it is to your liking.

苦 海 慈 航

Stuffed Bitter Gourd

(SERVES 4)
INGREDIENTS

6 Chinese mushrooms
1 bitter gourd (see NOTE)
1 tablespoon cornstarch
3 tablespoons green beans
½ cup water chestnuts
8 pieces spiced bean curds
⅓ cup corn oil

SEASONING A
½ teaspoon salt
1 tablespoon cornstarch
½ tablespoon sesame oil
⅓ teaspoon five-spice
  powder
½ teaspoon sugar

SEASONING B
1½ tablespoons light soy
  sauce
3 tablespoons clear soup
  stock (see p. 261)
½ tablespoon crushed garlic
1 tablespoon black fermented
  beans
1 tablespoon sugar
½ teaspoon salt

Soak the Chinese mushrooms in boiling water for 20 minutes. Drain. Cut off and discard the stems.

Cut off and discard the stem and top part from the bitter gourd, then chop it in sections. Scoop out the seeds and put the rings in a large pan of water. Bring to a boil and boil for 2 minutes. Drain and spread cornstarch around the insides. Put on a plate.

Wash the green beans and cook them for 5 minutes in boiling water. Drain and cover with cold water.

Peel the water chestnuts and mince them with the spiced bean curds and the Chinese mushrooms caps. Mix in seasoning **A**.

Heat ¼ cup oil in a wok and stir-fry the chopped ingredients for 1½ minutes. Remove from the wok with a slotted spoon and press into the bitter gourd rings. Put the plate into a steamer and steam over boiling water for 25 minutes.

Heat the remaining oil in a wok. Drain the green beans and stir-fry with seasoning **B** for 30 seconds. Spoon over the bitter gourds and serve.

NOTE
If you like, you could put the steamed bitter gourd into hot clear soup stock and serve this as a soup dish. Use summer squash in place of bitter gourd if the latter is unavailable.

清炒節瓜

Stir-Fried Fuzzy Melons

(SERVES 4)
INGREDIENTS

2 large or 4 small fuzzy
    melons
1/3 cup corn oil
1 tablespoon ginger juice (see
    NOTE)
1 tablespoon water
1 teaspoon salt
green stems of 2 scallions
2 teaspoons sherry

Peel the fuzzy melons and chop in slices.
    Heat 1/4 cup oil in a wok and add the ginger juice.
Stir-fry for 1 minute, then add the melon slices. Stir for
1 minute more, then add the water and salt and
simmer over a medium heat, covered, for 3 minutes.
Stir from time to time. Transfer to a serving dish.
    Chop the scallion stems and stir-fry them briefly in
the remaining 1 tablespoon oil. Sprinkle over the fuzzy
melons, add the sherry and serve.

NOTE
Ginger juice is a flavoring agent and also a tenderizer.
It is made from fresh ginger. If you cannot buy it, grate
some fresh ginger and press it through a tea-sieve to
extract the juice.

小家碧玉

Stir-Fried Angled Luffa

(SERVES 4)
INGREDIENTS

2 angled luffas
1/4 cup corn oil
1 tablespoon cornstarch
    mixed with 2 tablespoons
    water
1 1/2 teaspoons sesame oil

SEASONING A
1/2 tablespoon minced
    scallion
1/2 teaspoon crushed garlic

SEASONING B
1 teaspoon salt
2 tablespoons water

Peel the angled luffas. Wash them and chop in
triangular pieces.
    Heat the oil in a wok and stir-fry seasoning **A** until
lightly colored. Add the luffa along with seasoning **B**,
stir, then simmer for 1 1/2 minutes, stirring from time to
time.
    Add the cornstarch paste, stirring until the mixture
thickens. Just before serving, stir in the sesame oil.

NOTE
To make this dish more filling, you can add 1 piece of
dried bean curd sheet and 3 pieces (about 2 oz.)
fungus as shown in the top small picture (right). Soak
both these ingredients for 1 hour in cold water, then
shred and stir-fry them for 3-4 minutes before adding
the angled luffa.

蠔油菜心燴鮑魚菇

Abalone Mushrooms and Green Vegetables in Oyster Sauce

(SERVES 4)
INGREDIENTS

3-4 green-stemmed flat
   cabbages
8-10 abalone mushrooms
¼ cup corn oil
½ cup clear soup stock (see
   p. 261)
1 tablespoon cornstarch
   mixed with 1½
   tablespoons water
½ teaspoon sesame oil

SEASONING
1 teaspoon salt
1 tablespoon oyster sauce
   (see NOTE p. 279)
1½ tablespoons sugar

Cut off and discard the root and any withered leaves from the cabbages. Wash them and cut in half.

Cut off and discard the stems from the mushrooms. Wash and slice in large pieces.

Blanch the cabbage and mushrooms separately in boiling, salted water for 1 minute. Drain and plunge into cold water. Let cool, then drain again.

Heat the oil in a wok and stir-fry the cabbage and mushrooms. Add the seasoning, then the soup stock. Bring to a boil.

Stir in the cornstarch mixture to thicken the sauce. Just before serving, stir in the sesame oil.

NOTES
Plunging the cabbage and mushrooms into cold water after blanching helps to preserve their color.

Substitute 2 cups straw mushrooms for the abalone mushrooms.

三鮮豆苗

Stir-Fried Spinach with Fresh Vegetables

(SERVES 4)
INGREDIENTS

1 lb. spinach (see NOTE)
6 straw mushrooms
1 carrot
1 bamboo shoot
⅓ cup corn oil
1 teaspoon cornstarch mixed
   with 2 teapoons water

SEASONING
1 teaspoon salt
½ teaspoon white pepper

Discard the stems and any old leaves from the spinach. Wash it well and shake off the water.

Wash the straw mushrooms and chop in half. Peel the carrot; slice it and the bamboo shoot.

Heat the oil in a wok and stir-fry the mushrooms, carrot and bamboo shoot for 3 minutes. Add the spinach and seasoning and stir-fry for 30 seconds more. Stir in the cornstarch mixture to thicken the dish and serve at once.

NOTE
The spinach most usually used in this dish is also called pea shoots. It can be stir-fried on its own as a nourishing vegetable. If you cannot get pea shoots, use regular spinach.

佛手飄香

Chayotes with Red Chili Peppers

(SERVES 4)
INGREDIENTS

2 small chayotes (see NOTE)
3-4 red chili peppers
¼ cup corn oil
¼ cup water
1 teaspoon sherry

SEASONING
1 teaspoon salt
½ teaspoon white pepper

Peel the chayotes, then carefully cut away the white tissues. Cut in half and remove the seeds. Wash and slice.

Wash the red chili peppers and chop in fine slices.

Heat the oil in a wok and stir-fry the chili peppers until beginning to brown. Add the chayote slices with the seasoning. Stir and add the water. Simmer, covered, for 1½ minutes.

Stir the ingredients, add the sherry and serve.

NOTE
If chayote is unavailable, substitute 4-5 baby zucchini.

栗子燒香菇

Braised Chestnuts with Chinese Mushrooms

(SERVES 4)
INGREDIENTS

1 cup dried chestnuts
20 Chinese mushrooms
2 teaspoons sesame oil

SEASONING

3 tablespoons dark soy sauce
1 tablespoon rock sugar (see NOTE p. 114)
⅓ teaspoon salt
7-8 slices licorice (see NOTE)

Soak the dried chestnuts in cold water for at least 4 hours – the longer they are soaked, the quicker they cook and the more flavor they have. Drain and remove the red membrane. Wash them under cold running water.

Soak the Chinese mushrooms in boiling water for 20 minutes. Drain, reserving the soaking liquid. Cut off and discard the stems.

Put about 1¼ cups of the water used to soak the Chinese mushrooms in a saucepan and add the chestnuts, mushrooms and seasoning. Bring to a boil, then lower the heat and simmer for about 30 minutes until nearly all the liquid has been absorbed and the chestnuts are tender. Check the pan during cooking and add more water if necessary. Serve at once.

NOTE
Substitute peppermint leaves for licorice.

釀茄夾

Stuffed Eggplant Folders

(SERVES 4)
INGREDIENTS

½ tablespoon black moss
2 cakes bean curds
4 long eggplants
1 cup all-purpose flour
½ teaspoon salt
2 eggs
1 tablespoon corn oil
water (see recipe)
corn oil for deep frying

SEASONING A
½ teaspoon salt
½ teaspoon white pepper
1 egg white

SEASONING B
3 tablespoons oyster sauce
1½ tablespoons water
½ teaspoon salt
1 tablespoon minced scallion
½ tablespoon crushed garlic
2 tablespoons corn oil

Soak the black moss in cold water for 20 minutes.
Blanch the bean curds in boiling water for 3 minutes. Drain, cut off the hard edge and mash the remainder. Squeeze out any excess water.

Drain the black moss and mix with the mashed bean curd and seasoning **A**.

Wash the eggplants and discard the stem and top part. Chop in ½-inch slices, then cut almost through these to make the "folders". Press about ½ tablespoon of the bean curd mixture into each of these.

Mix the flour with the salt in a bowl. Make a well in the center and tip in the eggs beaten with the tablespoon corn oil. Gradually stir the flour into the eggs, adding sufficient water to make a smooth batter, the consistency of heavy cream. Let stand for 10 minutes.

Mix together all the ingredients for seasoning **B** except for the oil. Heat the oil in a wok and stir-fry the ingredients for 2-3 minutes. Serve this as a sauce.

Dip the eggplant folders into the batter to coat them and cook them in the pan of deep oil for about 4 minutes each, until puffed up and golden. Drain on paper towels and serve with the sauce.

Stir-Fried Mixed Vegetables

(SERVES 4)
INGREDIENTS

5 bean curd sheets
4 triangular-shaped fried
    bean curds
¼ cup corn oil
½ tablespoon minced
    scallion
3-4 small red chili peppers
    (optional)
1 lb. watercress
3 tablespoons clear soup
    stock (see p. 261)
1½ tablespoons cornstarch
    mixed with 2 tablespoons
    water

SEASONING
1 teaspoon salt
½ teaspoon sugar

Soak the bean curd sheets in cold water for about 20 minutes to soften them. Drain.

Discard all old or withered leaves from the watercress keeping only the tender, fresh leaves. Wash them thoroughly and drain. Chop in 1-inch sections.

Slice the fried bean curds and chop the bean curd sheets into big pieces. Chop the chili peppers, if using.

Heat the oil in a wok and stir-fry the scallion and chili peppers for 3-4 minutes. Add the watercress, fried bean curds, bean curd sheets, soup stock and seasoning. Cook, stirring for 3 minutes, then add the cornstarch mixture and stir until the sauce has thickened. Serve at once.

NOTE
Old leaves and stems from the watercress can be used to make soup. It is a very nutritious vegetable, said to be good for the lungs.

Fava Beans with Mustard Sauce

(SERVES 4)
INGREDIENTS

2 cups hulled fava beans
2 tablespoons minced
    scallion

SEASONING
½ teaspoon salt
2 tablespoons prepared
    English mustard
½ tablespoon sesame oil

Wash the fava beans but do not peel off the skins. Cook for 5-8 minutes in simmering water until tender. Drain.

Mix the minced scallion with the seasoning and stir into the fava beans. Serve at once.

NOTE
The beans should be quite well cooked for this dish, but not so over-cooked that they turn mushy when you mix them with the other ingredients.

千 里 飄 香

Steamed Spiced Bean Curd with Green Beans

(SERVES 4)

INGREDIENTS

4 cakes bean curd
½ cup green beans or salted vegetable
1 tablespoon sesame oil

SEASONING

1½ tablespoons light soy sauce
½ teaspoon salt
1 teaspoon sugar
½ teaspoon chili powder

Wash the bean curd and drain well. Dice.
Rub away the outer skin from the beans and mix them with the seasoning.
Put the diced bean curd on a plate and spoon the green beans on top. Steam over simmering water for 5-7 minutes. Stir in the sesame oil just before serving.

NOTE

If you use salted vegetable instead of green beans, it should be washed thoroughly and then chopped. Stir-fry the vegetable for 3 minutes before mixing with seasoning.

木 耳 順 風

Stir-Fried Fungus with Lettuce and Pineapple

(SERVES 4)

INGREDIENTS

½ lb. fungus (see NOTES)
1 head lettuce
2 pineapple slices, drained if canned
¼ cup corn oil
1 tablespoon cornstarch mixed with 2 tablespoons water

SEASONING

1 teaspoon salt
½ tablespoon sugar

Chop off and discard the fungus roots. Wash the fungus, then soak in cold water for 1 hour until softened. Chop in pieces.
Strip outer leaves from the head lettuce, wash it and chop in slices.
Heat the oil in a wok and stir-fry all the ingredients, except the cornstarch. Add the seasoning. Stir in the cornstarch mixture and cook, stirring, until the mixture has thickened slightly. Remove and serve at once.

NOTES

This is a delicious tasting sweet and sour dish.
Substitute 1 cup canned straw mushrooms for the fungus, and 3 celery stalks for the head lettuce.

烧素肉饼

Mixed Vegetable Patties

(SERVES 4)
INGREDIENTS

4 tablespoons fungus
2-3 tablespoons dried lily
4 tablespoons shredded
preserved vegetable
1 small onion
½ cup water chestnuts
1 bean curd
1 tablespoon minced scallion
11 tablespoons corn oil

SEASONING A
¼ cup cornstarch
½ teaspoon salt
½ teaspoon white pepper

SEASONING B
1½ tablespoons light soy
sauce
3 tablespoons clear soup
stock (see p. 261)
½ tablespoon sugar

Soak the fungus in cold water for 1 hour until softened. Shred finely. Soak the dried lily in cold water for 30 minutes. Chop roughly. Wash the preserved vegetables.

Peel the onion and chop off the ends. Mince the remainder. Peel the water chestnuts and mince finely.

Blanch the bean curd in boiling water for 3 minutes. Drain well and mash with seasoning **A** and all the other ingredients except for the scallion and the corn oil.

Heat 4 tablespoons oil in a wok and stir-fry the mixture for 2 minutes. Remove and leave to go cold. Form into round cakes about 1½ inches in diameter and ¼ inch thick.

Heat 6 tablespoons oil in a skillet and sauté the patties until golden brown on both sides. Arrange on a plate and sprinkle with the minced scallion.

Heat the remaining 1 tablespoon oil in a clean pan and add seasoning **B**. Bring to a boil, pour over the patties and serve.

煎茄絲餅

Eggplant Patties

(SERVES 4)
INGREDIENTS

3 long eggplants
⅓ cup cornstarch
⅓ cup corn oil

SEASONING A
⅓ teaspoon white pepper
½ teaspoon chili powder
½ teaspoon salt
½ tablespoon minced
scallion

SEASONING B
1 tablespoon malt vinegar
1 tablespoon light soy sauce
1 tablespoon clear soup stock
(see p. 261)
1 tablespoon crushed garlic
½ tablespoon sesame oil

Peel the eggplants and chop roughly. Soak in cold water for 15 minutes, then drain and steam for 7-8 minutes. Drain off any liquid and blend the eggplants with seasoning **A**. Let cool.

Stir the cornstarch into the cooled eggplants, mixing them together thoroughly.

Heat a third of the oil in a skillet over a medium heat. Drop in tablespoons of the eggplant mixture and cook until golden brown on one side. Turn over and press the pattie flat with a fish turner. Cook until golden brown on this side. Keep adding oil to the pan as necessary until all the mixture has been cooked. Serve with seasoning **B**, mixed well together.

NOTE
Sliced cucumber and tomato makes a tasty accompaniment to this dish. If you cannot find the long eggplants shown in small picture 1, right, regular eggplants are perfectly suitable.

四色沙拉

Salad of Four Colors

(SERVES 4)
INGREDIENTS

2 cucumbers
1 cup hulled fava beans
½ a small pumpkin
1 large potato
⅓ teaspoon white pepper
¼ cup yogurt dressing (see NOTE)

Wash the cucumbers and cut off and discard the end parts. Cut in fourths lengthwise and remove the seeds. Cut in chunks.

Wash the fava beans. Peel the pumpkin, cut in slices and remove the seeds. Wash the slices and cut in chunks. Peel the potato and wash, then cut in chunks, too.

Steam the fava beans, pumpkin and potato over gently boiling water for 15 minutes. Mix with the cucumber, pepper and dressing and serve.

NOTE

To make yogurt dressing, blend ¼ cup mayonnaise with 1 tablespoon natural yogurt, ¼ teaspoon superfine sugar, a large pinch of salt and ½ tablespoon each minced onion and celery. Beat well for about 1 minute. Keep in the refrigerator in a bowl covered with plastic wrap until wanted.

奶汁蘆筍

Asparagus with Milk

(SERVES 4)
INGREDIENTS

10 spears white asparagus
10 spears green asparagus
½ cup milk
½ tablespoon cornstarch
3 tablespoons light cream
2 tablespoons finely shredded carrot

SEASONING
1 teaspoon salt
½ teaspoon white pepper

Scrape away any old skin from the asparagus. Wash well and chop in 1½-inch sections.

Mix the milk with the cornstarch, keeping it smooth and free from lumps.

Blanch the asparagus in boiling water for 1½ minutes. Remove the green asparagus with tongs or a slotted spoon and leave the white asparagus for 1½ minutes more. Drain and put all the asparagus onto a plate.

Put the milk and cornstarch into a small pan with the cream and the seasoning. Bring to a boil, stirring all the time, and when the mixture has thickened pour it over the asparagus. Serve at once with the shredded carrot.

NOTES

Green asparagus will turn yellow if it is cooked for too long. A counsel of perfection would be to stand the asparagus upright so that the root part blanches for the full time, before turning them on their side so that the tips only blanch for 30 seconds.

If fresh asparagus is unobtainable, use canned or frozen asparagus.

滷塌棵菜

Spiced Chinese Flat Cabbage

(SERVES 4)
INGREDIENTS

1 lb. Chinese flat cabbage
3 tablespoons corn oil

SEASONING
½ teaspoon salt
½ tablespoon sugar
2 tablespoons dark soy sauce

Cut off and discard any old or withered leaves from the cabbage. Cut each one in 4 parts and wash these thoroughly.

Heat the oil in a wok and stir-fry the cabbage with the seasoning over a high heat for 1 minute. Put the lid on the wok and simmer for 1 minute more. Stir the cabbage and serve.

NOTE
If you prefer a thicker sauce, mix a little cornstarch and water into the cabbage.

酸辣洋葱

Hot and Sour Onions

(SERVES 4)
INGREDIENTS

2 onions
2-3 red chili peppers
¼ cup corn oil

SEASONING
1 teaspoon salt
½ tablespoon sugar
1 tablespoon white vinegar
½ tablespoon brown vinegar
pinch of white pepper

Peel the onions and cut off the ends. Cut the onions in half and then in square pieces.

Wash the chili peppers and slice diagonally.

Heat the oil in a wok and stir-fry the chili peppers for 1 minute. Add the onions and seasoning and stir-fry over a high heat for 2-4 minutes. The onions should still be crunchy. Serve.

NOTE
If you like the taste of raw onion, cook it for no more than 1 minute before serving.

糖醋高麗

Sweet and Sour Lettuce

(SERVES 4)
INGREDIENTS

½ head iceberg lettuce
¼ cup corn oil
½ tablespoon crushed garlic
½ tablespoon chopped red
   chili peppers

SEASONING
3 tablespoons sugar
¼ cup malt vinegar
1½ teaspoons salt

Discard outer withered leaves of the lettuce. Tear the remainder into large pieces and wash.

Heat the oil in a wok and stir-fry the garlic and chili peppers over a medium heat for about 1 minute. Raise the heat and add the lettuce. Cook for 3 minutes more, stirring all the time. Add the seasoning, stir to mix, then remove from the heat and serve.

涼拌四季豆

Cold Sauced Snap Beans

(SERVES 4)
INGREDIENTS

1 lb. snap beans
1 teaspoon salt
1 tablespoon grated fresh
   gingerroot
3 tablespoons sesame sauce
   (see NOTES)

Cut off and discard the ends and string from the beans. Wash under cold running water. Put into a pan of boiling water with the salt and grated ginger; cook for 2½ minutes.

Drain the beans and plunge them right away into a pan of ice water. Leave until cold. Drain well and mix with the sesame sauce.

NOTES
To make sesame sauce, blend together 1½ tablespoons raw sesame sauce, 2 tablespoons light soy sauce, ½ teaspoon salt, 3 tablespoons cold boiled water, 1 teaspoon sugar and 1 tablespoon sesame oil. If making the sauce to go with noodles, add more water and salt.

Plunging the cooked beans into cold water will help preserve their color. Choose even-size beans for this dish.

Three Tastes of Turnips

(SERVES 6)

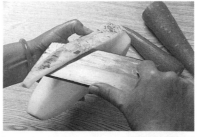

INGREDIENTS

1 lb. turnips
1 lb. carrots

SEASONING A

1½ tablespoons light soy
  sauce
½ tablespoon sesame oil
½ teaspoon white pepper
½ teaspoon salt

METHOD A

Peel the turnips and the carrots. Wash and chop in large chunks.

Cook in boiling water until just tender. Drain and mix with seasoning **A**. Serve.

INGREDIENTS

1 lb. green turnips

SEASONING B

3 tablespoons light soy sauce
½ tablespoon sesame oil

DRESSING

¾ teaspoon salt
1 tablespoon sugar

METHOD B

Wash the turnips well, but do not peel them. Chop in big slices and slice these almost down to the root (see picture opposite), so they resemble a comb.

Rub the slices with the dressing, stirring them with your hands constantly. After 20 minutes, rinse and squeeze out the juice. Mix with seasoning **B**; leave for 10 minutes, then serve.

INGREDIENTS

1 lb. green turnips

SEASONING C

1 tablespoon sugar
2 tablespoons white vinegar
½ teaspoon white pepper

DRESSING

¾ teaspoon salt
1 tablespoon sugar

METHOD C

Wash the turnips well and dry them, then shred finely.

Sprinkle the dressing over the turnips and leave for 30 minutes, stirring frequently with your hand. Rinse, squeeze out the juice, mix with seasoning **C** and serve.

NOTES

The dish in Method **B** is also known as Marinated Turnip. As it contains sesame oil it must be eaten the same day, but if you omit this ingredient, you can keep the turnip in a screw-top jar for several days.

The dish in Method **C** should be served as soon as it is prepared.

Substitute icicle radishes for the turnip. Jicama or regular turnips can be used in place of the green turnips.

咖哩豆腐

Curried Bean Curds

(SERVES 4)
INGREDIENTS

2 cakes bean curd
1½ tablespoons minced shallots
4 red or green chili peppers
¼ cup corn oil
about 3 tablespoons curry powder
¼ cup water
½ cup green beans
¼ cup milk
1 tablespoon cornstarch, mixed with 1½ tablespoons water

SEASONING
1½ teaspoons salt
1 tablespoon sugar

Wash the bean curd and blanch in boiling water for 3 minutes. Drain and cut in cubes.

Select the best parts of the shallots as you prepare them. Wash the chili peppers and mince.

Heat the oil in a wok and stir-fry the chopped shallot for 1 minute. Add the curry powder and cook for about 30 seconds, stirring. Add the bean curd, chili peppers, water and seasoning and cook for 3-5 minutes, covered, but stirring frequently.

Meanwhile cook the green beans for 5 minutes in boiling water. Drain.

Gradually stir the milk into the mixture in the wok, then add the cornstarch paste and cook, stirring until the mixture thickens. Serve at once with the green beans sprinkled on top.

NOTE
This is a very hot dish; if you prefer a milder taste reduce the amount of curry powder and replace the chilis with chopped green pepper.

小炒四季

Stir-Fried Snap Beans

(SERVES 4)
INGREDIENTS

½ lb. snap or snake beans
¼ cup corn oil
½ tablespoon shredded red chili peppers
1 tablespoon shredded fresh gingerroot

SEASONING
1 teaspoon salt
2 teaspoons light soy sauce
1 teaspoon sugar

Trim the beans. Wash them, then slice diagonally.

Heat the oil in a wok and stir-fry the chili peppers and ginger over a high heat for 30 seconds. Add the beans and seasoning and stir-fry for 1½ minutes more. Serve at once.

NOTE
If you like, add 1 crushed garlic clove, stir-frying it with the chili peppers.

芋　泥

Taro Mash

(SERVES 4)
INGREDIENTS

1 lb. taro (dasheen)
2 cups rich soup stock (see p. 261)
3 tablespoons light cream

SEASONING
1½ teaspoons salt
½ tablespoon sugar
½ teaspoon white pepper

Peel the taro and wash thoroughly. Chop in thick slices and steam over boiling water for 25 minutes until soft. Mash thoroughly.

Stir the soup stock into the mashed taro and add the seasoning. Rub through a strainer.

Put the taro purée into a pan and slowly bring to a boil. Stir in the cream and serve at once.

NOTE
You can substitute vegetable oil for the cream. This dish is commonly served with fried noodles as a snack.

辣　炒　軟　絲

Hot Bottle Gourd Shreds

(SERVES 4)
INGREDIENTS

1 bottle gourd
⅓ cup corn oil
2 tablespoons shredded red chili peppers
1 tablespoon minced garlic
1 tablespoon cornstarch mixed with 2 tablespoons water

SEASONING
1 teaspoon salt
1 teaspoon sugar

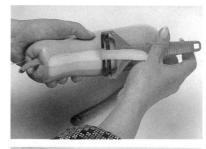

Peel the bottle gourd and wash it. Chop in slices, then shred these finely.

Heat the oil in a wok and stir-fry the chili peppers and garlic for 1 minute over a high heat. Add the shredded bottle gourd with the seasoning and stir-fry for a minute more.

Lower the heat and cook, stirring occasionally until the gourd is tender. Stir in the cornstarch paste and cook until the mixture has thickened. Serve at once.

NOTE
Look for a bottle gourd that feels heavy and looks fresh around the stem.

Vegetable String of Colors

(SERVES 4)

INGREDIENTS

6 large Chinese mushrooms
2 green peppers
12 water chestnuts
1 small yam
4 spiced bean curds
1 carrot
2 cucumbers

SEASONING

1 tablespoon crushed garlic
3 tablespoons light soy sauce
1½ tablespoons sugar
½ teaspoon salt
2 tablespoons water
2 tablespoons Hoisin sauce
1 teaspoon dry sherry

Soak the Chinese mushrooms in boiling water for 20 minutes. Drain. Cut off and discard the stems and cut the caps in half.

Wash the green peppers, cut in half and discard the seeds and stem part. Chop in chunks. Wash the water chestnuts. Peel the yam, wash and slice.

Wash the spiced bean curds and chop in 8 triangular shapes. Peel the carrot, wash and slice. Wash the cucumbers, cut off the end parts and slice.

Put the seasoning ingredients into a small pan and bring to a boil, stirring. Take off the heat.

Thread the vegetables alternately onto bamboo sticks, brush with the seasoning and broil for about 5 minutes on each side. Brush continually with the seasoning during broiling.

NOTE

An alternative method of cooking is to cook the skewered vegetables in corn oil for 3-5 minutes on either side. Serve them with the seasoning as a sauce.

烤素方

Deep-Fried Vegetable Folds

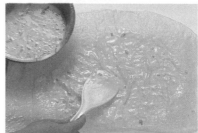

(SERVES 4)
INGREDIENTS

12 dried bean curd sheets
3 eggs
4 tablespoons minced
    scallions
1 teaspoon five-spice powder
½ teaspoon salt
1 tablespoon light soy sauce
vegetable oil for deep frying

Soak the bean curd sheets in cold water for 20-30 minutes to soften them. Pat dry with paper towels, taking care not to break or tear them.

Beat the eggs with the scallions, five-spice powder, salt and the soy sauce.

Lay 1 of the bean curd sheets flat and brush with the beaten egg mixture. Place another sheet on top and brush with the egg mixture. Fold up as shown in the small picture 3. Repeat this brushing and folding process with the remainder of the bean curd sheets.

Cut the folded sheets into squares or triangles being very careful not to tear them.

Heat the oil and deep-fry the bean curd folds for 4-5 minutes. Remove with a slotted spoon and drain on paper towels before serving.

腐衣香菜

Bean Curd Rolls with Basil

(SERVES 4)
INGREDIENTS

10 dried bean curd sheets
1½ cups (about 2 oz.) fresh
    basil leaves (see NOTE)
2 tablespoons all-purpose
    flour mixed with 1½
    tablespoons water
corn oil for deep frying

SEASONING
1 teaspoon salt
2 teaspoons sugar
½ teaspoon white pepper

Soak the bean curd sheets in cold water for 20-30 minutes to soften them. Pat dry with paper towels, taking care not to break or tear them.

Pick off and discard any old or withered leaves from the basil, and wash the remainder. Dry, then chop with 4 of the bean curd sheets. Mix in the seasoning.

Lay 2 sheets of bean curd flat, one on top of the other. Put a third of the basil mixture on one end, then roll up the bean curd as shown in the small picture 2. Brush the end with the flour paste to seal. Make 2 more rolls with the remaining 4 sheets of bean curd and the basil mixture.

Heat the oil and deep-fry the rolls for about 5 minutes. Remove and drain on paper towels and let cool. When cold cut in sections and serve.

NOTES
You could substitute white wormwood, scissored chives or bean sprouts for the basil.

If you prefer, serve the rolls hot, cutting them in sections as soon as they are cooked.

扑 双 冬

Stir-Fried Bamboo Shoots with Chinese Mushrooms

(SERVES 4)
INGREDIENTS

12 Chinese mushrooms
3 bamboo shoots
¼ cup corn oil

SEASONING
⅔ teaspoon salt
2 tablespoons soy sauce
½ tablespoon sugar

Soak the Chinese mushrooms in boiling water for 20 minutes. Drain, reserving 3 tablespoons of the soaking water. Cut off and discard the stems and cut the caps in half if they are very large.

Peel the bamboo shoots and cut in half. Cook in boiling water for 20 minutes, drain and plunge in cold water, leaving to cool completely. Drain and cut in ½-inch thick slices.

Heat the oil in a wok and stir-fry the bamboo for 3 minutes. Add the Chinese mushrooms, seasoning and the reserved water from the Chinese mushrooms. Stir everything together, put the lid on the wok and simmer for 5 minutes. Serve.

炒 珍 珠 菜

Stir-Fried White Wormwood

(SERVES 4)
INGREDIENTS

1 lb. white wormwood (see NOTE)
¼ cup corn oil

SEASONING
1 teaspoon salt

Tear off and discard any old or withered leaves from the white wormwood. Wash and dry, then tear into sections.

Heat the oil in a wok and stir-fry the white wormwood with the seasoning for 1½ minutes. Serve at once.

NOTE
If white wormwood is uavailable, use Chinese cabbage or bean sprouts instead.

莧 菜 糠

Stir-Fried Chinese Red Spinach

(SERVES 4)

INGREDIENTS

2 lb. Chinese red spinach
7 tablespoons corn oil
2 tablespoons chopped garlic
1 tablespoon cornstarch
   mixed with 2 tablespoons
   water

SEASONING
1 teaspoon salt
½ teaspoon white pepper
2 teaspoons sugar

Tear off and discard any old or withered parts from the spinach. Wash the remainder, rubbing it together to clean it throughly.

Heat the oil in a wok and stir-fry the garlic for 1 minute. Add the spinach and seasoning and stir. Put the lid on the wok and simmer the spinach until it is well cooked and tender. Stir in the cornstarch to thicken and serve at once.

NOTE
Substitute 1 lb. broccoli for the red spinach.

鍋 貼 絲 瓜

Sponge Gourd Pan Sticks

(SERVES 4)

INGREDIENTS

1 medium sponge gourd (see
   NOTE)
¼-⅓ cup corn oil
1 tablespoon chopped
   preserved vegetable
   (optional)
½ teaspoon salt
½ tablespoon minced
   scallion
6 tablespoons cornstarch

SEASONING
2 tablespoons light soy sauce
3 tablespoons clear soup
   stock (see p. 261)
½ tablespoon minced red
   chili peppers
1 tablespoon minced garlic
3 tablespoons sesame oil

Peel the sponge gourd and cut off the stem. Wash, chop in half and slice thinly.

Heat 2 tablespoons oil in a wok and stir-fry the gourd slices and preserved vegetable (if used) for a few minutes. Remove and mix with the salt and scallion. When cool, mix carefully with the cornstarch.

Heat half the remaining oil in a skillet and cook tablespoonfuls of the gourd mixture, pressing flat with a fish turner. Cook over a medium heat until brown on both sides. Repeat until the mixture is finished, adding more oil as necessary. Serve hot with the seasoning ingredients mixed together, as a dip.

NOTE
Substitute cocozelle for the sponge gourd. Instead of the sauce suggested, serve with chili sauce or prepared English or Jamaican mustard.

高風亮節

Stir-Fried Baby Bamboo Shoots with Red Chili

(SERVES 4)

INGREDIENTS

1 lb. baby bamboo shoots
4 red chili peppers
¼ cup corn oil
½ tablespoon crushed garlic
¼ cup clear soup stock (see p. 261)

SEASONING

1 teaspoon salt
1½ tablespoons light soy sauce
1 tablespoon sugar

Tear off the old stems and skins from the baby bamboo shoots and wash. Wash the chili peppers and slice finely.

Heat the oil in a wok and stir-fry the chili peppers and garlic for 1 minute. Add the baby bamboo shoots and the seasoning, and stir thoroughly. Pour in the soup stock and simmer, covered, until most of the liquid has been absorbed. Serve at once.

NOTES

Baby bamboo shoots are sweet and crispy.

If you would rather the dish is not too hot, substitute sweet red peppers for the chilis.

留芳百世

Stir-Fried Taro Stem with Peanuts

(SERVES 4)

INGREDIENTS

1 lb. taro (dasheen) stems (see NOTE)
6 tablespoons peeled peanuts
⅓ cup corn oil
1 tablespoon crushed garlic

SEASONING

1 teaspoon salt
1 teaspoon sugar
½ tablespoon soy sauce

Tear the taro stems apart and peel away the stringy skin. Chop off the end part, then wash the stems and chop in 1-inch diagonal slices.

Put the peanuts in a strong plastic bag and crush them with the back of the chopper.

Heat the oil in a wok and stir-fry the garlic for 1 minute. Add the taro slices and stir-fry for 3 minutes more. Add the seasoning and the crushed peanuts, and cook, covered for 3 minutes or until the taro is tender. Stir once more and serve.

NOTE

Look for tender young taro stems for this recipe and be sure to cook them until they are quite soft. If they are unavailable, use snow peas instead.

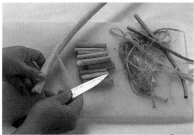

麻菇鶏湯
Soup of Assorted Shreds

(SERVES 4)

INGREDIENTS

1 oz dried bean curd sheets
2 cups (about 2 oz.) fungus
5-6 Chinese mushrooms
1 piece (about 2 oz.) bamboo
   shoot
4 cups clear soup stock (see
   p. 261)

SEASONING

1½ teaspoons salt
½ teaspoon white pepper

Soak the dried bean curd sheets and the fungus in cold water for about 20 minutes until softened. Drain and shred finely.

Soak the Chinese mushrooms in boiling water for 20 minutes. Drain. Cut off and discard the stems and shred the caps finely.

Peel the bamboo shoot. Wash it and shred finely.

Put all the shredded ingredients into a bowl (see picture opposite). Add the seasoning and carefully pour in the soup stock, taking care not to disarrange the vegetables. Steam over gently boiling water for 40 minutes. Serve right away.

香菌鴨
Bean Curd Rolls with Mushrooms

(SERVES 4)

INGREDIENTS

16 pieces of dried bean curd
   sheets
4 Chinese mushrooms
7 tablespoons light soy sauce
2½ tablespoons sugar
1 teaspoon five-spice powder
½ teaspoon salt
1 tablespoon sesame oil
1¼ cups clear soup stock
   (see p. 261)
1 tablespoon rock sugar
8 pieces of licorice or
   peppermint leaves
1 stick cinnamon

Soak the dried bean curd sheets in cold water for 20-30 minutes. Pat dry with paper towels, taking care not to tear the sheets.

Soak the Chinese mushrooms in boiling water for 20 minutes. Drain. Cut off and discard the stems and finely chop the caps. Mix with 4 tablespoons soy sauce, the sugar, five-spice powder, salt and sesame oil. Put in a small pan, bring to a boil, lower the heat and simmer for 1 minute.

In a separate pan, put the soup stock, the rest of the soy sauce, rock sugar, licorice or peppermint leaves and the cinnamon. Bring to a boil, lower the heat and simmer for 20 minutes. Discard the cinnamon stick.

Lay a sheet of bean curd flat and brush with the Chinese mushroom mixture. Repeat, layering and brushing 8 bean curd sheets together. Roll up, then repeat with the remaining 8 sheets of bean curd.

Wrap the bean curd rolls in unbleached muslin and tie with strings to secure. Steam for 25 minutes. Remove, cool slightly, then discard the string and muslin. Serve in slices with the soup stock sauce.

木耳燒素肉

Stir-Fried Glutens with Fungus

(SERVES 4)
INGREDIENTS

½ lb. gluten puff
2 tablespoons light soy sauce
corn oil for deep frying
2 cups (about 2 oz.) fungus
small piece fresh gingerroot
3 tablespoons oil
3 tablespoons clear soup
    stock (see p. 261)

SEASONING
1 teaspoon salt
1½ tablespoons sugar
½ teaspoon white pepper

Tear the gluten puff into pieces. Mix with the soy sauce and leave for 20 minutes.

Heat the oil and deep fry the gluten puff for 30 seconds. Remove with a slotted spoon and drain on paper towels.

Cut off and discard the roots from the fungus. Wash and slice.

Pare the ginger and cut in slices.

Heat the 3 tablespoons oil in a wok and stir-fry the fungus and ginger. Add the fried gluten puff and the seasoning. Stir-fry for a minute, then add the soup stock and simmer, covered, for 1-2 minutes more. Serve at once.

NOTE
You could add shredded cucumber and carrot to this dish to give it a bit of color.

糟香麵筋

Marinated Glutens with Red Fermented Sauce

(SERVES 4)
INGREDIENTS

½ lb. gluten puff
1½ tablespoons red
    fermented grain sauce or 2
    red fermented bean curds
¼ cup corn oil

SEASONING
1 tablespoon sugar
3 tablespoons clear soup
    stock (see p. 261)

Wash the gluten puff and dry on paper towels. Cut in slanting pieces.

Blend the red fermented grain sauce or the fermented bean curds with the seasoning, mashing them together. Add the glutens and leave for 20 minutes.

Heat the oil in a wok and stir-fry the marinated glutens over a medium heat for 3 minutes. Serve at once.

NOTE
Any fermented bean curd sauce could be used instead of the red fermented grain sauce.

鄉味肉豆

Home-Town Style Snow Peas

(SERVES 4)
INGREDIENTS

¾ lb. snow peas (see NOTE)
¼ cup corn oil
½ tablespoon minced fresh
    gingerroot
⅓ tablespoon crushed garlic
⅓ tablespoon minced red
    chili peppers

SEASONING
1 teaspoon salt
½ teaspoon sherry

Trim the snow peas, removing any strings. Wash.
    Heat the oil in a wok and stir-fry the ginger, garlic
and chili peppers for 1 minute. Add the snow peas and
stir. Cook over a medium heat, covered, for 1 minute,
then add the seasoning, and cook, stirring, for a
further minute. Serve at once.

NOTE
Snow peas are also known as sugar peas.

金針香菇炒白菜

Stir-Fried Chinese Cabbage with Chinese Mushrooms

(SERVES 4)
INGREDIENTS

5 Chinese mushrooms
2 cups (about 2 oz.) dried lily
    flowers
1 medium Chinese cabbage
¼ cup corn oil
½ tablespoon cornstarch
    mixed with 2 tablespoons
    water

SEASONING
1 teaspoon salt
½ tablespoon sugar

Soak the Chinese mushrooms in boiling water for
20 minutes. Drain. Cut off and discard the stems and
shred the caps.
    Cut off and discard the hard stem parts from the
dried lily flowers. Tie a knot in each of the flowers,
wash them and soak in cold water for about 30
minutes. Drain and squeeze dry.
    Cut off and discard the root part and any old or
withered leaves from the cabbage. Wash the leaves
and cut in wide shreds.
    Heat the oil in a wok and stir-fry the mushroom
shreds for 1-2 minutes. Add the cabbage and lily
flowers and stir. Lower the heat, and cook covered,
until the cabbage is soft.
    Stir in the seasoning and the cornstarch paste, and
cook until the mixture has thickened. Serve at once.

福壽暖鍋

Pot of Assorted Vegetables

(SERVES 4)
INGREDIENTS

1 cup (about 1 oz.) dried lily
    flowers
½ a small cabbage
1 carrot
1 turnip
½ a medium cauliflower
1 small taro (dasheen)
1 cup all-purpose flour
½ teaspoon salt
1 teaspoon chili powder
4 eggs
¼-⅓ cup water
⅓ cup corn oil
3 tablespoons shredded
    preserved vegetable
5 cups clear soup stock (see
    p. 261)

SEASONING
1½ teapoons salt

Cut off and discard the hard stem parts from the dried lily flowers. Tie a knot in each of the flowers, wash them, then soak in cold water for about 30 minutes. Drain and squeeze dry.

Cut off and discard the root and any old or withered leaves from the cabbage. Wash the leaves and shred them.

Peel the carrot and turnip, wash and dice. Wash the cauliflower, cut off and discard any tough stems and cut into small flowerets. Peel the taro and shred it.

Mix together the flour, salt and chili powder and mix to a smooth batter with the eggs, water and 1 tablespoon oil. Coat the cauliflower, cabbage and taro with this batter.

Heat the remaining oil and deep-fry the battered vegetables until golden brown. Remove and keep warm. Pour off all but 1 tablespoon of the oil.

Stir-fry the preserved vegetable in the oil for a few minutes, then add the seasoning, soup stock, carrot, and turnip. Bring to a boil, lower the heat and simmer for 5 minutes. Stir in the dried lily flowers and the fried battered vegetables. Serve at once.

全福暖鍋

Family Pot

(SERVES 4)
INGREDIENTS

8 Chinese mushrooms
9 pieces of dried bean curd
    sheets
10 water chestnuts
2 tablespoons corn oil
1 carrot
2 pieces of fried bean curd
    sheet
2-3 water bamboos
8 seaweed rolls
9 tablespoons minced
    preserved vegetable
2 tablespoons shredded
    bamboo shoot
6 tablespoons chopped
    fungus
12 pieces wonton skin
1 slice fresh gingerroot
5 cups clear soup stock (see
    p. 261)
1 cup bean sprouts

SEASONING
1½ tablespoons salt
½ tablespoon sugar
2 tablespoons soy sauce

Soak the Chinese mushrooms in boiling water for 20 minutes. Drain. Cut off and discard the stems.

Soak the dried bean curd sheets in cold water for 20 minutes until soft. Drain and shred 1 of them finely.

Peel and wash the water chestnuts and cook them in the oil for 2 minutes. Remove with a slotted spoon.

Peel the carrot and chop in chunks. Divide each fried bean curd sheet into 4 pieces.

Discard the skins from the water bamboos and cut off the stems. Chop in chunks and wash. Wash the seaweed rolls.

Mix 3 tablespoons of chopped preserved vegetable with the shredded dried bean curd sheet and the bamboo shoots. Mix in the dried bean curd sheets.

Mix the rest of the preserved vegetable with the fungus and wrap in the wonton skins.

Put the ginger and soup into a large saucepan and bring to a boil. Add the carrot, Chinese mushrooms, water bamboo, water chestnuts, seaweed rolls and the dried bean curd sheet mixture. Bring to a boil, lower the heat and simmer gently for 20 minutes. Add the seasoning, the wonton packages and bean sprouts, and serve.

双菇扒芥菜

Mustard Greens with Mushrooms

(SERVES 4)
INGREDIENTS

1 lb. mustard greens (or a
  crisp lettuce)
1 cup straw mushrooms
1 cup button mushrooms
½ teaspoon baking soda
¼ cup corn oil
½ tablespoon crushed garlic
1 teaspoon minced fresh
  gingerroot
½ cup clear soup stock (see
  p. 261)
1 tablespoon cornstarch
  mixed with 2 tablespoons
  water
1 teaspoon sesame oil

SEASONING
1 teaspoon salt
2 teaspoons sugar

Cut off and discard any withered or old parts from
the mustard greens. Wash and chop in chunks.

Wash the straw mushrooms and the button
mushrooms. Cut off and discard any muddy stems and
cut them all in half. Blanch in boiling water for 1
minute, drain (reserving the water) and plunge in cold
water. Let cool.

Add the soda to the boiling water used to blanch
the mushrooms. Add the mustard greens and cook for
1½ minutes. Drain and rinse under cold running
water.

Heat the oil in a wok and stir-fry the garlic and
ginger for 1 minute. Add the mustard greens and half
of the seasoning. Stir-fry for 1 minute, then remove
with a slotted spoon.

Add the soup stock, and the straw and button
mushrooms to the pan. Bring to a boil, stir in the rest of
the seasoning and cook for 1 minute. Stir in the
cornstarch mixture, and when the sauce has
thickened, pour it over the mustard greens. Dribble
over the sesame oil and serve.

農家樂

The Farmer's Joy

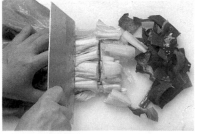

(SERVES 4)
INGREDIENTS

½ lb. vermicelli
¾ lb. white Chinese cabbage
1 large fungus
1 large carrot
¼ cup corn oil
1 tablespoon chopped
  scallion
¼ cup clear soup stock (see
  p. 261)

SEASONING
⅔ teaspoon salt
1½ tablespoons soy sauce
1 teaspoon sugar

Soak the vermicelli in cold water for 15 minutes
until softened. Cut in sections.

Cut off and discard the root and any old or
withered leaves from the Chinese cabbage. Wash and
chop in 1-inch slices. Wash the fungus and slice.

Peel the carrot and chop in large slices.

Heat the oil in a wok and stir-fry the scallion for 1
minute. Add the fungus and carrot slices and stir-fry
for 1 minute more. Add the white cabbage and cook,
stirring, for a few minutes.

Add the drained vermicelli, the soup stock, and the
seasoning, mixing everything together well. Bring to a
boil, lower the heat and simmer, covered for 1 minute
and serve.

NOTE
Add bamboo shoot, Chinese mushrooms and bean
curd sheets to this dish if you want to make it more
substantial.

豆絲春濃

Stir-Fried Bean Cake Shreds with Snap Beans

(SERVES 4)
INGREDIENTS

1 cup green bean starch
½ cup rice flour
water (see recipe)
8-10 snap beans
2 cups (about 2 oz.) fungus
1 cup bean sprouts
⅓ cup corn oil
⅔ teaspoon chili powder
2 tablespoons clear soup
    stock (see p. 261)

SEASONING
1 teaspoon salt
1 tablespoon dark soy sauce

Blend the green bean starch and the rice flour with sufficient water to make a pliable dough. Knead it, then press it out thinly. Put it in a skillet and cook on both sides over a medium heat until beginning to brown. Remove and chop in fine shreds.

Trim the beans, removing any strings. Chop in diagonal slices. Wash the fungus and shred. Wash the bean sprouts.

Heat the oil in a wok and cook the chili powder for 30 seconds. Add the beans, fungus and bean sprouts and stir-fry for 1 minute. Add the shredded cooked dough and the soup stock and simmer, covered, for 1 minute. Serve at once.

脆味瓜片

Pickled Cucumber Slices

(SERVES 4)
INGREDIENTS

1 lb. cucumbers
2 tablespoons white vinegar
3 tablespoons sesame oil

SEASONING
2½ teaspoons salt
¼ cup sugar

Wash the cucumbers, cut off and discard end parts and then slice finely.

Mix the cucumber slices with the seasoning, mixing them together well. Put in a dish and chill.

Just before serving, squeeze out the excess liquid from the cucumbers and blend with the vinegar and sesame oil. Pour over cucumbers and serve.

NOTE
You can keep the sliced cucumbers in the refrigerator for up to 2 days. Cover with plastic wrap or their flavor will permeate other foods in the refrigerator.

炸洋蔥餅

Onion Cakes

(SERVES 4)
INGREDIENTS

2 large onions
1 cup all-purpose flour
⅓ teaspoon salt
3 eggs
¼ cup water
9 tablespoons corn oil

SEASONING
1 teaspoon salt
¼ tablespoon mild paprika

Peel the onions, chop off end parts, then wash and slice finely.

Mix together the flour and salt, and then mix to a batter with the eggs, water and 1 tablespoon oil.

Heat ¼ cup corn oil in a wok and stir-fry the sliced onions for 2 minutes. Remove with a slotted spoon, cool slightly, then mix with the batter.

Heat the remaining oil in a skillet and cook spoonfuls of the onion and batter, until golden brown on both sides.

Mix the salt and paprika with a tablespoon of the oil used for cooking and serve with the hot onion cakes.

NOTE
You could serve the onion cakes with homemade tomato sauce instead of the paprika mix if you prefer.

炸紫菜素捲

Crispy Laver Rolls

(SERVES 4)
INGREDIENTS

1 carrot
½ a cucumber
1 piece (about 2 oz.) bamboo shoot
2 cups (about 2 oz.) fungus
½ teapoon salt
2 tablespoons all-purpose flour
4½ tablespoons water
3 pieces of laver
3 tablespoons light soy sauce
2 teaspoons cornstarch
½ teaspoon chili powder
1½ tablespoons corn oil

Peel the carrot and shred finely. Wash the cucumber, peel and wash the bamboo shoot and wash the fungus. Shred all these vegetables finely. Put in a colander and sprinkle with the salt.

Mix the flour to a paste with 1½ tablespoons water.

Lay the pieces of laver out flat and arrange a third of the shredded vegetables on each piece as shown in the small picture 2. Roll up and seal the ends with the flour paste.

Put the soy sauce, cornstarch, chili powder and the remaining 3 tablespoons water into a small saucepan. Bring to a boil, stirring, then remove from the heat.

Heat the oil in a skillet and cook the laver rolls over a medium heat for 5 minutes, turning them constantly. Remove, cut in diagonal pieces and serve with the soy sauce mixture.

凉拌海蜇

Cold Sauced Jellyfish

(SERVES 4)

INGREDIENTS

1 lb. jellyfish, shredded (see NOTES).
½ teaspoon salt
2 tablespoons light soy sauce
3 tablespoons shredded carrot
3 tablespoons shredded Chinese celery or scallions
1 teaspoon sugar
1 tablespoon sesame oil

Cover the jellyfish with cold water and let soak for 20 minutes. Wash under cold running water, place in a colander and scald with boiling water. Immediately plunge in cold water and let soak for 4-5 hours (or until you want to serve it).

When ready to serve, drain the jellyfish and squeeze out the water. Mix the salt and half the soy sauce into the jellyfish and let stand for 10 minutes. Drain again very thoroughly.

Mix the jellyfish with the shredded carrot and Chinese celery or scallions. Mix in the rest of the soy sauce with the sugar and sesame oil. Serve.

NOTES

You can use dried, fresh or frozen jellyfish for this recipe. Dried jellyfish must be soaked in cold water until it has softened. Frozen should be thoroughly thawed before use.

When scalding the jellyfish, tip spoonfuls of boiling water over it rather than plunging it into a pan of boiling water. Stir the jellyfish as you pour on the water; the shreds should roll up.

黄瓜粉皮

Cucumbers with Mung Bean Sheets

(SERVES 4)

INGREDIENTS

3 cucumbers
2 tablespoons crushed garlic
1 package (about 8 slices) mung bean sheets

SEASONING
1 tablespoon sesame oil
1½ tablespoons white vinegar

DRESSING
2 teaspoons salt
2 tablespoons sugar

Wash the cucumbers; cut off the stems and end pieces. Wipe them dry, then crush them slightly with the chopper. Chop in 1-inch sections and mix with the garlic and dressing. Put into a bowl, cover with plastic wrap and refrigerate for at least 4 hours.

Meanwhile, soak the mung bean sheets in cold water to soften them. Chop in 1-inch sections.

Squeeze the juice from the cucumbers and mix with the strips of mung bean sheets. Stir in the seasoning and serve.

NOTES

If you like a hot taste, substitute chili oil for the sesame oil and add 2 or 3 small chopped chili peppers.

Use mung bean sheets on the day that you buy them.

花生麵筋

Peanuts with Gluten Puff

(SERVES 4)
INGREDIENTS

1 cup raw peanuts
3 oz. gluten puff
½ cup water

SEASONING
2 tablespoons light soy sauce
½ teaspoon salt
½ tablespoon powdered rock
    sugar
1 tablespoon brown sugar
2 star anises

Wash the peanuts thoroughly and soak them in cold water for 4 hours.

Put the gluten puff into a pan and cover with boiling water. Simmer until it is soft – about 5 minutes. Drain.

Drain the peanuts and mix with the seasoning in a saucepan. Add the water and bring to a boil. Lower the heat and simmer for 10 minutes. Add the drained gluten puff and cook for 5 minutes more. Serve at once.

NOTE
You can use cooked peanuts for this dish, in which case soak them first in boiling water containing 2-3 star anises for 1 hour (see small picture 3).

滷豆乾

Spiced Bean Curds

(SERVES 4)
INGREDIENTS

1 pack of spices (see NOTES)
2½ cups water
10 oz. spiced bean curds (see
    NOTES)
2 tablespoons light soy sauce
½ tablespoon rock sugar

Boil the pack of spices in the water for 30 minutes. Wash the spiced bean curds under cold running water. Add them to the pan with the soy sauce and the rock sugar. Bring to a boil, then lower the heat and simmer for 10 minutes. Remove from the heat, but leave the bean curds in the liquid until ready to serve.

NOTES
A pack of spices should contain star anise, fennel, dried orange peel, cinnamon and licorice.

If you do not cook the spiced bean curds on the day you have bought them, put them in a pan with some salt and cover with water. Bring to a boil and cook for 3 minutes. This will preserve them for up to 3 days. Keep in the refrigerator.

炒三色丁
Stir-Fried Cubes in Three Colors

(SERVES 4)
INGREDIENTS

½ a salted cabbage, cubed
½ a preserved vegetable, cubed
¼ cup corn oil
1 piece (about 2 oz.) bamboo shoot, cubed

SEASONING
1 tablespoon sugar
½ tablespoon light soy sauce
½ teaspoon white pepper
¼ cup water

Soak the salted cabbage and preserved vegetable in cold water for 20 minutes. Drain well.

Heat the oil in a wok and stir-fry all the vegetables together for 1 minute. Add the seasoning, cover the pan and cook for 2 minutes. Serve.

NOTES
This makes an ideal stuffing for steamed dumplings.

If you like, mix in 2 teaspoons sesame oil just before serving.

滷桶筍
Marinated Bamboo Shoots

(SERVES 6)
INGREDIENTS

1 lb. pickled bamboo shoots
2 star anises
2 sweet red peppers, seeded
4 cloves garlic, minced
¼ cup corn oil
¼-⅓ cup water

SEASONING
1 teaspoon salt
2 tablespoons light soy sauce
1½ tablespoons powdered rock sugar (see NOTE p. 251)

Tear the pickled bamboo shoots into long shreds. Wash them thoroughly, then squeeze out all the water.

Put the bamboo shreds into a saucepan and cover with water. Add the star anises, bring to a boil and boil for 5 minutes. Drain and rinse under running water. Squeeze out the water again.

Crush the peppers thoroughly with the back of the chopper then stir-fry with the garlic in the oil for 2 minutes. Add the bamboo shreds with the seasoning and the water. Stir for a few minutes, then simmer for about 20 minutes, stirring occasionally until the bamboo shoot is tender and most of the liquid has evaporated. Serve at once.

NOTE
A large quantity of this dish can be prepared at one time as it will keep for up to 3 days in the refrigerator. Reheat as you want to serve it. This is why it is called *Marinated* Bamboo Shoots.

Spiced Sour Cabbage

(SERVES 4)
INGREDIENTS

1 lb. sour cabbage
¼ cup corn oil
2 cups water or clear soup
    stock (see p. 261)

SEASONING
2 tablespoons light soy sauce
1 tablespoon powdered rock
    sugar (see NOTE p. 251)
1 tablespoon brown sugar
½ teaspoon white pepper

Wash the sour cabbage very thoroughly, discarding any old leaves. Squeeze out the liquid, then shred the cabbage and soak in cold water for 10 minutes. Drain.

Heat the oil in a wok. Mix the seasoning into the cabbage and stir-fry over a high heat for a few minutes. Add the water or soup stock, bring to a boil, then lower the heat, and simmer, covered for 15 minutes, stirring occasionally. Drain off most of the liquid and serve at once.

NOTES

A large quantity of this dish can be prepared at one time as it will keep in the refrigerator for up to 5 days. Do not drain off the excess liquid until you heat it up to serve. The liquid helps to preserve the dish.

If you like a hot taste, add 2 minced chili peppers to the seasoning ingredients.

Marinated Chives

(SERVES 4)
INGREDIENTS

5 bunches (about 10 oz.)
    chives
1½ tablespoons salt

SEASONING
white wine vinegar
sesame oil

Discard any old leaves from the chives. Wash the remainder and dry in a clean cloth.

Sprinkle the salt over the chives, then rub them with your hands until they have softened. Rinse the chives and squeeze out the liquid. Mince the chives and put into a dish.

Serve spoonfuls at a time, passing the white vinegar and sesame oil for each person to help themselves.

NOTE
This dish comes from northern China, where garlic is usually added to it.

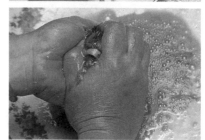

Soup of Five Blessings

(SERVES 4)
INGREDIENTS

½ cup longan pulp
½ cup red dates
½ cup fresh lotus seeds
½ cup ginkgo fruits
½ cup fresh lily
5 cups water
½ cup crushed rock sugar

Wash the longan pulp and the red dates. Soak the dates in cold water for 1-2 hours.

Wash the lotus seeds and the ginkgo fruits. Wash the lily and remove the outer membrane.

Put all the ingredients together with the water and crushed rock sugar into a saucepan. Bring to a boil, then lower the heat and simmer for 1 hour. Serve.

NOTE
If fresh lily and lotus seeds are not available, buy dried ones and soak them in cold water for 2-3 hours and overnight respectively.

Lotus Root with Red Dates

(SERVES 4)
INGREDIENTS

2 sections of lotus root
(renkon)
1 teaspoon salt
1 cup red dates, soaked
overnight in cold water
2-4 tablespoons rock sugar
4 cups water

Peel the lotus root and chop it in bite-size pieces. Wash thoroughly, adding the salt to the water. Drain.

Wash the red dates under running water after their soaking.

Put the lotus root pieces into a large saucepan with the dates, rock sugar and water. Bring to a boil, then lower the heat and simmer for 1-1½ hours until the mixture smells sweet. Keep an eye on the pan and add more water if it evaporates too much.

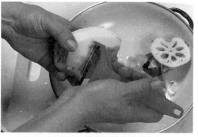

如意帶玉

Stir-Fried Green Celery with Bean Sprouts

(SERVES 4)
INGREDIENTS

1 lb. bean sprouts
2 spiced bean curds
3 stems Chinese celery
⅔ cup oil

SEASONING

1 teaspoon salt
1 tablespoon light soy sauce
1 tablespoon clear soup stock
(see p. 261)
1 teaspoon sugar

Wash the bean sprouts and drain thoroughly. Chop the spiced bean curds in shreds.

Cut off and discard the old stems and leaves from the celery. Wash and cut in 1-inch sections.

Heat the oil in a wok and stir-fry the bean sprouts, bean curds and celery together with the seasoning for about 10 minutes. Cover and simmer for 2 minutes more, then serve.

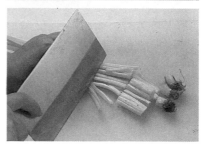

堆金積玉

Golden Glutens with Emerald Peppers

(SERVES 4)
INGREDIENTS

½ lb. gluten puff
2 tablespoons dark soy sauce
6 green chili peppers
corn oil for deep frying, plus
¼ cup extra oil

SEASONING

1 teaspoon salt
1 tablespoon sugar
2 tablespoons clear soup
stock (see p. 261)

Chop the gluten puff in diagonal slices and marinate with the soy sauce for 20 minutes.

Crush the green chili peppers gently with the chopper, then slice them in 1-inch sections.

Heat the pan of oil for deep frying and deep-fry the gluten until browned. Remove with a slotted spoon and drain on paper towels.

Heat the ¼ cup oil in a wok and stir-fry the chili peppers, fried glutens and seasoning over a high heat for 1 minute. Serve at once.

NOTE
If this dish is going to be too hot for you, substitute green peppers for the chilis.

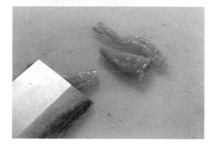

Green-Stemmed Flat Cabbage with Chinese Mushrooms

(SERVES 4)
INGREDIENTS

8 large Chinese mushrooms
1 teaspoon salt
3 tablespoons corn oil
1 lb. green-stemmed flat
  cabbage
½ cup clear soup stock (see
  p. 261)
1½ tablespoons cornstarch
  mixed with 1½
  tablespoons water

SEASONING
1 teaspoon salt
1 teaspoon sugar

Soak the Chinese mushrooms in boiling water for 20 minutes. Drain. Cut off and discard the stems and chop the caps in half.

Remove the outer withered leaves of the cabbage and wash the remainder. Chop in 2½-inch pieces, then chop these in half lengthwise. Blanch in boiling water mixed with the 1 teaspoon salt for 1-1½ minutes. Drain and soak in cold water until cold. Drain and squeeze out the water, then arrange the cabbage on a plate.

Heat the oil in a wok and stir-fry the mushrooms for 1-2 minutes. Add the stock and seasoning and cook for 5 minutes. Stir in the cornstarch mixture and when the stock has thickened, spoon it and the mushrooms carefully over the cabbage. Serve at once.

Shredded Water-Bamboo Shoots

(SERVES 4)
INGREDIENTS

4 water-bamboo shoots
  (about 10 oz.)

SEASONING
1 teaspoon salt
½ tablespoon light soy sauce
½ teaspoon white pepper
3 teaspoons sesame oil
1 teaspoon sugar
1 teaspoon white vinegar

Cut away the outer skin of the water-bamboo shoots and chop off the end part. Slice each piece in half lengthwise. Steam these pieces over boiling water for 12 minutes.

Remove from the steamer and shred the shoots finely. Mix with the seasoning and serve.

NOTES
You can keep this in the refrigerator for up to 3 days. It makes a refreshing summer dish.

Substitute 2½ cups shredded Chinese cabbage or lettuce for the water-bamboo shoots.

芝蔴腐竹片

Bean Curd Sheets with Black Sesame Seed

(SERVES 4)

INGREDIENTS

6 dried bean curd sheets
corn oil for deep frying
1 tablespoon black sesame
  seeds
1 tablespoon corn oil
2 tablespoons garlic soy
  sauce (see NOTE)

Use scissors to cut the bean curd sheets in thin strips and drop them, a few at a time, into a pan of oil, heated until it is smoking. Deep-fry until they turn crispy. Remove and drain on paper towels while you cook the remainder.

Pick out and discard any impurities in the black sesame seeds, then stir-fry them with the 1 tablespoon oil for 1-2 minutes over a gentle heat. Remove.

Mix the garlic soy sauce with the fried bean curd sheets and sprinkle the black sesame seeds over the top.

NOTE
To make garlic soy sauce, mix together 3 tablespoons light soy sauce, 1 tablespoon crushed garlic and ½ teaspoon white pepper. Keep in a screw-top jar.

蒜豉苦瓜

Bitter Gourd with Fermented Beans

(SERVES 4)

INGREDIENTS

1 bitter gourd
½ tablespoon salt
1 tablespoon fermented black
  beans (see NOTE p. 54)
⅓ cup corn oil
½ tablespoon crushed garlic
½ tablespoon minced chili
  peppers
3 tablespoons water

SEASONING
1 tablespoon soy sauce
½ teaspoon salt
1 tablespoon sugar
½ teaspoon white pepper

Chop the bitter gourd in half lengthwise. Remove the seeds and cut off the peel, the stem and the end part. Slice the flesh and sprinkle it with the salt. Leave for 20 minutes, stirring the pieces with your hand frequently, then squeeze out the juice. Blanch in boiling water for 30 seconds and drain.

Crush the fermented beans with the back of the chopper.

Heat the oil in a wok and stir-fry the beans, garlic and chili peppers over a medium heat for 2-3 minutes. Add the bitter gourd and stir everything together. Add the seasoning and the water and simmer, covered, for 3-5 minutes. Serve.

核桃酪

Sweet Walnut Soup

(SERVES 4)
INGREDIENTS

½ cup large red dates
1 cup walnut halves
½ tablespoon powdered rock
   sugar (see NOTES)
4 cups water

Wash the red dates, then soak them in cold water for 4 hours. Cut open and remove the seeds. Wrap the pieces in a square of unbleached muslin and rub together by tapping with the back of a knife to loosen the skins. Let soak in water for 10 minutes more to remove the skins, then mash the dates.

Grind the walnut halves to a powder. Mix together with the dates, rice flour and rock sugar powder. Tip into a pan and gradually stir in the water. Bring to a boil, stirring over a medium heat and serve.

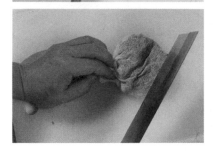

NOTES

Walnuts are very nutritious and said to be particularly good for the elderly.

If you cannot get hold of powdered rock sugar, use crystal rock sugar and crush it with the back of the chopper.

芝麻糊

Sesame Paste

(SERVES 2)
INGREDIENTS

3 tablespoons sesame
   powder
3 tablespoons brown sugar
2 cups boiling water

Mix the sesame powder with the sugar in a bowl. Gradually add the boiling water, stirring to keep the mixture smooth. Serve at once.

NOTES

There are two kinds of sesame powder on the market. One is pure sesame powder, the other a mixture of sesame powder and rice powder or cornstarch. If using the pure one, add 1 tablespoon cornstarch, stirring this in with the sugar.

This dish is traditionally served as a dessert.

脆皮豆腐

Crispy Bean Curds

(SERVES 4)
INGREDIENTS

¾ lb. fresh bean curd
1 egg, beaten
1½ cups all-purpose flour
corn oil, for deep frying
1 scallion, minced, for
   garnish

SEASONING
3 tablespoons light soy sauce
1 garlic clove, crushed
½ teaspoon sugar
2 teaspoons sesame oil

Cut the bean curd in 1 x 2 inch pieces. Place in a bowl and scald with boiling water for 1 minute.

Dip each rectangle of bean curd first in the beaten egg and then in the flour, shaking off any excess flour.

Heat the oil in a deep-fat fryer and deep-fry the bean curd pieces for 3-4 minutes until golden. Remove with a slotted spoon and place on a serving platter.

Mix the seasoning ingredients together to make a dipping sauce and place in a small bowl.

Sprinkle the bean curd with a little minced scallion and serve with the dipping sauce.

炒皮笛

Stir-Fried Bamboo Shoots

(SERVES 4)
INGREDIENTS

4 spiced bean curds
1 can (4 oz.) bamboo shoots,
   drained
4 Chinese mushrooms,
   soaked (see NOTE)
3 tablespoons sesame oil
1 inch piece fresh gingerroot,
   sliced
2 fresh red chili peppers,
   seeded and thinly sliced
3 tablespoons clear soup
   stock (see p. 261)
1 tablespoon cornstarch

SEASONING
½ teaspoon salt
½ tablespoon light soy sauce
½ teaspoon sugar

Slice the bean curd, slice the bamboo shoots and cut the mushrooms in small pieces.

Heat the sesame oil in a wok or skillet and stir in the ginger. Stir-fry for 30 seconds and then remove the ginger with a slotted spoon and discard.

Add the red chili peppers and cook for 15 seconds. Stir in the bamboo shoots, mushrooms, spiced bean curd and the soup stock. Cook for 1 minute and then lower the heat and simmer for a further minute.

Mix the cornstarch with a little water and stir in the mixture. Cook for about 1 minute until thickened and serve.

NOTE
Soak the Chinese mushrooms in warm water for 30 minutes before using and remove stems.

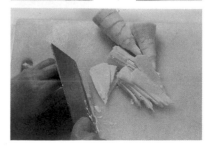

芝麻蘆筍

Asparagus with Black Sesame Seeds

(SERVES 4)
INGREDIENTS

1 lb. fresh asparagus
1 teaspoon salt
2 tablespoons black sesame seeds (see NOTE)
1 tablespoon corn oil

SEASONING
½ teaspoon salt
1 tablespoon light soy sauce
½ teaspoon white pepper

Cut off the ends and peel away the tough skin from the ends of the asparagus. Cut in 1 inch pieces.

Bring a large saucepan of water to a boil. Add the salt and throw in the asparagus. Cover and cook over a moderate heat for 5 minutes.

Drain the asparagus and let soak in cold water for 5 minutes. Drain thoroughly.

Dry-fry the black sesame seeds in a wok or skillet for 30 seconds. Remove and set aside.

Heat the oil in the wok or skillet, add the asparagus and stir-fry for 10 seconds. Add the seasoning ingredients along with the black sesame seeds and stir well.

Spoon onto a serving platter and serve at once.

NOTE
Black sesame seeds have the same flavor as white sesame seeds and these can be used if the black ones are not available.

芋泥

Creamed Taro

(SERVES 4)
INGREDIENTS

1 taro (dasheen), (about 10 oz. in weight)
5 cups chicken stock (see p. 149)

SEASONING
1½ teaspoons salt
½ teaspoon white pepper
2 teaspoons sugar

Peel the taro and cut in large pieces. Place in a colander or steamer and steam, covered, over a high heat for 30 minutes. Mash with a fork or potato masher.

Bring the chicken stock to a boil and stir in the mashed taro and the seasoning ingredients.

Lower the heat and simmer for 20 minutes and then spoon into a serving dish.

NOTE
Taro, or dasheen as it is also known, is a tuber. It has a mealy texture, and gray or pale lilac-colored flesh. It is available year round.

枸杞渾元

Medlar with Egg

(SERVES 1)
INGREDIENTS

4 tablespoons fresh medlar
   leaves
1¼ cups water or clear soup
   stock (see p. 261)
1 egg
⅓ teaspoon salt

    Pick the medlar leaves off the stems. Wash them
and wipe dry on a clean cloth. Put into a soup bowl.
    Put the water or soup into a small saucepan and
bring to a boil. Ladle out about ½ cup and put this into
a small bowl.
    Break the egg into the small bowl and let it stand
for about 30 seconds. Then stand the bowl in the
saucepan of simmering liquid. Cook for 3-5 minutes
until the white of the egg is setting. Pour the egg with
the liquid over the medlar leaves. Add the salt and
serve.

NOTE
Choose young tender medlar leaves for this dish; they
will lose their bright green color as soon as they come
into contact with the boiling liquid.

奶蛋

Steamed Milk Egg

(SERVES 1)
INGREDIENTS

1 egg, beaten
⅔-¾ cup milk
1 tablespoon superfine sugar

    Strain the beaten egg, then stir in the milk and
sugar. Pour into a small bowl.
    Place the bowl in a steamer and steam, covered,
over gently boiling water for 5 minutes. Remove the lid
and steam for 5 minutes more. Serve.

NOTE
Use 1 tablespoon honey instead of superfine sugar.

奶汁冬瓜帽

Winter Melon Pieces with Milk

(SERVES 4)
INGREDIENTS

1 lb. winter melon
8-10 Chinese mushrooms
3 spiced bean curds
6-8 button mushrooms
3 tablespoons corn oil
½ cup milk
1½ tablespoons cornstarch

SEASONING A
¼-⅓ cup clear soup stock
   (see p. 261)
1 slice fresh gingerroot
½ teaspoon salt
½ teaspoon white pepper

SEASONING B
1 teaspoon salt
1 teaspoon sugar
½ teaspoon white pepper

Cut away the skin from the winter melon and discard the seeds. Chop the flesh in rectangular pieces about ¼ × 1½ inches. Place these in a large bowl and add seasoning **A**. Put the bowl in a steamer and steam for 20 minutes. Drain off the liquid and reserve it, but discard the ginger.

Soak the Chinese mushrooms in boiling water for 20 minutes. Wash the bean curds and button mushrooms. Cut off and discard the stems from the Chinese mushrooms, then mince the caps with the bean curds and button mushrooms. Sprinkle over seasoning **B** and mix everything together well.

Heat the oil in a wok and stir-fry the Chinese mushroom mixture for 2 minutes. Press this on top of the winter melon. Steam for 15 minutes more, then remove and invert the bowl on a plate.

Mix together the milk, the liquid drained from the melon and the cornstarch. Pour into a small pan and bring to a boil slowly, stirring all the time. Let the mixture bubble for a minute or so until it thickens, then pour it over the winter melon and serve at once.

冰 心 玉 潔

Crystal Beauty

(SERVES 4)
INGREDIENTS

1 section lotus root (renkon)
½ package condensed agar-
   agar powder
2 cups clear soup stock (see
   p. 261)
Maraschino cherries, to serve

SEASONING
1½ teaspoons salt
½ teaspoon white pepper

Peel the lotus root and chop in small pieces. Soak these in water for 30 minutes.

Put the agar-agar powder into a pan with the stock and the seasoning. Simmer gently for 30 minutes, then remove from the heat. Pour through a strainer lined with a piece of unbleached muslin.

Drain the lotus root and put it into the strained liquid. Tip back into the rinsed-out pan and bring to a boil. Pour into a square loaf pan, cover with plastic wrap, and when cool, put in the refrigerator.

When ready to serve, remove the pan from the refrigerator – it should have set into a firm gelatin. Cut in strips and serve with ice cubes and Maraschino cherries.

NOTE
This dish is a delightfully fresh one to serve on a hot summer's day.

Clear Soup Stock

INGREDIENTS

1 medium-size parsnip
1 medium-size turnip
2 onions
4 celery stalks
2 tablespoons corn oil
4 tablespoons chopped
    button mushroom stems
6¼ cups water
2 teaspoons salt
bouquet garni (see NOTES)
3 black peppercorns

Wash the parsnip and turnip but do not peel. Chop them in chunks. Peel the onions, wash the celery and chop these in chunks, too.

Heat the oil in a large saucepan and add all the chopped vegetables and the mushroom stems. Cook, stirring occasionally, for 5-7 minutes over a medium heat.

Add the water, salt, bouquet garni and peppercorns to the pan. Bring to a boil, then lower the heat and simmer for 30 minutes.

Strain the liquid into a bowl, pressing the vegetables with the back of a wooden spoon to extract as much liquid as possible. Discard the vegetables left in the strainer.

Let the stock cool completely, then cover with plastic wrap and put in the refrigerator.

NOTES

Make a bouquet garni by tying together 2 sprigs of parsley, 1 sprig of thyme and 1 bay leaf.

Keep the stock for 2-3 days in the refrigerator, or freeze it in small quantities (ice cube trays or small yogurt pots make ideal containers) and use as required.

Rich Soup Stock

INGREDIENTS

1 large carrot
1 small turnip
1 cup button mushrooms
2 onions
4 celery stalks
1 small tomato
2 tablespoons corn oil
5 cups water
2 teaspoons salt
bouquet garni (see NOTES
    above)
3 black peppercorns

Wash the carrot and turnip but do not peel. Wipe the mushrooms with damp paper towels. Peel the onions and wash the celery and the tomato. Chop all these vegetables in chunks.

Heat the oil in a large saucepan and add all the chopped vegetables. Cook, stirring occasionally, for 8-10 minutes, over a medium heat.

Add the water, salt, bouquet garni and peppercorns to the pan. Bring to a boil, then lower the heat and simmer for 30 minutes.

Finish off as outlined above in Clear Soup Stock.

RICE AND NOODLES

Except in the northern, wheat-producing regions, rice is undoubtedly the single most important food in China. The Chinese phrase implying "to eat a meal" when literally translated means "to eat cooked rice" and all the meals of the day concern eating rice. For instance, the Chinese word for "breakfast" means "morning cooked rice" when literally translated.

Consequently, unless you plan to cook a typical northern-style dinner, no Chinese meal would be complete without rice. Somewhat surprisingly, the Chinese do not tend to serve their rice in very elaborate forms. *Fried Rice* is far more common in Western restaurants than in China itself. Plain long-grain rice which is boiled until tender and then served in individual bowls is the most common way of eating rice. While the accompanying dishes add flavor to the meal, rice is still considered the centerpiece and it's a common belief that, if necessary, a man could survive on nothing else.

Noodles are frequently eaten in the north, where wheat is widely grown. Wheat noodles can be bought fresh or dried and are made with or without eggs. There are also several other types of noodle available, principally rice noodles, made from rice flour, and cellophane noodles or transparent vermicelli, made from ground mung beans.

Unlike rice, noodles tend to be cooked with other ingredients – they can be steamed, stir-fried or stirred into soups. Cellophane noodles, particularly, are eaten more as a vegetable or bean curd, since they absorb the tastes of other ingredients and add a slippery texture. Other grains, such as oatmeal, are also included in this chapter, since, like rice, they provide bulk and substance in a meal.

炒 飯 三 式

Fried Rice

SIMPLE FRIED RICE

(SERVES 4)
INGREDIENTS

4 cups cooked long-grain
rice (see NOTE)
3 tablespoons corn oil
6 eggs, beaten
4 tablespoons minced
scallions
1 teaspoon salt
½ teaspoon rice wine or dry
sherry

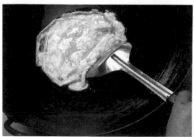

Break up the cooked rice with chopsticks or a fork.
Heat the oil in a wok, add the beaten eggs and
cook for 1 minute. Add the rice and stir thoroughly.

Stir in the minced scallions and salt and stir-fry the
mixture for 3 minutes until the eggs are cooked and
the rice is loose and dry.

Stir in the rice wine and cook for a further minute
and then serve.

NOTE
To make 4 cups cooked rice: place 1 cup long-grain
white rice in a bowl, cover with cold water and stir to
loosen the grains. Strain off the cloudy water and
repeat this two more times. Place the rice in another
bowl of cold water and let stand for 5 minutes. Bring a
large saucepan of salted water to a boil, add the rice
and the soaking water and cook over a medium heat
for 10-12 minutes or until the rice is tender. Pour the
rice through a strainer and leave to drain. Place in a
serving dish, cover with a lid and keep warm in a
gently heated oven.

Noodles with Ground Pork Sauce

(SERVES 6)

INGREDIENTS

2½ cups bean sprouts
4 leeks, sliced
1¼ lb. fresh egg noodles
1½ tablespoons sesame oil
3 cups clear soup stock (see p. 261)
6 slices of cooked lean pork
12 cooked shelled shrimp

PORK SAUCE

¼-⅓ cup corn oil
6 scallion bulbs, chopped (reserving the tops for a garnish)
1 tablespoon ginger juice
⅔ cup soy sauce
½ lb. lean ground pork
3 tablespoons rice wine or dry sherry
½ tablespoon salt
1 tablespoon rock sugar
3 cups water

Make the pork sauce: Heat the oil in a skillet or wok, then add the scallions and sauté for 2 minutes until browned. Add the ginger juice and stir-fry for a few seconds. Stir in the soy sauce and ground pork and cook for 2-3 minutes, stirring constantly.

Add the rice wine, the salt and the rock sugar along with the 3 cups water. Bring to a boil and then lower the heat, cover and simmer for 40 minutes.

Bring a saucepan of water to a boil, add the bean sprouts and leeks and scald for 2 minutes. Drain and place the vegetables in 6 soup bowls.

Cook the noodles in plenty of salted boiling water for 3-5 minutes or until the noodles are just tender. Drain. Stir in the sesame oil and toss.

Place the noodles in the soup bowls containing the bean sprouts and leeks.

Bring the soup stock to a boil in a saucepan, and pour over the noodle mixture in each soup bowl. Add to each bowl 2 tablespoons of the ground pork sauce, and garnish with 1 slice of lean cooked pork, 2 cooked shelled shrimp and the chopped scallion tops. Serve.

腊腸飯糰

Rice Dumplings with Pork Sausage

(SERVES 4)
INGREDIENTS

1 teaspoon corn oil
4 Chinese pork sausages (see
    NOTE)
4 cups cooked long-grain
    rice (see NOTE p. 264)
4 teaspoons Worcestershire
    or Sweet and Sour Sauce

Heat the oil in a wok or skillet and cook the sausages for 5 minutes, turning occasionally. Cut in half lengthwise.

Take four pieces of cellophane, about 8 × 10 inches each and place one piece on top of a piece of damp cloth or unbleached muslin. Arange one-fourth of the cooked rice in an oval shape on top of the cellophane.

Place two sausage halves in the center of the rice (see small picture 2, right) and sprinkle with a little Worcestershire or Sweet and Sour sauce.

Slide your hands under the damp cloth. Bring them around to fully enclose the rice mixture, using your thumbs to push the cellophane over the rice. Mold the rice into a sausage shape and twist the ends of the cellophane to seal tightly.

Wrap the rice "sausage" in foil and repeat to make four dumplings.

Place the rice packages in a colander or steamer, cover and steam over a high heat for 15 minutes. Tie a ribbon around each dumpling, if liked, and serve.

咖哩飯糰

Curry-flavored Rice Dumplings

(SERVES 4)
INGREDIENTS

3 tablespoons corn oil
1 pearl onion or scallion bulb,
    minced
1 carrot, diced
2 garlic cloves, minced
1-2 tablespoons Chinese
    curry powder (see NOTE
    p. 145)
½ cup diced cooked pork
2 cups cooked long-grain
    rice (see NOTE p. 264)

SEASONING
1½ teaspoons sugar
1 teaspoon white pepper
pinch of salt

Heat the oil in a wok or skillet and sauté the onion for 1 minute. Add the diced carrot and sauté for 30 seconds and then add the garlic, curry powder and pork and stir-fry for 1 minute.

Stir in the seasoning ingredients, stir-fry for 2 minutes and add the cooked rice, stirring thoroughly.

Take four large (8 × 10 inch) or eight small (5 × 6 inch) pieces of cellophane. Divide the rice among the pieces, bring the edges together and twist, and then wrap each cellophane ball in foil.

Place the rice balls in a colander or steamer and steam over a high heat for 15 minutes.

Unwrap the foil and tie the neck of the cellophane with ribbon. Serve hot or cold.

腊鴨飯

Rice with Duck and Ginger

(SERVES 4)
INGREDIENTS

½ cooked duck
1 cup raw long-grain rice
fresh parsley or marjoram, for
garnish

SEASONING
1 tablespoon ginger juice
(see NOTES)
1 tablespoon rice wine or dry
sherry
½ teaspoon white pepper
1 tablespoon shortening

Remove excess fat from the duck and cut in bite-size pieces.

Wash the rice and place in a large saucepan. Add the duck pieces and the seasoning ingredients and sufficient water to come about 1 inch above the surface of the rice.

Bring to a boil, lower the heat, cover and cook very gently for 10-12 minutes or until all the water has been incorporated and the rice is tender.

Garnish with fresh parsley or marjoram and serve.

NOTES

To make ginger juice, finely grate a section of fresh gingerroot into a saucer. Squeeze the grated ginger with the back of a spoon and the juice will run off. Alternatively, place the ginger in a garlic press and squeeze over a cup to catch the juice.

If you have a rice steamer, use this to cook the rice. Follow the package directions.

腊味飯

Rice with Assorted Meat

(SERVES 4)
INGREDIENTS

2 Chinese pork sausages (see
NOTE p. 267)
2 pieces of dried chicken or
duck
½ cup cubed ham
1 cup raw long-grain rice
1 tablespoon dried shrimp
(see NOTE)
⅓ cup garden peas
scallion curl, for garnish (see
NOTE p. 82)

SEASONING
½ tablespoon minced fresh
gingerroot
1 tablespoon rice wine or dry
sherry
1 tablespoon shortening
1 teaspoon salt
½ teaspoon white pepper

Cut the sausage and dried chicken or duck in small cubes. Place in a small pan with the ham, cover with boiling water, lower the heat and simmer for 5 minutes. Drain.

Rinse the rice and place in a large saucepan. Add the diced meats, the shrimp, the peas and the seasoning ingredients. Stir in enough water to come 1 inch above the surface of the rice.

Bring to a boil, lower the heat, cover and cook very gently for 10-15 minutes or until the water has been absorbed and the rice is tender. Serve at once, garnished with a scallion curl.

NOTE
Soak the dried shrimp in warm water for 30 minutes before use.

Pekinese Noodles in Special Sauce

(SERVES 4)
INGREDIENTS

1¼ lb. fresh egg noodles
2 tablespoons sesame oil
⅓ cup corn oil
2 scallions, minced
½ small cucumber, cut in
   thin shreds
2 cups diced cooked pork
2 carrots, diced
⅓ cup diced bamboo shoots

SEASONING

2 tablespoons yellow bean
   sauce
2 tablespoons sweet bean
   sauce
½ tablespoon dark soy sauce
½ tablespoon sugar

Bring a large saucepan of water to a boil, add the noodles and cook for 2 minutes. Drain thoroughly and place in a serving bowl. Stir in the sesame oil and mix thoroughly. Cover and keep warm while making the sauce.

Place the corn oil in a wok or skillet. Add the scallions and the seasoning ingredients and stir-fry for 1 minute.

Reserve a few cucumber shreds for garnishing and add the remainder with the pork, carrots and bamboo shoots to the wok. Mix thoroughly and cook for 3-4 minutes until hot and bubbly.

Pour the sauce over the noodles and garnish with the reserved cucumber shreds.

Shanghainese Thick Noodle Soup

(SERVES 4)
INGREDIENTS

2 cups Chinese mushrooms
⅓ cup corn oil
2 scallions, minced
2 garlic cloves, crushed
1 cup sliced Nappa cabbage
½ lb. cooked pork, thickly
   sliced
2½ cups clear soup stock
   (see p. 261)
2 tablespoons cornstarch
¼ cup water
2 eggs, beaten
1 lb. fresh egg noodles

SEASONING A

1½ tablespoons light soy
   sauce
1 teaspoon salt

SEASONING B

3 teaspoons sesame oil
1 teaspoon white pepper

Soak the Chinese mushrooms in warm water for 30 minutes. Discard stems. Drain and cut caps in large pieces.

Place the oil in a large Dutch oven and stir-fry the scallions and garlic for 1 minute.

Add the Nappa cabbage, the sliced pork, the mushrooms and seasoning **A** and cook, stirring for 2 minutes.

Add the soup stock and bring to a boil. Mix the cornstarch with the water and stir into soup. Cook for a few minutes until it is slightly thickened and then remove from the heat and stir in the eggs using chopsticks or a fork.

Bring a large saucepan of water to a boil, add the noodles and cook for 5 minutes. Drain and place the noodles in a soup tureen. Pour the soup over the noodles and sprinkle with seasoning **B**. Serve immediately.

Chicken E-Mein Soup

(SERVES 4)

INGREDIENTS

2 chicken legs
4 cups boiling water
1 tablespoon ginger wine
  (see Glossary)
1½ teaspoons salt
pinch of white pepper
10 oz. fresh E-Mein noodles
  (see NOTE)
cilantro, for garnish, optional

Chop the chicken legs into large pieces. Place in boiling water for 1 minute to scald and then drain and place in a bowl.

Add the boiling water and the ginger wine. Place the bowl in a steamer, cover and steam over a medium-high heat for 40 minutes or until the chicken is cooked. Stir in the salt and pepper and set aside while cooking the noodles.

Place the noodles in a large bowl, cover with boiling water and scald for 30 seconds. Drain and stir into the soup. Garnish with cilantro, if liked.

NOTE
E-Mein noodles are a type of egg noodles which are flat and twice as wide as regular egg noodles. They are mainly used for festivals, birthdays and banquets. Regular thin noodles can be used (pictured left, center). If using dried egg noodles, soak in boiling water for 5 minutes.

Homemade Bean Threads

(SERVES 4)

INGREDIENTS

1 cup green bean flour
2⅔ cups rice flour
shortening, for greasing
¼ cup corn oil
2 scallions, minced
2 slices cooked pork, cut in
  thin strips
1 dried squid, soaked (see
  NOTE)
2 dried black mushrooms,
  soaked
1 small piece (about 1 oz.)
  bamboo shoot, cut in thin
  strips
1 large carrot, grated
2½ cups clear soup stock
  (see p. 261)
carrot strips, for garnish

SEASONING
1 tablespoon light soy sauce
1 teaspoon rice wine or dry
  sherry
1½ teaspoons salt
½ teaspoon white pepper

Mix the green bean flour with the rice flour and slowly add enough cold water to make a thick paste.

Grease a large skillet with the shortening. Smooth a thin layer of paste over the pan, spreading it out toward the edges to make a large pancake.

Place the pan over a low to medium heat and cook gently until the underside is lightly brown. Flip over and cook the other side until lightly brown. When cooked, slide the pancake onto a platter and cut in long strips. Repeat until all the mixture is used. These are the green bean threads.

Heat the oil in a wok, add the scallions and stir-fry for 1 minute. Add the pork, squid, mushrooms, bamboo shoot and carrot and stir-fry for 2 minutes.

Add the soup stock and bring to a boil. Stir in the seasoning ingredients and the green bean threads and cook for 5 minutes. Garnish with carrot strips and serve at once.

NOTE
Soak the dried squid in cold water overnight before use. Then remove head and tentacles and cut in thin pieces.

江西辣味米粉

Spicy Rice Noodles

(SERVES 4)

INGREDIENTS

1 package (11 oz.) thin rice
    vermicelli
¼ lb. pork tenderloin
1 cup small dried fish
2 or 3 red chili peppers
⅓ cup corn oil
⅔ cup clear soup stock (see
    p. 261)
1½ cups shredded Nappa
    cabbage
salt and pepper

SEASONING

1 tablespoon light soy sauce
large pinch of five-spice
    powder
½ tablespoon rice wine or
    dry sherry
1 teaspoon cornstarch

Place the noodles in a bowl and cover with boiling
water. Let soak for 10 minutes, stirring occasionally
with chopsticks or a fork to loosen and then drain.
Rinse under cold water.

Cut the pork in thin strips. Mix the seasoning
ingredients in a bowl, add the pork and marinate for
10 minutes.

Rinse the dried fish in cold water and shake off
excess water. Cut the chili peppers thinly, discarding
the seeds.

Heat the oil in a wok, add the dried fish and chilis
and stir-fry for 5 seconds. Add the pork and stir-fry for
another 2 minutes.

Stir in the soup stock and Nappa cabbage, lower
the heat to medium and cook for 3 minutes or until the
cabbage is soft.

Add the rice noodles and salt and pepper. Cover
and simmer for 3-4 minutes and then remove cover
and stir-fry over a higher heat. Serve hot.

台式炒米粉

Stir-Fried Rice Noodles

(SERVES 4)

INGREDIENTS

¼ lb. pork tenderloin
1 package (11 oz.) thin rice
    vermicelli
⅓ cup corn oil
2 red chili peppers, seeded
    and finely sliced
½ cup cooked shelled shrimp
2½ cups bean sprouts
½ cup clear soup stock (see
    p. 261)
3 or 4 chives or scallion tops,
    chopped

Cut the pork in thin strips and marinate in
seasoning **A** for 20 minutes.

Soak the vermicelli in boiling water for 10 minutes.
Drain thoroughly.

Heat the oil in a wok, add the chili peppers and
stir-fry for 5 seconds. Stir in the pork and cook for 3
minutes, stirring all the time. Add the shrimp, bean
sprouts, soup stock, vermicelli and seasoning **B** and
cook rapidly for 3-5 minutes or until almost dry.

Add the chopped chives or scallion tops and stir.
Serve at once.

SEASONING A

½ tablespoon light soy sauce
2 teaspoons cornstarch
½ tablespoon ginger wine
    (see Glossary)

SEASONING B

3 tablespoons light soy sauce
1 teaspoon salt
½ teaspoon white pepper
½ teaspoon sugar

干 絲 素 麵

Noodles of Dried Bean Curd Shreds

(SERVES 2)
INGREDIENTS

3 Chinese mushrooms
2 cups dried bean curd
   shreds
5 cups boiling water
1 teaspoon baking soda
2 tablespoons corn oil
1 tablespoon shredded
   bamboo shoot
1 tablespoon shredded carrot
1 tablespoon shredded celery
1 tablespoon straw
   mushrooms (see NOTE
   p. 133)
2 cups clear soup stock (see
   p. 261)

SEASONING
⅔ teaspoon salt
2 teaspoons sesame oil

Soak the Chinese mushrooms for 30 minutes in warm water. Drain. Cut off and discard the stems and shred the caps.

Chop the dried bean curd shreds in sections and cook in the boiling water mixed with the soda for 5 minutes. Drain and wash under cold running water.

Heat the oil in a wok and stir-fry the shredded Chinese mushrooms for 2 minutes. Add the bamboo shoot, carrot, celery and straw mushrooms and stir-fry for 3 minutes more. Add the seasoning and the soup. Bring to a boil, add the dried bean curd shreds, bring back to a boil and boil for 3 minutes. Serve at once.

NOTE
Substitute 2 cups white vermicelli for the dried bean curd shreds.

Chicken with Sweet Rice

(SERVES 4–6)
INGREDIENTS

1 tablespoon oyster sauce
  (see NOTES)
1 broiler-fryer (about 3 lb. in
  weight)
2 cups glutinous rice (see
  NOTES)
⅔-¾ cup corn oil
½ cup chopped cooked ham
2 Chinese dried mushrooms,
  soaked and chopped (see
  NOTES)
1 tablespoon light soy sauce
1 teaspoon sugar
1 tablespoon rice wine or dry
  sherry
5 cups water
2 eggs, beaten
3 tablespoons cornstarch
cherry tomatoes, for garnish

Pour the oyster sauce over the chicken, and marinate for 30 minutes.

Wash the rice in cold water several times, until the water runs clear. Place the rice in a bowl and cover with boiling water. Let stand for 1 minute, then drain.

Heat 2 tablespoons of the oil in a wok or skillet. Add the rice, and stir-fry for 1 minute. Add the ham, mushrooms, soy sauce, sugar and rice wine and continue stir-frying for a few more minutes.

Add the water to the rice mixture, bring to a boil, lower the heat, cover and simmer for 30 minutes or until the water is absorbed.

Stuff the rice mixture in the body cavity of the chicken, and place in a large steamer. Put 1 inch boiling water in a large saucepan. Set the steamer over the saucepan, cover with a tight-fitting lid and steam for 2 hours.

Remove the stuffing from the chicken, and place on a serving dish.

Cut the chicken in bite-size pieces and then coat with the beaten eggs. Dust thoroughly with the cornstarch. Heat the remaining oil in a skillet, add the chicken and cook for 5 minutes.

Arrange the chicken pieces around the rice on the serving dish, garnish with cherry tomatoes and serve.

NOTES

Oyster sauce is made from oysters cooked in soy sauce and brine, and is available from some supermarkets and from Chinese delicatessens.

Glutinous rice, which is also known as sweet rice, is available from Chinese delicatessens. Stickier and sweeter than regular rice, it should be washed and soaked before cooking.

Before using the Chinese dried mushrooms, soak them in warm water for 20-30 minutes or until they are soft. Remove the stems, then chop.

牛肉湯刀削麵

Noodles in Beef Brisket Soup

(SERVES 4)
INGREDIENTS

1½ lb. beef brisket
4 cups water
3 tablespoons rice wine or
    dry sherry
5 cups all-purpose flour
1½ teaspoons salt
2 or 3 Nappa cabbage leaves,
    cut in 4 pieces
1 red chili pepper, for
    garnish, optional

SEASONING A

½ inch piece fresh gingerroot
1 scallion, sliced
½ tablespoon aniseeds or 3
    caraway seeds
½ tablespoon cumin seeds
1 teaspoon salt

SEASONING B

3 tablespoons rice wine or
    dry sherry
1 teaspoon salt

Cut the beef in thin 1 inch slices. Place in a Dutch oven, cover with boiling water and simmer for 1 minute. Drain and return beef to the pot.

Wrap all the seasoning **A** ingredients in a piece of cloth or unbleached muslin, tie the end securely with string and add to the pot along together with the water and the rice wine.

Add seasoning **B** and bring the pot to a boil. Lower the heat and simmer for 1-1½ hours or until the beef is tender. Remove the spice pack.

Place the flour in a bowl and add sufficient water to make a dough. Knead slightly and then cover and set aside for 20 minutes. Knead again until smooth and shape into a fat sausage.

Bring a saucepan of water to a boil, add the salt and throw in the Nappa cabbage leaves. Remove the leaves with a slotted spoon and add to the beef soup. Reserve the boiling water.

Hold the dough in one hand and, using a sharp knife, cut off the thin "noodles" (see small picture, right). Bring the cabbage water back to a boil and drop the noodles into the water. Cook for 1 minute and then carefully remove and stir into the beef soup.

Cook for a further 2-3 minutes and serve, garnished with red chili pepper, if liked.

辣肉醬炒通心粉

Pasta in Pork Sauce

(SERVES 4)
INGREDIENTS

2 cups pasta shells
¼ cup corn oil
1 cup ground pork
2 scallions, chopped
⅓ cup clear soup stock (see
    p. 261)
onion rings, baby cucumbers
    and red chili peppers,
    sliced, for garnish

SEASONING

½ tablespoon hot bean paste
    (see NOTE)
2 teaspoons cayenne
½ tablespoon ginger wine
    (see Glossary)
1 teaspoon salt
1 teaspoon sugar
½ teaspoon white pepper

Bring a large pan of salted water to a boil, add the pasta and cook for 8-10 minutes or until the pasta is tender. Drain and rinse in cold water.

Heat the oil in a skillet, add the ground pork, scallions and the seasoning ingredients. Stir thoroughly and pour in the soup stock. Cook for 2 minutes and stir in the pasta.

Stir-fry for a further 2 minutes until evenly mixed. Spoon onto a serving platter and garnish with onion rings, sliced baby cucumbers and sliced chili peppers, if liked.

NOTE

Hot bean paste should be used carefully as it is very hot. It is made from crushed soybeans, chili and sugar and is usually sold in jars from most Chinese groceries.

281

Pork Congee

(SERVES 4)
INGREDIENTS

3 slices lean pork
2½ cups clear soup stock
   (see p. 261)
1 carrot, diced
⅓ cup garden peas
½ cup oatmeal
1 teaspoon salt

Cut the pork in small pieces. Pour the soup stock into a saucepan and add the pork, carrot and peas. Bring to a boil and add the oatmeal.

Boil gently for 10-12 minutes and then remove from the heat, cover and let stand for 5 minutes.

Serve with a sprinkling of salt.

Sweet Congee

(SERVES 4)
INGREDIENTS

2½ cups milk
2 tablespoons sugar
½ cup oatmeal

Warm the milk in a saucepan and add the sugar. Heat, stirring, until the sugar dissolves and add the oatmeal.

Bring to a boil, stirring, and then lower the heat and simmer gently for 4-5 minutes until the oatmeal is cooked. Serve.

Rice Dumplings with Tomato Sauce

(SERVES 4)
INGREDIENTS

3 tablespoons corn oil
1 garlic clove, crushed
3 tablespoons garden peas
4 cups cooked long-grain
   rice (see NOTE p. 264)
¾ cup diced cooked ham
3 tablespoons tomato sauce
1½ teaspoons salt
½ teaspoon white pepper

Heat the oil in a wok and stir-fry the garlic for 10 seconds. Add the peas, cook for 1 minute and then stir in the rice and diced ham.

Stir in the tomato sauce, salt and pepper and mix thoroughly.

Take 8 pieces of cellophane, measuring approximately 4 × 5 inches and place a tablespoon of the rice mixture in the center of each. Gather up and twist the top securely and then wrap each in a piece of foil.

Place in a steamer, cover and steam for approximately 15 minutes over a high heat.

Unwrap the foil, tie the neck of the packages with a ribbon and serve.

Rice Dumplings with Beef

(SERVES 4)
INGREDIENTS

¾ lb. rump steak
3 tablespoons corn oil
4 cups cooked long-
   grain rice (see
   NOTE, p. 264)

SEASONING
1 tablespoon light soy
   sauce
½ tablespoon rice
   wine or dry sherry
½ teaspoon salt
½ teaspoon baking
   soda
1 tablespoon sugar
½ teaspoon white
   pepper
1½ teaspoons
   cornstarch

Slice the beef against the grain in long strips. Mix the seasoning ingredients in a bowl, add the steak and marinate for 30 minutes.

Heat the oil in a wok and stir-fry the beef for 3 minutes. Remove.

Take four pieces of cellophane, about 8 × 10 inches, and place one piece on top of a piece of damp cloth or unbleached muslin. Arrange about one-fourth of the cooked rice in an oval shape on top of the cellophane and place two or three strips of beef in the center of the rice (see small picture 1, p. 267).

Slide your hands under the damp cloth. Bring them around to fully enclose the rice mixture, using your thumbs to push the cellophane over the rice. Mold the rice into a sausage shape and twist the ends of the cellophane to seal tightly.

Wrap the rice "sausage" in foil and repeat this process another three times until all the rice and beef has been used.

Place the rice packages in a colander or steamer, cover and steam over a high heat for 15 minutes. Tie a ribbon around each dumpling, if liked, and serve.

玉米筍湯

Baby Corn Soup

(SERVES 4)
INGREDIENTS

6 Chinese mushrooms
12 baby corn cobs
3 salted bamboo shoots
4 tablespoons green beans
2½ cups clear soup stock
(see p. 261)
½ teaspoon salt
1 teaspoon sesame oil

Soak the Chinese mushrooms in boiling water for 20 minutes. Drain. Cut off and discard the stems and chop each cap in half.

Wash the baby corn cobs and chop them in half. Rinse the salted bamboo shoots under cold water and chop off the stems and end parts. Wash again and chop in square sections. Wash the green beans.

Put all ingredients into a large bowl. Add the soup stock and salt and place the bowl in a steamer. Steam over boiling water for 20 minutes. Drizzle the seasame oil over the soup before serving.

NOTE
Salted bamboo shoots can be bought at Chinese markets but you could substitute ⅓ cup of any salted vegetable for them.

韭菜干絲

Stir-Fried Dried Bean Curd Shreds with Chives

(SERVES 4)
INGREDIENTS

1 bunch (about 2 oz.) chives
2½ cups dried bean curd
shreds or fresh egg noodles
¼ cup corn oil
¼-⅓ cup clear soup stock
(see p. 261)

SEASONING
1 teaspoon salt
1½ teaspoons sugar
½ tablespoon light soy sauce
½ teaspoon white pepper

Discard any old or withered leaves from the chives. Wash the remainder and chop in 1½-inch sections. Chop the dried bean curd shreds in 1-inch sections and wash in salted water.

Heat the oil in a wok. Add the soup stock with the dried bean curd shreds or noodles and the seasoning. Stir-fry over a gentle heat for 5-7 minutes, until the liquid has been absorbed. Add the chives and stir-fry for 30 seconds. Serve at once.

NOTE
A Chinese proverb runs "Chive is the chicken of the poor" and herbalists endorse that it is a very nutritious vegetable. It is easy to grow; do not neglect it.

麻油麵線

Egg Noodles with Sesame Oil

(SERVES 2)
INGREDIENTS

1 package (bundle) fresh egg
   noodles
3 tablespoons sesame oil
2 eggs, beaten
1 tablespoon minced fresh
   gingerroot
1 slice fresh gingerroot
1½ cups clear soup stock
   (see p. 261)
1 teaspoon salt

Wash the noodles very thoroughly.
   Heat the oil in a wok and stir-fry the eggs over a
medium heat. When set, remove the eggs and stir-fry
the minced ginger and the slice of ginger for 1 minute
or so. Remove the slice of ginger and put on one side.
Pour the soup into the pan and add the salt. Bring to a
boil and add the noodles and fried egg. Bring to a boil
again and serve at once with the slice of ginger for
garnish.

NOTES
   This is a famous dish from the Fuchow style of
cooking.
   Fresh egg noodles are sold in bundles.

清湯銀耳

Soup of White Fungus

(SERVES 4)
INGREDIENTS

1 cup (about 1 oz.) white
   fungus
4½ tablespoons rock sugar
   (see NOTE p. 114)
4 cups clear soup stock (see
   p. 261)
4 Maraschino cherries, for
   decoration

Soak the white fungus in cold water for 4-6 hours.
Remove the root and any hard pieces and wash the
fungus until it is quite clean. Soak for a further 2 hours
in hot water to let it expand. Drain off the water.
   Put the fungus and rock sugar into a bowl with the
clear soup. Place in a pan of hot water and simmer
very gently for 45 minutes to 1 hour until the soup
becomes glutinous. Check the pan from time to time
to make sure it does not burn dry. Serve the soup in
individual bowls with a cherry in each one.

海鮮烏龍麵
Noodles in Seafood Soup

(SERVES 4)
INGREDIENTS

4 crab claws
¼ lb. squid
8 clams
3 dried black mushrooms,
   soaked (see NOTES)
¼ lb. pork tenderloin
5 cups clear soup stock (see
   p. 261)
3 tablespoons fish stock or 1
   fish bouillon cube
4 quail eggs, optional
1 package (10 oz.) u-dong
   noodles (see NOTES)
8 cooked shrimp in shells

SEASONING
1 teaspoon salt
1 tablespoon ginger wine
   (see Glossary)
½ teaspoon white pepper

Crack the crab claws with a heavy rolling pin or mallet.

Pull away the head and entrails from the squid. Feel inside the body and remove the transparent cartilage. Peel off and discard the mottled skin from the body, and rinse the squid under running water. Cut in 1 inch pieces.

Split the clams open with a knife, and rinse clean.

Remove the stem from the dried black mushrooms and slice.

Cut the pork in slices.

Place the soup stock in a saucepan. Add the fish stock, sliced pork, black mushrooms and quail eggs if using. Bring to a boil.

Add the noodles and seasoning, and cook rapidly for 2 minutes.

Add the crab, squid and clams and cook for a further 3 minutes. Finally add the shrimp and cook for 3 minutes. Skim the surface if necessary and then serve.

NOTES
Soak the black mushrooms in warm water for 20-30 minutes. Drain.

U-dong noodles are dried noodles made of wheat flour and water. They are straight, flat and quite thick. Soak in cold water for 10 minutes before using.

麻油鷄麵線
Thin Noodles in Chicken Soup

(SERVES 4-6)
INGREDIENTS

4 chicken legs
1 inch piece fresh gingerroot,
   cut in 4 pieces
1 bundle (10 oz.) mein-tsein
   noodles (see NOTES)
⅓ cup sesame oil
2 tablespoons rice wine or
   dry sherry
5 cups water

Using a cleaver or meat ax, cut the chicken legs in 4 pieces.

Using a meat mallet, pat the slices of gingerroot flat.

Rinse the noodles and cut them in 4 inch long sections. Lay on a piece of unbleached muslin or a clean dish towel and place on a heatproof plate. Place the plate in a steamer or large colander, cover and steam for 2 minutes.

Heat a wok or skillet with the oil and stir-fry the ginger for 10 seconds. Add the chicken and stir-fry for 8 minutes, until cooked and lightly browned.

Add the rice wine and the water, and bring to a boil. Add the noodles, bring back to a boil and serve.

NOTE
Mein-tsein are thin dried egg noodles. They are sold either in bundles or coiled in packages.

廣式炒麵

Chow-Mein, Cantonese-Style

(SERVES 6)
INGREDIENTS

1 cup corn oil
2 chicken breasts cut in bite-size pieces
1 lb. fresh egg noodles
1½ teaspoons salt
½ teaspoon white pepper
4 cups shredded collard greens
4 black mushrooms soaked (see NOTE 1, p. 291) and sliced
¼ cup cooked shelled shrimp
2 roasted duck breasts
10 slices cucumber
4 slices bamboo shoot
4 quail eggs, optional
1 tablespoon sherry

SEASONING
½ teaspoon salt
½ teaspoon soy sauce
⅓ cup clear soup stock (see p. 261) or water
2 tablespoons cornstarch

Heat 3 tablespoons of the oil in a pan and sauté the chicken for 8 minutes. Remove and set aside.

Cook the noodles in plenty of boiling salted water for 3-5 minutes or until just tender.

Heat 6 tablespoons of the remaining oil in a wok. Add the noodles and stir to separate. Add the salt and pepper, and stir-fry for 4-5 minutes.

Arrange the noodles in a coil. Swirl 4 tablespoons of the remaining oil slowly around the rim of the wok, just above the noodles. Cover and cook for about 4-6 minutes, or until the noodles are browned on one side.

When the noodles no longer stick to the base, turn them over. Splash the remaining oil around the rim, and fry till browned. Remove and place on a serving dish.

Re-heat the wok and stir-fry the collard greens, mushrooms, shrimp, chicken, duck, cucumber, bamboo shoot and quail eggs, if using, adding a little more oil if necessary. Add the seasoning ingredients, stirring continually and bring to a boil. Cook for 1 minute. Sprinkle with the sherry, and remove from the heat. Pour over the noodles and serve.

咖哩牛肉炒麵

Curried Beef Chow Mein

(SERVES 6)
INGREDIENTS

10 oz. rump steak
1 package (10 oz.) buckwheat noodles
⅓ cup corn oil
3 scallions, chopped
1 tablespoon grated fresh gingerroot
3 garlic cloves, crushed
1 large onion, cut in wedges
1½ cups clear soup stock (see p. 261)
½ cup snow peas

SEASONING A
1 tablespoon cornstarch
1 egg white
1 tablespoon ginger wine (see Glossary)

SEASONING B
5 tablespoons Chinese curry powder
½ cup milk
½ teaspoon salt
1½ tablespoons sugar

Cut the steak in thin 1 inch long slices. Mix seasoning **A** ingredients in a bowl, add the sliced beef and marinate for 20 minutes. Drain.

Bring a large saucepan of salted water to a boil and cook the noodles for 1½-3 minutes. Drain.

Heat the oil in a wok or skillet and stir-fry the scallions, ginger and garlic for 1-2 minutes. Add the onion and seasoning **B** ingredients, cook for 2 minutes and then add the beef slices. Stir-fry for 2-3 minutes, or until the meat is evenly brown.

Add the noodles and the soup stock, and bring to a boil. Boil for 2 minutes, then add the snow peas and stir-fry for 1 minute. Remove from the heat and serve.

Taiwanese-Style Noodles

(SERVES 6)
INGREDIENTS

2½ cups bean sprouts
1 lb. fresh egg noodles
1 tablespoon sesame oil
¼ cup corn oil
2 scallions, chopped
½ lb. lean pork, sliced
1½ cups shredded Nappa
cabbage

SEASONING
1 tablespoon ginger juice
¼ teaspoon five-spice
powder
1½ teaspoons salt
1 tablespoon soy sauce
½ teaspoon white pepper
½ teaspoon rice wine or dry
sherry
½ cup clear soup stock (see
p. 261)

Rinse the bean sprouts in cold water and drain.

Cook the noodles in a large saucepan of boiling salted water for 3-5 minutes. Drain, then toss in the sesame oil.

Heat the corn oil in a wok or skillet, then add the scallions and stir-fry for 20 seconds. Add the pork slices and stir-fry for 3 minutes. Add the Nappa cabbage, stir-fry for 2 minutes until softened, and then add the bean sprouts, noodles and seasoning ingredients.

Cook for 1 minute, uncovered, and then cover and simmer for 1 minute. Remove the lid and stir-fry for a further 2 minutes. Serve immediately.

Rice Noodles with Lettuce

(SERVES 4-6)
INGREDIENTS

1 lb. fresh rice noodles
1 head Romaine or Boston
lettuce
5 cups chicken stock (see
p. 149)
1 teaspoon salt
2 tablespoons rice wine or
dry sherry
1 teaspoon sesame oil

Cook the noodles in a large saucepan of boiling, salted water for 1 minute, or until the noodles are just tender. Drain, and place in a serving dish.

Break the lettuce into individual leaves and rinse in cold water. Shred in even-size pieces.

Heat the stock to boiling. Add the salt and rice wine and then throw in the lettuce leaves. Cook for 2 minutes and pour over the noodles. Sprinkle with Sesame oil and serve.

DIM SUM

Dim Sum are the little snacks that are extremely popular in China. They are eaten in the morning and sometimes all afternoon as well! They frequently consist of little steamed or deep-fried breads or pastries with savory or sweet fillings.

The wrappers that enclose these mouth-watering snacks are made from various types of dough. The dough is normally made of all-purpose flour, although occasionally recipes will call for rice flour when a specially light texture is required. The fillings themselves usually consist of meat – pork and beef are popular – and they are often flavored with a sweet and sour seasoning, such as red bean paste. This strong, distinctive flavor contrasts particularly well with the slightly sweet flavor of the dough.

In Chinese restaurants, you can eat a complete meal composed of Dim Sum, but this may be unrealistic to attempt at home. However, one, or possibly two, Dim Sum snacks, such as Steamed Pork Buns (p. 299) or Salted Vegetable Patties (p. 313) would be delicious to serve at the start of a meal or as a light lunch dish.

Steamed Pork Buns

(SERVES 4)
INGREDIENTS

2½ cups all-purpose
   flour
½ cup lukewarm water
1 teaspoon active dry
   yeast
½ teaspoon sugar
1 tablespoon
   shortening

FILLING
2½ cups lean ground pork
1 teaspoon salt
1 tablespoon ginger
   wine (see Glossary)
½ tablespoon sesame
   oil
pinch of white pepper
¼ cup water

Make leavened dough with the flour, water, yeast, sugar and shortening as directed on p. 345.

Make the filling: Mix all filling ingredients with the water to make a smooth paste.

Break the dough into 20 small pieces, rolling each piece between floured hands to make a small ball.

Roll out the ball to make a round, about 3½ inches in diameter. Place 1 tablespoon of filling in the center of each round. Bring the edges together over the meat and press together firmly. Stand for 3-5 minutes.

Place a layer of unbleached muslin over the base of a bamboo or metal steamer, place the buns on top and steam them, covered, for 10 minutes. Serve at once.

NOTE
Steamed buns can be served in a soup, if liked. Stir a little light soy sauce into chicken stock or rich soup stock, heat the soup and then float the steamed buns on top.

Steamed Pork and Vegetable Buns

(SERVES 4)
INGREDIENTS

5 cups all-purpose
   flour
1 cup lukewarm water
1½ teaspoons active
   dry yeast
1 tablespoon sugar

FILLING
1½ cups lean ground
   pork
3 cups finely shredded
   Nappa cabbage
½ tablespoon soy
   sauce
½ tablespoon ginger
   wine (see Glossary)
½ tablespoon sesame
   oil
1 teaspoon salt
pinch of white pepper

Make leavened dough with the flour, water, yeast and sugar, as directed on p. 345. Place the filling ingredients in a large bowl and mix thoroughly.

Break the dough in 10 even-size pieces and roll each piece in a ball to make a round, about 5 inches in diameter. Place 2 tablespoons of filling in the center of each and fold the edges over the filling, pressing together firmly to seal.

Cover the buns with a damp cloth and let stand for 20 minutes.

Lay a piece of damp unbleached muslin over the base of a bamboo or metal steamer and place the buns on top. Steam, covered, over a high heat for 25 minutes and then serve at once.

NOTE
Both of these steamed buns are delicious served with a dipping sauce. Make a sauce by mixing 3 tablespoons finely grated fresh gingerroot, 3 tablespoons light soy sauce and 3 tablespoons Chinese white (or cider) vinegar.

Cantonese-Style Congee

(SERVES 4)
INGREDIENTS

1¼ cups ground pork
1⅓ cups white glutinous rice
6¼ cups clear soup stock
    (see p. 261)
1-2 yiu-tiao (see NOTES)
3 fresh parsley sprigs
1 teaspoon white pepper
salt

Tie the ground pork in a piece of unbleached muslin.

Wash and drain the rice thoroughly. Put in a large saucepan with the soup stock and pork and bring to a boil.

Meanwhile, chop the yiu-tiao and put in a bowl. When the rice mixture – known as congee – is ready, discard the pork and pour the congee over the yiu-tiao. Mince the parsley and sprinkle on top. Season to taste with pepper and salt. Serve at once.

NOTES

Yiu-tiao is also known as twisted doughnut and is available in Oriental markets. It is a long stick of deep-fried dough.

Beef, fish or pork liver can also be used to flavor the congee.

Taro Congee

(SERVES 4)
INGREDIENTS

1⅓ cups white glutinous rice
4 cups clear soup stock (see p. 261)
6 tablespoons dried shrimp
½ large taro (dasheen)
3 tablespoons corn oil
3 shallots, minced
⅔ cup lean ground pork
2 tablespoons spiced preserved vegetable root, minced
3 tablespoons water
1 scallion, chopped, for garnish

Wash and drain the glutinous rice and simmer in the soup stock for about 1 hour.

While the rice is cooking, soak the dried shrimp in cold water for 10-15 minutes, then drain. Peel the taro and cut in large cubes.

Heat the oil in a wok or large skillet and stir-fry the shallots for a few seconds. Add the soaked shrimp, pork and preserved vegetable and cook, stirring for 3-5 minutes. Add the taro cubes with the water. Cover and simmer for 5 minutes.

Add the rice mixture to the wok, stir well and bring to a boil. Lower the heat and simmer for 15 minutes. Add the seasoning ingredients, garnish with scallions and serve right away.

SEASONING
2 teaspoons salt
1 teaspoon white pepper
2 scallions, minced

NOTE
Dried squid can be used instead of dried shrimp. Soak it in cold water overnight, then cut in small pieces. Dried squid is available at Chinese markets and can be stored for some months in a dry place.

碎肉煎餅
Pork and Onion Pancakes

(SERVES 4)
INGREDIENTS

2 small onions
½ cup corn oil
5 cups all-purpose flour
⅔ cup ground pork or beef
approx. 2½ cups boiling
    water
2 tablespoons chopped fresh
    parsley

SEASONING
2 teaspoons salt
½ teaspoon sugar
1 teaspoon white pepper

Slice the onions very finely and cook them in 1 tablespoon of the oil for about 2 minutes. Remove with a slotted spoon and mix with the flour, ground meat and seasoning ingredients. Stir in sufficient boiling water to make a thick smooth paste. Stir in the chopped parsley.

Add 3-4 tablespoons oil to a pancake pan and heat gently. Add large spoonfuls of the mixture and cook on both sides until golden brown and crisp. Remove from the pan and keep warm while you cook the remainder of the pancakes in the same way, adding more oil to the pan as necessary.

家常菜餅
Cabbage and Bean Curd Patties

(SERVES 4)
INGREDIENTS

1 lb. Chinese cabbage or
    Nappa cabbage
2 teaspoons salt
1 fresh bean curd
1 cup ground pork
5 cups all-purpose flour
approx. 2½ cups boiling
    water
⅔ cup corn oil

SEASONING
½ tablespoon light soy sauce
½ tablespoon sugar
1 teaspoon white pepper
1 tablespoon cornstarch
½ tablespoon sesame oil

Remove old or withered leaves from the outside of the cabbage, then wash and drain the remainder. Rub the leaves with the salt and leave for 10 minutes. Wash off the salt, gently squeeze out excess water and chop cabbage finely.

Mash the bean curd, then mix with the chopped cabbage, pork and seasoning ingredients.

Prepare the scalded dough (see p. 344) using the flour and the boiling water. Knead the dough until smooth and shiny, then divide into 8 pieces. Roll each of these out to a circle about 4 inches in diameter and place 1-2 tablespoons of the bean curd mixture in the center. Wrap the dough around the filling using your hands and seal the edges firmly.

When the filling is enclosed in the dough, flatten the patties slightly with a rolling pin.

Heat the oil in a wok or skillet and cook the patties for about 20 minutes, until lightly golden on both sides. Serve.

Steamed Dumplings

(SERVES 4)
INGREDIENTS

1¾ cups ground pork
5 cups all-purpose flour
approx. 2½ cups boiling
    water

SEASONING
1 tablespoon ginger wine
    (see Glossary)
½ teaspoon white pepper
1½ teaspoons salt
2 teaspoons sesame oil
3 tablespoons clear soup
    stock (see p. 261)

Mix the ground pork with the seasoning ingredients and keep stirring until the mixture is very sticky and well-blended.
Prepare the scalded dough (see p. 344) using the flour and boiling water. Knead well, then shape into a long roll and cut in 12 sections. Roll each section to a thin round.
Place 1 tablespoon of the filling in the center of each dough round, then pinch the edges of the dough around the filling (see small picture 2, right).
Put a piece of damp unbleached muslin or cheesecloth in the base of the steamer and carefully place the dumplings on top. Steam, covered, over rapidly boiling water for 8-10 minutes and serve at once.

NOTE
Make sure the water is boiling hard before placing the dumplings in the steamer.

Doubled Pancakes

(SERVES 4)
INGREDIENTS

3½ cups all-purpose flour
1½ cups self-rising flour
approx. 2½ cups boiling
    water
2 tablespoons melted
    shortening

Sift the flours together and mix with boiling water to make scalded dough (see p. 344). Divide the dough in 12 pieces, shape into balls and flatten each one.
Brush one side of each piece of dough with melted shortening and place them together in pairs, greased side inside. Roll out to a thin round.
Dry-fry each pancake in a heavy-bottomed pan over medium heat until beginning to brown. Turn the pancake over and cook the other side, then remove and keep warm while you cook the remainder in the same way.
Separate each pair of pancakes for serving.

NOTE
Serve these pancakes with slices of crispy duck.

湖州肉粽

Glutinous Rice Dumplings

(SERVES 4)

INGREDIENTS

¾ lb. pork
3 cups white glutinous rice
large pinch of salt
bamboo leaves and straw
　(see NOTES)

SEASONING
½ cup dark soy sauce
1 tablespoon rice wine or dry
　sherry
1 teaspoon white pepper

Cut the pork in 2 inch wide strips. Mix the seasoning ingredients together and pour over the pork. Coat thoroughly, cover and leave in a cool place overnight. Drain the pork, reserving the marinade.

Wash and drain the rice and add to the reserved marinade with the salt. Mix well, leave for about 10 minutes, then mix again.

Place the wrong sides of two bamboo leaves together and fold down the top fourth, tucking it inside the "cupped" shape. Put 2 tablespoons of the rice into the second fourth of the leaves and place 2 meat strips on top. Cover with another 2 tablespoons of rice, pressing it down well.

Fold the bottom half and the sides of the leaves over the rice, wrapping neatly and tightly. Tie with straws to secure packages.

Put the packages in a large saucepan and cover with cold water to come about 3 inches above the packages. Bring to a boil, then lower the heat and simmer very gently for about 4 hours.

Off heat, let the packages stand in the pan, covered, for 1 hour more before serving.

NOTES

Fresh and dried bamboo leaves are available in some Oriental markets, along with the straw for tying the tsung-tzu. You could tie the packages with fine string if you prefer.

These rice dumplings are traditionally served around the time of the Dragon Boat Festival which occurs on May 5th each year.

Red Bean Dumplings

(SERVES 4)
INGREDIENTS

scant 1 cup ground pork
¾ cup sugar
1¼ cups red bean paste
¼ cup melted shortening
3 cups white glutinous rice
bamboo leaves and straw
　(see NOTE above)

Mix the pork with the sugar and let stand, covered, overnight.

Mix the red bean paste with the shortening, then wrap 2 tablespoons of this around the pork mixture. Press into an oval shape.

Wash and drain the rice, then assemble and cook the dumplings as outlined above, from Step 3.

Ho-Fun Soup

(SERVES 6)
INGREDIENTS

¾ lb. sirloin steak
1 head (about 10 oz.) Chinese
    cabbage
4 scallions
1 lb. rice noodles or Ho-Fun
¼ cup corn oil
5 cups clear soup stock (see
    p. 261)

SEASONING A
½ tablespoon ginger wine
    (see Glossary)
½ teaspoon five-spice
    powder
1 teaspoon sesame oil
1 tablespoon cornstarch
    mixed with ⅓ cup water
½ teaspoon salt

SEASONING B
1½ teaspoons salt
½ tablespoon light soy sauce
2 teaspoons corn oil

Cut the beef thinly and mix thoroughly with seasoning **A**. Leave for 20 minutes.

Discard any old or withered leaves from the Chinese cabbage, wash and drain the remainder and chop roughly. Mince the scallions and cut the rice noodles in short lengths.

Heat the oil in a wok or skillet and stir-fry the scallions for a few seconds. Add the shredded beef and stir-fry for 1-2 minutes, until the beef is browned.

Add the soup stock to the pan along with the noodles and seasoning **B**. Bring to a boil, then lower the heat, add the cabbage and simmer for 5 minutes. Serve at once.

Two Different Styles of Sushi

(SERVES 4)
INGREDIENTS

⅓ cup glutinous rice
2 eggs
1 tablespoon butter
4-6 pieces laver or 20 dried
    bean curd sheets
½ cucumber
½ cup chopped cooked pork

SEASONING A
3 tablespoons white vinegar
¼ cup sugar
1½ tablespoons water

SEASONING B
½ teaspoon pepper
1½ tablespoons light soy
    sauce
½ teaspoon five-spice
    powder

Cook the rice in boiling water until just tender (see p. 264). Drain and put in a bowl.

Beat the eggs together; melt the butter in a small pancake pan and add the eggs. Cook over a medium heat until the egg is set. Cool and cut in shreds.

Place seasoning **A** ingredients in a small saucepan and heat gently until sugar has dissolved. Pour slowly over the cooked rice, stirring it in thoroughly.

If using laver, place it under a hot broiler for 5 seconds, then spread thinly with the rice. Finely shred the cucumber and sprinkle over the rice along with the egg shreds and pork. Roll the laver around the filling to form a long roll. Cut in 1 inch sections and serve.

If using dried bean curd, put the sheets in a saucepan with seasoning **B**. Bring to a boil, lower the heat and then simmer for 5 minutes. Drain and gently squeeze dry. Cut each one in half, open up and carefully remove the soft inside. Stuff with the rice filling and serve.

Pork-Stuffed Balls

(SERVES 6)
INGREDIENTS

5 Chinese mushrooms
2 cups dried turnip shreds
10 oz. lean pork
1 cup green shrimp in shells
¼ cup corn oil
½ cup diced bamboo shoot
5 cups sweet potato flour
approx. 4 cups lukewarm
    water
vegetable oil, for deep frying

SEASONING
1½ teaspoons salt
1 tablespoon cornstarch
    mixed with a little water
½ tablespoon ginger wine
    (see Glossary)
½ teaspoon white pepper
½ tablespoon light soy sauce

    Soak the Chinese mushrooms in warm water for 30 minutes. Drain. Cut off and discard the stems and dice the caps.
    Soak turnip shreds in hot water for 20 minutes. Drain and squeeze dry.
    Dice the pork.
    Shell the shrimp and remove the thin "vein" or intestinal cord that runs down the spine.
    Heat 3 tablespoons of the oil in a wok or skillet and stir-fry the mushrooms, turnip shreds, pork and bamboo shoots with the seasoning ingredients for 5 minutes.
    Place the potato flour in a bowl and gradually add lukewarm water to make a thick paste.
    Brush the insides of 4 rice bowls with the remaining oil and pour in about 2½ tablespoons of the paste. Add 2-3 tablespoons of the pork filling and sprinkle a few shrimp on top. Cover with another spoonful of paste.
    Place the bowls in a steamer and steam over rapidly boiling water for about 10 minutes. Remove and let stand for 5 minutes.
    Heat the oil in a deep-fat fryer to medium hot. Carefully remove the balls from the dishes and place them in the hot fat. Cook for a few seconds, so that the outside is very slightly crisp. Serve with a little soy sauce as a dip.

Oyster Omelet

(SERVES 4)
INGREDIENTS

¾ pint fresh oysters or clams
1 head (about 10 oz.) lettuce
    or Chinese spinach
1 cup cornstarch
1¼ cups water
⅓ cup corn oil
4 eggs

SEASONING
¼ cup ketchup
½ cup peanut powder or
    ground peanuts

    Wash the oysters or clams and dry on paper towels. Wash and dry the lettuce or Chinese spinach and chop or tear roughly into pieces.
    Mix the cornstarch with the water to make a smooth paste.
    Heat 1½ tablespoons of the corn oil in a pancake pan and add one fourth of the oysters or clams. Immediately spoon 6 tablespoons of the cornstarch mixture on top. Break an egg into the pan next to the oysters, and stir to break the yolk. Add some lettuce or spinach and 1 more tablespoon oil.
    Switch up the heat, add a little more of the cornstarch mixture and cook for 5 minutes more. Turn the omelet over and cook for 2 more minutes. Remove and keep warm while you cook a further three omelets in the same way.
    Mix the seasoning ingredients and serve with the omelets.

鹹菜餅

Salted Vegetable Patties

(SERVES 4)
INGREDIENTS

5 cups all-purpose flour
approx. 1 cup water
½ cup finely shredded lean
    pork
⅔ cup corn oil
⅔ cup finely shredded salted
    vegetable

SEASONING A
1 tablespoon light soy sauce
large pinch salt
½ teaspoon sugar
2 teaspoons ginger wine (see
    Glossary)
1½ teaspoons cornstarch

SEASONING B
½ teaspoon white pepper
2 tablespoons cornstarch
    mixed with 3 tablespoons
    water

Sift the flour into a large bowl and gradually stir in sufficient water to make a smooth, quite firm dough (see p. 343). Divide into 8 pieces.

Mix the pork with seasoning **A**, stir well and let stand for 20 minutes.

Heat 3 tablespoons of the oil in a wok or skillet and add pork. Stir-fry for 3 minutes, then remove with a slotted spoon. Set aside.

Add the salted vegetable to the oil in the wok and cook for 2 minutes, stirring. Return the pork to the wok with seasoning **B**, and cook for 2 minutes, stirring all the time.

Roll the dough out into thin rounds and place 1 tablespoon filling in the center of each. Pinch the edges together over the filling, then carefully flatten each patty slightly.

Heat the remaining oil in a skillet and cook the patties over a medium heat, until they are golden brown and crispy on both sides. Drain on paper towels and serve at once.

燒賣

Steamed Pork Dumplings

(SERVES 4)
INGREDIENTS

5 cups all-purpose flour
approx. 1 cup water
1½ cups ground pork
24 green shrimp, in shells
1½ inch piece fresh
    gingerroot, thinly sliced
light soy sauce, to serve

SEASONING A
1 teaspoon salt
½ tablespoon ginger wine
    (see Glossary)
½ teaspoon white pepper

SEASONING B
1½ teaspoons ginger wine
2 teaspoons cornstarch

Make the dumpling wrappers with the flour and the water as outlined in the recipe above.

Mix the pork with seasoning **A** and let stand for 20 minutes. Shell the shrimp and remove the thin "vein" or intestinal cord that runs down the spine. Mix them with seasoning **B** and let stand for 20 minutes.

Roll the dough out into thin rounds and place about 1½ tablespoons filling in the center of each. Pinch the edges to look like the top of a flower, leaving a small opening in the center. Place a shrimp in this.

Place the dumplings in a steamer lined with unbleached muslin or lettuce leaves, and steam for 25 minutes.

Finely shred the ginger lengthwise and serve with the cooked dumplings. Serve some soy sauce as a dip.

NOTE
If you prefer you could buy wonton wrappers and use them instead of making the dumpling dough.

鍋貼

Pan Sticks Dumplings

(SERVES 4)
INGREDIENTS

5 cups all-purpose flour
approx. 1 cup water
1¼ cups ground pork
4 tablespoons chopped
   chives
¼ cup corn oil

SEASONING A
½ teaspoon salt
½ teaspoon white pepper
1½ teaspoons ginger wine
   (see Glossary)
1½ teaspoons sesame oil

SEASONING B
⅓ cup malt vinegar
½ teaspoon chili oil

Make a dough with the flour and water (see p. 343) and knead until smooth. Roll into a sausage shape, approximately 1 inch in diameter and cut in 1 inch lengths. Flatten these slightly, then roll each one out to a round, slightly thicker in the center than at the edges. Dust lightly with flour.

Mix the pork and chives together with seasoning **A**. Place about 2 teaspoons of this mixture in the center of each dough round and fold the edges together to form a long "stick". Press lightly to flatten the bottom.

Heat the oil in a skillet and place all the dumplings in the pan. Cook for 1 minute over a medium heat, then raise the heat and add about 2 tablespoons water to the pan. Cover and cook until the water has evaporated. Remove the lid and continue cooking until the dumplings are slightly scorched on the bottom.

Blend seasoning **B** together, sprinkle over the dumplings and serve.

水餃

Boiled Pork Dumplings

(SERVES 4)
INGREDIENTS

5 cups all-purpose flour
approx. 3 cups water
1 head (about 10 oz.) Chinese
   cabbage (see NOTE)
1½ cups ground pork

SEASONING
1 teaspoon salt
1 teaspoon sugar
½ teaspoon white pepper
1 tablespoon ginger wine
   (see Glossary)
½ tablespoon sesame oil
2 tablespoons clear soup
   stock (see p. 261)

Make a dough with the flour and 1 cup of the water (see p. 343) then follow the directions outlined in the recipe above to form dumpling wrappers.

Cut off and discard any old or withered leaves from the Chinese cabbage, then wash the remainder. Place in a saucepan of boiling water, lower the heat and simmer for 10 minutes, then drain thoroughly and chop finely. Mix with the ground pork and seasoning ingredients beating together thoroughly.

Place a small tablespoon of the filling in the center of each dumpling skin and pinch the edges together to make a boat shape (see main picture).

Bring 1¼ cups water to a boil in a saucepan. Add the dumplings one by one, stirring gently to ensure they do not stick to the base of the pan. Simmer for 5 minutes, then add the remainder of the cold water. Bring to a boil again, lower the heat and then simmer for 5 minutes. Serve at once.

NOTE
If you are unable to find Nappa cabbage, use Chinese leaves or collard greens.

韭菜盒子
Scallion Ho-Tsu

(SERVES 4)
INGREDIENTS

1 lb. scallions
1 soft spiced bean curd
1 small piece (about 1 oz.)
  bamboo shoot
2½ cups all-purpose flour
approx. 1¼ cups boiling
  water
¼ cup corn oil

SEASONING
2 teaspoons salt
½ teaspoon white pepper
1 teaspoon sesame oil

Discard any withered leaves from the scallions and wash and dry the remainder thoroughly. Mince. Mash the bean curd and chop the bamboo shoot. Place together in a bowl and mix with the seasoning ingredients.

Make scalded dough with the flour and boiling water (see p. 344). Divide in 4 pieces and roll each one to a 6-8 inch diameter round.

Divide the filling among the rounds, then fold the dough over to make semi-circles. Press edges together, and seal well.

Heat the oil in a skillet and cook the scallion ho-tsu slowly for about 15 minutes, until golden brown. Turn over and cook the other side until golden brown. Drain on paper towels and keep warm while cooking the remainder. Serve at once.

蔥油餅
Scallion Pancakes

(SERVES 4)
INGREDIENTS

5 cups all-purpose flour
approx. 2½ cups boiling
  water
6 scallions
½ cup corn oil
2 teaspoons salt

Make scalded dough with the flour and the boiling water (see p. 344) and divide in 4 pieces.

Mince the scallions.

Roll out each piece of dough to a round ⅛ inch thick. Brush with a little oil, then sprinkle with scallions and salt. Roll up the dough, bring the ends together and pinch them to seal. Roll into a rough ball, then roll this out with a rolling pin to a 6 inch diameter circle.

Heat 1 tablespoon of the remaining oil and cook each pancake over a medium heat until golden brown on both sides. Drain on paper towels and keep warm while cooking the remainder. Add more oil to the pan as necessary. Serve at once.

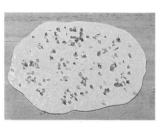

Steamed Dough Twists

(SERVES 6)
INGREDIENTS

5 cups all-purpose flour
1¼ cups self-rising flour
approx. 1¼ cups lukewarm
 water
2 teaspoons active dry yeast
1½ tablespoons sugar
2 tablespoons melted
 shortening
1½ teaspoons white vinegar

SEASONING
2 tablespoons shortening
green part of 2 scallions,
 minced
½ tablespoon salt

Make the leavened dough using all the ingredients except the seasoning (see p. 345).

Roll out the dough into two large thin rounds, about ¼ inch thick. Mix the seasoning ingredients together and spread evenly over each round. Roll the two sides of the dough, into the middle (see small picture 1 right).

Cut the roll in half, then fold the edges of each into the center and fold in half again (see small picture 2). Place them side by side and press down in the centers with a chopstick (see small picture right 3). Place the squares on a plate, cover with a damp piece of unbleached muslin or a dish towel and let stand for 20 minutes.

Place the twists in a steamer and steam over rapidly boiling water for 20-30 minutes. Serve at once.

NOTE
Serve these dough twists hot with meat and fish dishes, such as Salted Shrimp (see p. 25).

Steamed Bread

(SERVES 6)
INGREDIENTS

5 cups all-purpose flour
1¼ cups self-rising flour
2 teaspoons active dry yeast
1½ tablespoons sugar
2 tablespoons melted
 shortening
1½ teaspoons white vinegar
approx. 1 cup lukewarm
 water

Make a leavened dough following directions on p. 345. Knead well and shape into a roll about 3 inches in diameter. Cut in 2 inch pieces, cover with a damp piece of unbleached muslin and let stand for 20 minutes.

Place the flat cakes in a steamer and steam over rapidly boiling water for 20-30 minutes. Serve at once.

NOTES
The Chinese name for these dumplings is man-tou. It is similar to the Dough Twists (above) but makes a better accompaniment to such dishes as Spiced Brisket (see p. 125).

The secret of making good man-tou is to knead the dough really well. It will take about 20 minutes to do this properly.

Huo-Shao

(SERVES 6)
INGREDIENTS

2½ cups all-purpose flour
2½ cups self-rising flour
approx. 1 cup water

Sift the flours together into a bowl and add sufficient water to make a firm dough. Knead, then cover and let stand for about 25 minutes. Knead again to make a smooth dough – it should feel quite stiff.

Divide the dough into 6 pieces and shape each one into a round, roughly 2½-3 inches in diameter. Flute the edges by pinching the dough with your thumb and index finger.

Place the huo-shao on a baking sheet and bake in a preheated hot oven (450°F) for 15-20 minutes until golden brown. Turn the buns once or twice to ensure they brown evenly.

NOTE
Hard and crispy, huo-shao is a very popular "dry" bread in China. If you find it too hard, serve it dipped in a soup.

Pork and Vegetable Buns

(SERVES 4)
INGREDIENTS

5 cups all-purpose flour
1½ teaspoons active dry
  yeast
1 tablespoon sugar
approx. 1 cup lukewarm
  water
1¼ lb. Chinese cabbage
1¾ cups lean ground pork
3 tablespoons black or white
  sesame seeds
3 tablespoons corn oil
½ cup water

SEASONING A
1½ teaspoons salt
1 tablespoon ginger wine
  (see Glossary)
1 teaspoon white pepper
½ teaspoon sesame oil
¼ cup clear soup stock (see
  p. 261)

SEASONING B
1 inch piece fresh gingerroot,
  minced
3 tablespoons light soy sauce
3 tablespoons malt vinegar

Make a dough with the flour, yeast, sugar and water (see p. 345). Divide into 8 pieces.

Discard any old or withered leaves from the Chinese cabbage and wash the remainder. Drain thoroughly, then chop finely. Mix with the pork and seasoning **A**.

Roll the dough pieces into 3-4 inch rounds, slightly thicker in the center than around the edges. Place 2 tablespoons of the pork filling in the center and bring the dough up around the filling. Pinch the tops to close.

Cover the buns with a damp piece of unbleached muslin or a dish towel and let stand for 30 minutes. Then put a wet piece of unbleached muslin in the base of a steamer, put the buns on top and steam over rapidly boiling water for 20 minutes.

While the buns are steaming, dry-fry the sesame seeds for 2 minutes to roast them. Remove the buns from the steamer and sprinkle with the sesame seeds.

Heat the oil in a large skillet and cook the buns for 2 minutes. Add the water, cover the pan with a lid and cook for 10 minutes.

Serve the buns at once with seasoning **B** mixed together.

蘇州月餅
Moon Cakes

(SERVES 4)
INGREDIENTS

1 quantity watered and oiled
   dough with oiled dough
   filling (see p. 347)
2 tablespoons peanut oil
corn oil, for deep frying

PORK FILLING
1¾ cups lean ground pork
4 tablespoons preserved
   vegetable
½ tablespoon ginger wine
   (see Glossary)
½ tablespoon cornstarch
½ teaspoon salt
1 teaspoon white pepper
½ tablespoon sesame oil

Prepare the watered and oiled dough and roll out
into rounds as directed on p. 349.

Mix the pork thoroughly with the preserved
vegetable, the ginger wine, cornstarch, salt and
pepper and sesame oil.

Heat the peanut oil in a wok or skillet. Add the
pork filling ingredients, and cook, stirring, for a few
minutes, until the pork has lost all its pinkness.

Place 2 tablespoons of the filling in the center of
each wrapper and seal the dough around the filling. If
you like, make decorative cuts around the cakes.

Heat the oil in a deep-fat fryer and deep-fry the
cakes until they are golden brown all over. Drain on
paper towels and serve.

豆沙酥
Red Bean Pastries

(SERVES 4)
INGREDIENTS

1 lb. red bean paste (see
   NOTE p. 61)
1 quantity oiled dough (see
   p. 346)
¼-⅓ cup corn oil

Divide the red bean paste into 16 balls and roll into
oval shapes.

Make the dough as directed on p. 346. Divide
into 16 pieces and roll each of these to an oval shape
large enough to encase the red bean paste.

Wrap the paste in the dough and place on a baking
sheet. Brush with a little oil and bake in a preheated
hot oven (450°F) for about 30 minutes, brushing with
more oil from time to time. Serve hot.

一口酥
E Kuo Pastries

(SERVES 4)
INGREDIENTS

1 quantity oiled dough (see
   p. 346)
1 quantity moon cake pork
   filling (see above)
corn oil, for deep frying

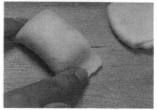

Prepare the oiled dough as direced on p. 346 and
roll into several small oval shapes.

Place about 2 tablespoons of the cooked filling onto
each dough shape and secure filling as shown in
pictures on the right.

Heat the oil in a deep-fat fryer and deep-fry the
cakes until they are golden brown all over. Drain on
paper towels and serve at once.

Chinese Breads

(MAKES ABOUT 8)
INGREDIENTS

3½ cups all-purpose flour
1¾ cups self-rising flour
¼ quantity oiled paste filling
   (see p. 348)
approx. 1 cup water
½ cup black or white sesame
   seeds
3 tablespoons corn oil

Sift the flours together into a bowl and add 2 tablespoons oiled paste. Mix together, then add sufficient water to make into a dough. Knead lightly, cover with a damp piece of unbleached muslin or a dish towel and let stand for 20 minutes. Knead again until smooth and shiny.

With your hands, roll the dough into a long roll about 1½ inches in diameter. Cut into 8 pieces and roll each of these into a thin oval shape. Spread the oiled paste onto each oval and top with another oval piece of dough. Roll out lightly, then fold into three as shown in small picture 3 on the right.

Brush each package with a little water and sprinkle with sesame seeds. Place the packages, sesame side down on the board or working surface and roll out to an oval shape measuring 6 × 4 inches.

Heat the oil in a wok or skillet and cook the breads over a low to medium heat for about 8-10 minutes until lightly browned. Turn over and cook the other side for the same time. Serve hot.

NOTE
Chinese Breads make an excellent accompaniment to cold bean curd drinks or soup. Alternatively they are delicious served with crisp, deep-fried pastries.

Shao-Ping Sandwiches

(MAKES ABOUT 15)
INGREDIENTS

3½ cups all-purpose flour
1¾ cups self-rising flour
¼ quantity oiled paste filling
   (see p. 348)
approx. 1 cup water
½ cup white sesame seeds
⅓ cup corn oil
7-8 slices roast beef or pork,
   halved to serve.

Sift the flours together into a bowl and add about 3 tablespoons of oiled paste filling. Mix together, then add sufficient water to make into a dough. Knead lightly, cover with a damp piece of unbleached muslin or a dish towel and let stand for 20 minutes. Knead again until smooth and shiny.

Roll out the dough to a large round about ¼ inch thick. Spread half the remaining oiled paste on top and roll up the dough into a long "stick". Roll this out again and spread the remaining filling on top.

Roll the dough into a long "stick" once more and cut in 15 pieces. Roll each of these into a small round about ¾ inch thick and brush with water. Sprinkle with the sesame seeds.

Heat the oil in a wok or skillet and add the shao-ping rolls, sesame seed side down. Cover the pan and cook over medium heat for about 5 minutes. Turn the cakes over and cook the other side for a further 5-10 minutes, until brown.

Remove the rolls from the oil. Quickly split them open and put a little roast beef or pork into each one. Serve hot.

台式香菇肉粽
Bamboo Wrapped Pork and Rice Dumplings

(SERVES 4)
INGREDIENTS

⅔ cup unsalted peanuts
8-10 dried Chinese mushrooms
4 tablespoons dried baby shrimp
10 oz. pork
3 cups white glutinous rice
4 shallots
¼ cup melted shortening or corn oil
⅔ cup clear soup stock (see p. 261)
bamboo leaves and straw

SEASONING

1½ tablespoons light soy sauce
½ teaspoon black pepper
½ teaspoon salt

Soak the peanuts in cold water overnight, then drain. Soak the Chinese mushrooms in warm water for 30 minutes. Drain, cut off and discard the stems and dice the caps finely. Soak the shrimp in warm water for 30 minutes, then drain.

Cut the pork in ½ inch cubes. Wash and drain the rice thoroughly and mince the shallots.

Heat the shortening or corn oil in a wok or skillet and stir-fry the shallots for 1 minute. Add the pork and seasoning and stir-fry for 2 minutes. Remove.

Stir the peanuts and rice into the oil left in the wok and stir-fry over medium heat for 2 minutes. Gradually stir in the stock, then simmer, covered, over a very low heat until the rice is cooked.

Return the pork to the pan with the mushrooms and shrimp and mix well. Off heat, let cool.

Wrap about 3 tablespoons of the rice mixture in each bamboo leaf as described in Glutinous Rice Dumplings, p. 307, but make a little smaller.

Steam the dumplings for 1-1½ hours and serve.

筒仔米糕   油飯
Oiled Rice

(SERVES 4)
INGREDIENTS

4 Chinese mushrooms
4 tablespoons dried baby shrimp
¾ lb. pork
3 cups white glutinous rice
6 shallots
3 tablespoons corn oil
⅓ cup clear soup stock (see p. 261)
2 teaspoons rock sugar

SEASONING

½ teaspoon salt
½ teaspoon white pepper

Soak the Chinese mushrooms in warm water for 30 minutes. Drain. Cut off and discard the stems and shred the caps. Soak the shrimp in warm water for 30 minutes, then drain. Cut the pork in thin slices, about 1 inch wide.

Wash and drain the rice, then cook in a large saucepan of boiling water for about 10 minutes. Drain.

Finely chop the shallots. Heat the oil in a wok or large skillet and stir-fry the shallots for a few seconds. Add the mushrooms, shrimp and pork and the seasoning ingredients and cook for 5 minutes, stirring frequently. Remove from the wok using a slotted spoon.

Add the rice to the wok and stir-fry over a medium heat for a few seconds. Gradually stir in the stock and rock sugar, then cook over a low heat for about 15 minutes until the rice is very tender. Mix in the pork mixture and serve in small bowls.

Fried Nien-Kao

(SERVES 4-6)
INGREDIENTS

1¼ lb. nien-kao (see p. 341 and NOTE)
⅓ cup corn oil
2 tablespoons water
4 sprigs fresh parsley

SEASONING A
2 tablespoons sweet and hot sauce
1 tablespoon dark soy sauce
1 tablespoon Hoisin sauce

SEASONING B
2 garlic cloves, crushed
3 tablespoons light soy sauce
½ tablespoon chili sauce

Cut the nien-kao into slices.

Heat 1 tablespoon of the oil in a skillet and add seasoning **A**. Stir well, then add seasoning **B** along with the water. Bring to a boil. Mince the parsley and add to the pan, stir for a few seconds, then remove the pan from the heat. Spoon into a serving dish.

Heat the remaining oil in a clean skillet and add the nien-kao in a single layer. Cook over a medium heat until both sides are golden brown.

Serve hot with the seasoning sauce.

NOTE
Ready-made nien-kao can be bought in Chinese markets in the spring. It is one of the traditional dishes of the Chinese New Year.

Stir-Fried Nien-Kao with Vegetable

(SERVES 4-6)
INGREDIENTS

1¼ lb. nien-kao (see NOTE above)
20 dried Chinese mushrooms
10 oz. green-stemmed flat cabbage (see NOTE)
¼ cup corn oil
2 teaspoons sesame oil

SEASONING
3 tablespoons light soy sauce
½ tablespoon sugar
½ teaspoon salt
½ cup clear soup stock (see p. 261)

Cut the nien-kao in thin slices. Soak the Chinese mushrooms in warm water for 30 minutes. Drain. Cut off and discard the stems and cut the caps in half. Wash the cabbage and chop in 1 inch sections.

Heat the oil in a wok or skillet, add the mushrooms and stir-fry for 2 minutes. Add the seasoning ingredients and cook, covered, for about 2 minutes.

Add the nien-kao and cabbage and cook, stirring frequently, for about 10 minutes, until the cabbage is tender.

Serve hot with the sesame oil sprinkled on top.

NOTE
If you are unable to buy Chinese flat cabbage, use kale or collard greens instead.

Po-Su Buns

(SERVES 4)
INGREDIENTS

1 quantity leavened dough
  (see p. 345)
1 quantity scalded dough
  (see p. 344)
1 quantity oiled dough filling
  (see p. 347)
2 boneless chicken breasts
10 oz. lean pork
6 tablespoons minced
  canned bamboo shoot

SEASONING
1½ teaspoons salt
½ teaspoon white pepper
½ teaspoon sugar

Make the leavened, scalded and oiled dough filling as directed on p. 345, p. 344 and p. 347.

Knead the leavened and scalded doughs together, cover and let stand for 30 minutes. Roll out to a large round. Roll out the oiled dough filling and place on top. With your hands, roll all the doughs together to make a long sausage. Cut this in 8 pieces.

Mince the chicken and mince or grind pork. Mix with the minced bamboo shoot and seasoning ingredients.

Roll out the pieces of dough to rounds about 5 inches in diameter, slightly thicker in the middle than at the edges. Place about 2 tablespoons filling in the center, then bring the dough up around the filling and pinch the edges to seal. Cover with a damp piece of unbleached muslin or a dish towel and let stand for 20 minutes.

Steam the buns over rapidly boiling water for 20 minutes and serve at once.

Easy-To-Make Bread Rolls

(SERVES 4)
INGREDIENTS

2 teaspoons active dry yeast
1 teaspoon sugar
¼ cup lukewarm water
1 teaspoon salt
5 tablespoons butter
½ cup milk
2 eggs, plus 2 extra yolks
2½ cups all-purpose flour

Mix the yeast with the sugar and water and let stand for 10 minutes.

Put the salt into a saucepan with 3 tablespoons of the butter and the milk. Stir over a low heat until the butter has melted. Off heat, beat in 1 whole egg and the 2 extra yolks. Pour into a large bowl.

Sift the flour twice onto a plate, then beat into the egg mixture. Beat in the yeast mixture. Remove the mixture from the bowl and knead on a lightly floured surface for about 15 minutes, until the dough is shiny and smooth.

Place dough into a large oiled plastic bag. Tie the opening tightly and put into the refrigerator overnight.

Divide the dough into 8 pieces and form each one into a bun shape. Melt the remaining butter and brush the rolls with it. Place in the refrigerator for 10 minutes, then lightly dust with flour. Cover with waxed paper and let stand in a cool place for 30-40 minutes.

Remove the waxed paper and place the rolls on a baking sheet. Sprinkle lightly with water, then bake in a preheated hot oven (425°F) for 15-20 minutes.

Beat the remaining egg and brush over the top of the rolls. Return to the oven for 5 minutes more, until golden and shiny. Serve warm or cold.

Turnip Cakes

(SERVES 4)
INGREDIENTS

4 tablespoons dried baby
   shrimps
¾ lb. turnips
¼ lb. lean pork
2 garlic cloves
1 cup corn oil
5 cups all-purpose flour
approx. ⅞ cup water

SEASONING A
1½ teaspoons salt
1 teaspoon sugar

SEASONING B
1 teaspoon salt
½ teaspoon white pepper

Soak the shrimp in warm water for 30 minutes. Drain and chop roughly.

Peel the turnips and grate into a bowl of water. Wash, then drain and squeeze dry. Mix with seasoning **A** and let stand for 20 minutes.

Mince or grind the pork and slice the garlic thinly.

Heat 2 tablespoons of the oil in a skillet and sauté the shrimp and pork for 2 minutes. Add the turnip, garlic and seasoning **B** and cook, stirring for a further 1-2 minutes.

Make a fairly soft dough with the flour and water (see p. 343) and divide in 8 pieces. Roll each one out to a thin round.

Divide the filling among the rounds and fold the dough up over the filling. Flatten with a heavy rolling pin into large patties.

Heat half the remaining oil in a skillet and cook 4 of the patties over a medium to low heat. Cook for about 3 minutes, until golden brown. Turn over and cook the other side until golden brown. Drain on paper towels and keep warm while you cook the remainder of the patties in the same way, using the remaining oil.

Milk Pancakes

(SERVES 4)
INGREDIENTS

1¼ cups milk
¼ cup sugar
2½ cups whole wheat flour
butter, for cooking
jam, cream and candied
   cherries, to serve

Place the milk and sugar in a saucepan and heat gently to dissolve the sugar. Still on the heat, gradually beat in the flour. Off heat, beat until the mixture is really smooth. Let stand for 20 minutes, then beat again.

Heat a knob of butter in a skillet and swirl to grease the base of the pan. Spoon 3-4 tablespoons of the batter into the pan and tip the pan to form a round of batter. Cook until the batter is lightly set.

Turn the pancake over and cook the other side until lightly browned. Remove and keep warm while you cook the remainder of the batter in the same way.

Serve with jam or cream, decorated with candied cherries.

Sweet Potatoes in Syrup

(SERVES 6)
INGREDIENTS

2 lb. sweet potatoes
1⅔ cups packed light brown sugar
½ cup superfine sugar
2-3 tablespoons rock sugar (see NOTE p. 114)
½ cup water
3 tablespoons corn oil
½ cup light corn syrup

Peel the sweet potatoes and cut in 2 inch sections.
Place all the brown sugar in a saucepan along with the superfine and rock sugars, water and oil. Heat gently until the sugars have all dissolved, then bring to a boil.

Add the potatoes, bring back to a boil, then lower the heat and simmer gently for 30-35 minutes, until the potatoes are shiny and transparent-looking.

Heat the corn syrup until it thins. Put the sweet potatoes in a serving dish and pour the syrup over the top. Serve at once.

Seafood Rolls

(SERVES 4)
INGREDIENTS

1 pint fresh oysters or clams, shucked
4 cups fresh bean sprouts
¼ lb. lean pork
2 celery stalks
½ teaspoon salt
½ teaspoon chili powder
8 pieces fresh bean curd sheet
2 tablespoons all-purpose flour
2 tablespoons water
corn oil, for deep frying
3 garlic cloves

SEASONING
1 tablespoon Hoisin sauce
2 tablespoons sugar
2 tablespoons vinegar
½ teaspoon white pepper
2 teaspoons cornstarch mixed with ¼ cup water

Wash the oysters or clams and dry on paper towels. Wash the bean sprouts and drain thoroughly. Cut pork in tiny cubes and chop the celery. Mix all these together with the salt and chili powder.

Cut each bean curd sheet in 3 equal-size pieces. Mix the flour and water to a paste and brush around the outside of the bean curd sheet pieces.

Place 2 tablespoons of filling in the center of each bean curd wrapper and roll up. The flour paste should seal the edges.

Heat the oil in a deep-fat fryer and fry the rolls until they are golden brown and crispy all over. Drain on paper towels and keep warm.

Chop the garlic roughly. Heat 2 tablespoons of oil in a clean skillet and sauté the garlic for 1 minute. Add the seasoning ingredients and bring to a boil. Pour this over the seafood rolls and serve.

335

Rice Triangles

(SERVES 4-6)
INGREDIENTS

3 cups white glutinous rice
1 tablespoon baking soda
bamboo leaves and straw

Wash and drain the rice thoroughly. Mix with the soda and let stand for 1-2 hours.

Pack the rice into the bamboo leaves as for Glutinous Rice Dumplings, see p. 307, but make these dumplings quite small and shape them into small triangles (see small pictures, right). Tie the packages securely with straw or string.

Place the rice triangles in a large saucepan and cover with water. Bring to a boil, lower the heat and simmer very gently for about 4 hours. Keep the pan topped up with boiling water to cover the dumplings during this time. Switch off the heat, but let the dumplings stand in the water for an hour more before serving.

NOTE
These dumplings can be served as a sweet or savory dish. For a sweet dish, serve them with sugar; for a savory one – with soy sauce or salt.

Spiral Dumplings

(SERVES 4)
INGREDIENTS

1 cup dried red beans (see NOTES)
3 cups white glutinous rice
½ teaspoon salt
bamboo leaves and straw

Wash the beans and soak in cold water for 2 hours. Wash and drain the rice and mix with the salt.

Drain the beans and stir into the rice.

Place the underside or rough side of 2 bamboo leaves together and fold into a cone shape. Push 2-3 tablespoons rice and bean mixture into the case and then fold the leaves over the filling to make a triangular shape with a flat bottom. Tie securely and repeat with all the filling.

Bring a large pan of water to a boil and drop the dumplings into it - the water should cover them completely. Lower the heat and simmer very gently for 6 hours. Switch off the heat and let the dumplings stand in the pan for an hour more before serving.

NOTES
Dried red beans are available from some Oriental markets. Red bean sauce can be used instead, if preferred, but do not use kidney beans.

These dumplings can also be served as a sweet or savory dish. Dip in sugar for a sweet dish, and into hot bean or soy sauce for savory.

An alternative way of serving the dumplings, is to let them go cold, then unwrap them, coat lightly in flour and deep fry in hot oil until golden brown.

337

Smiling Muffins

(SERVES 4)
INGREDIENTS

5 cups self-rising flour
1¼ cups whole wheat flour
1 teaspoon baking soda
½ tablespoon baking powder
2 eggs
1½ tablespoons melted
   shortening
⅔ cup sugar
approx. 1 cup water
½ cup white or black sesame
   seeds
corn oil, for deep frying

Sift the flours, soda and baking powder into a large bowl. Make a well in the center.

Beat eggs together. Pour into the well and add the shortening and sugar. Add sufficient water to make a firm dough. Knead lightly, then cover with a damp piece of unbleached muslin or a dish towel and let stand for 20 minutes.

Shape the dough into a long roll and cut in 1 inch sections. Roll each of these into a ball, then coat them with the sesame seeds.

Heat the oil in a deep-fat fryer and deep-fry the balls, turning them over in the oil, until they are slightly split and golden brown in color.

Remove from the oil and drain on paper towels. Serve at once.

Sesame Snacks

(SERVES 4)
INGREDIENTS

2½ cups whole wheat flour
2 tablespoons melted
   shortening
½ cup lukewarm water
2 tablespoons sugar
½ teaspoon salt
1½ tablespoons black
   sesame seeds
corn oil, for frying

Sift the flour and mix to a dough with the shortening, water, sugar and salt. Knead lightly, then cover with a damp piece of unbleached muslin or a dish towel and let stand for 20 minutes.

Roll out the dough to a large round, about ¼ inch thick and sprinkle with the sesame seeds. Cut in 1 inch strips and cut these into diamond shapes.

Make a lengthwise slit in the center of the diamond shapes and push one end of the diamond through the slit to give a braided effect.

Heat the oil in a deep fat fryer and cook the twists, a few at a time, until golden brown all over. Drain on paper towels and serve.

NOTE
These crunchy twists are delicious served with cocktails.

Sweet Nien-Kao

(SERVES 6-8)

INGREDIENTS

1⅔ cups packed light brown
    sugar
4 cups water
1 lb. sweet rice flour
1 cup rice flour
3 tablespoons melted
    shortening
vegetable oil, for brushing
5 red dates or prunes, soaked
    (see NOTES)

Place the sugar and water in a saucepan and set over a medium heat. When the sugar has dissolved, bring to a boil. Let cool.

Mix the flours together and gradually stir in the sugar syrup, keeping the mixture smooth all the time. Stir in the shortening and mix well.

Place a large piece of plastic wrap in the base of a steamer and brush with oil. Pour the flour paste into the steamer and place the dates or prunes on top.

Steam over rapidly boiling water for 2 hours. Test for doneness by inserting a knife or chopstick into the nien-kao; if it comes out clean, the cake is done.

NOTES

Soak the red dates for 4 hours before using. Soak the prunes overnight.

There are two types of nien-kao – brown and white, the difference being in the color of the sugar used. Brown nien-kao is more popular.

Steam the nien-kao over a large pan of boiling water; it is better not to have to add any water to the pan during the steaming process.

Cantonese Turnip Cake

(SERVES 6-8)

INGREDIENTS

1 cup dried baby shrimp
4 lb. white turnips
6 tablespoons shortening
2 teaspoons salt
1 piece (about 3 oz.) smoked
    ham
2 Chinese sausages (see
    NOTE)
1½ teaspoons white pepper
1 tablespoon sugar
3⅓ cups rice flour
1-1¼ cups water
1 tablespoon chopped fresh
    parsley

Soak the shrimp in warm water for 30 minutes, then drain. Peel the turnips and grate finely in a food processor.

Heat 4 tablespoons of shortening in a wok or skillet and stir-fry the shrimp for 1 minute. Add the shredded turnip and salt and cook for a further 5 minutes stirring frequently.

Mince the smoked ham and sausages and add to the wok with the pepper and sugar. Stir well and cook for 5 minutes, then remove from the heat.

Mix the flour with water to make a thick, smooth paste. Stir this into the turnip mixture, mixing together well.

Place a large piece of plastic wrap in the base of a steamer. Melt the remaining shortening and brush over the plastic wrap. Spoon the turnip mixture on top, and steam over boiling water for 2 hours. Test for doneness by inserting a knife into the cake – it should come out clean. Let cool. Sprinkle with parsley. Serve.

NOTE

Chinese sausages are sweet, mildly seasoned cured sausages, around 6 inches long and ½ inch thick. Sold in Oriental markets, they should be steamed for 30 minutes before use.

General directions for making dough

1 Measure the ingredients carefully. Generally speaking, 1 cup flour is sufficient for one person. Sift flour into a bowl.

2 Make a well in the center of the flour. Gradually pour in the water and mix it into the flour, adding sufficient water to bring the mixture together.

3 Use a knife or chopstick to combine the mixture. To make the dough shiny, add a little melted shortening.

4 When you have added sufficient water to make the dough, flour your hands lightly and begin kneading.

5 Work the dough in the bowl, pressing it with the palm of your hand and turning it frequently. Continue until the dough is smooth.

6 Soak a piece of unbleached muslin, cheesecloth or a dish towel in cold water, then squeeze it out very firmly.

7 Place the cloth over the bowl containing the dough and let stand for 20-30 minutes. This lets the dough rest.

8 If you want the dough to be quite chewy and "elastic", knead the dough vigorously for a short time by pulling and pushing it apart.

9 For a smoother pastry, knead the dough in the usual way. The longer you knead it, the smoother it will be.

10 If the dough feels sticky as you are kneading, flour the surface liberally and work a little into the dough.

11 If the dough feels too dry and is difficult to knead, cut it in pieces and sprinkle with water. Knead together again.

12 Knead the dough until it is quite smooth. If you do not want to use it right away, cover it with a damp cloth.

How to make scalded dough

INGREDIENTS

2½ cups all-purpose flour
1 tablespoon melted
    shortening (optional)
approx. 1¼ cups water

This is the dough most commonly used for steamed dim sums. Melted shortening may be added to make the dough shiny.

1   Measure the flour and sift into a large bowl. Stir in the melted shortening if using.

2   Boil the water and measure out the required quantity.

3   Gradually pour the water into the flour, stirring all the time.

4   Keep stirring to mix thoroughly but do not bring the mixture together.

5   Cover the bowl with a damp cloth and let stand for about 10 minutes.

6   Knead the mixture to bring it together to a rough dough. Remove from the bowl.

7   If necessary, add more flour or water – it should feel damp but not wet. Cover with a damp but not wet cloth; let stand for 20 minutes.

8   Knead the dough vigorously by pulling and pushing it apart.

9   Finish off by kneading it with the palm of your hand until it is really smooth.

10   The kneading process will take 15-20 minutes. The dough is then ready for use.

11   If you do not want to use it immediately, put in a bowl and cover with a damp cloth.

How to make leavened dough

INGREDIENTS

2½ cups all-purpose flour
½ cup lukewarm water
1 teaspoon sugar
1 teaspoon active dry yeast

This dough can be used for baking as well as steaming and boiling. If it is to be used for cakes and cookies, it is usual to add baking powder to the mixture. Vinegar and shortening can also be added to the flour for some recipes, and occasionally milk is substituted for the water.

1 Ingredients used in making leavened dough. The yeast mixture is shown in the glasses and bowls (right).

2 Test the temperature of the water by pouring a little onto your wrist. It should be lukewarm. i.e. blood heat.

3 Pour the water into a small bowl and add the sugar.

4 Stir until the sugar has dissolved. It is necessary to make the yeast work.

5 Sprinkle the dry yeast into the bowl but do not stir it in. Let stand for 7-10 minutes.

6 The yeast mixture is ready to use when small bubbles have appeared on the surface.

7 Sift the flour three times to make it as light as possible. Add the yeast mixture and stir, adding a little more warm water if necessary.

8 Mix the flour and liquid thoroughly, then knead into a rough dough.

9 Using a finger, make holes all over the dough. Sprinkle the surface with water.

10 Cover the bowl with a damp cloth and leave for 3 hours at room temperature.

11 The dough will expand and rise. This picture was taken after the dough had stood for 2 hours.

12 Knead the dough until completely smooth and shiny. Use immediately or let stand, covered, for another 20 minutes.

How to make oiled dough

INGREDIENTS

1 cup all-purpose flour
2¼ cups self-rising flour
½ cup melted shortening

Oiled dough is most commonly used for deep-frying dim sums. It is easy to work and can be used to make various shapes and patterns, which look very pretty and decorative when cooked. Some patterns can be made by cutting into the dough, but care should be taken not to cut so deep that the filling is exposed during cooking. If you want the dough to be shiny after cooking, brush it with some beaten egg. You can also add color and flavor to the dough by adding soy sauce to it.

1   Sift the two types of flour together into a large bowl.

2   Add the melted shortening, stirring it into the flour.

3   Add sufficient water to bring the flour together in small lumps.

4   Not enough water has been added here to form a smooth dough. A little more is needed.

5   Knead the dough until it is smooth and shiny. This will take about 15 minutes. Let stand for 20 minutes, then knead again before use.

How to make watered and oiled dough

WATERED AND OILED WRAPPING

INGREDIENTS

1¼ cups all-purpose flour
1¼ cups self-rising flour
⅔ cup water
2 tablespoons melted
   shortening
1 tablespoon sugar, optional

This pastry is made by combining a watered and oiled dough wrapping with a dough or paste filling. It is used when a layered effect is required.

You can color and flavor the pastry by adding curry powder to it. Replace ½ tablespoon of the flour mixture with 2 tablespoons curry powder.

1 Sift the two types of flour together into a bowl. Stir in the water and then the shortening.

2 Add the sugar, if using, and mix the ingredients together with your hands.

3 Knead the dough thoroughly until smooth. Let stand for 20 minutes, then knead again.

OILED DOUGH FILLING

INGREDIENTS

½ cup all-purpose flour
1¾ cups self-rising flour
⅔ cup melted shortening
1 teaspoon sugar, optional

Sugar is added to the filling and wrapping dough to give the dough a crisper, browner finish. Omit the sugar if you are intending to cut the dough in shapes.

1 Sift the two types of flour together. Stir in the shortening and sugar, if using.

2 Mix together thoroughly. This is particularly important if sugar has been added as it has to dissolve into the other ingredients.

3 Knead the dough well, then let stand for 20 minutes. Knead again before use.

OILED PASTE FILLING

INGREDIENTS

1 cup shortening
2 cups all-purpose flour,
   1 tablespoon pepper and
   salt, mixed
1 tablespoon ground
   cinnamon

Oiled paste filling is used rather than the oiled dough filling when making cakes such as Chinese Breads (see p. 325).

1 Melt the shortening in a wok or heavy-bottomed saucepan, and stir in the flour, keeping the mixture smooth.

2 Cook the mixture over a high heat until it begins to turn brown and become slightly "scorched".

3 Add the pepper, salt and cinnamon. Stir for 1 minute more, then pour into a bowl to cool slightly.

HOW TO COMBINE WRAPPING AND FILLING

INGREDIENTS

1 quantity watered and
oiled wrapping (see p. 347)
1 quantity oiled dough or paste
filling (see p. 347 and 348)

There are two ways of combining the wrapping and filling to make
the complete dough.

METHOD 1

The quickest way is to roll out the wrapping to a large piece about
¼ inch thick. Place the filling on top and fold the wrapping around
it. Roll out the dough again to a rectangle again about ¼ inch
thick. Fold the bottom third up over the dough and the top third
down. Press the ends with the rolling pin to seal and roll out again.
Repeat the folding process and roll out the dough again. Using your
hands, roll up the dough to a long sausage shape, then cut in 1 inch
pieces and roll these out to thin rounds to use as dumpling skins.

METHOD 2

1 Knead the wrapping and
filling separately and roll
each one into a long sausage
shape using your hands. Cut
in small sections.

2 Flatten the wrapping
dough to a rough round. Roll
the filling into a small ball.

3 Place the filling ball on the
wrapper and fold the wrapper
around it to enclose filling
completely.

4 Repeat with all the dough,
then flatten the balls slightly in
the palms of your hands.

5 Roll each piece out to an
oval shape. Roll these up from
one end then repeat the rolling
out and folding up process
once more.

6 Roll out the balls to a
thin round if required for
dumplings.

7 Alternatively, the dough
can be shaped into decorative
patterns and shapes.

8 To make "shell" shapes,
roll up the thin rounds and
mold each roll into a shell"
with a fluted edge.

9 Mold two "shells" together
to make a "wheel" shape. The
finished dough shapes are
deep fried.

ENTERTAINING

One of the most notable and exciting features of a Chinese meal is that it contains so many different dishes.

For day-to-day eating in China, the general practice is to serve one savory dish per person in addition to a rice dish. Appetizers, soups and noodle dishes are also served, according to individual taste.

When planning a Chinese meal, choose dishes that will give a good balance of flavor, richness, texture and color. Harmony of taste and texture is an all important element of Chinese cuisine and a well-balanced menu will provide a gastronomic treat that few will forget! Any of the recipes from this chapter will make perfect dishes for a dinner party, but to add variety you can also select one or two dishes from some of the other chapters in the book. To help you grasp the basic principles of planning a Chinese dinner party, try following any of the menu ideas featured on p. 384.

All the recipes in the book need to be served in conjunction with several other dishes, in order to make a reasonably complete meal. However, if time is short and authenticity is not strictly essential, simply double the ingredients in selected recipes to create an instant Western compromise.

Cantonese Fried Chicken

(SERVES 4)
INGREDIENTS

4 chicken pieces
2 tablespoons light soy sauce
2 egg whites, lightly beaten
1 cup all-purpose flour
½ cup corn oil
fresh parsley, for garnish

SEASONING
2 tablespoons rice wine or
   dry sherry
1 tablespoon ketchup
2 teaspoons Worcestershire
   sauce
½ teaspoon sugar
pinch of salt

Chop the chicken pieces in halves or fourths and pound with the back of a cleaver. Place the soy sauce in a bowl and add the chicken pieces. Let stand for 30 minutes.

Drain the chicken. Coat with the egg whites and then dust with the flour.

Heat the oil in a large wok and add the chicken. Stir-fry for 6-7 minutes until the chicken is cooked and golden brown.

Drain the oil and add the seasoning ingredients. Stir thoroughly and serve, garnished with parsley.

Shredded Chicken and Pepper

(SERVES 4)
INGREDIENTS

6 oz. boneless chicken
   breasts, skinned
1 egg white, lightly beaten
½ green pepper, seeded
½ sweet red pepper, seeded
½ cup corn oil
1 small onion, chopped
1 tablespoon light soy sauce

SEASONING
1 tablespoon rice wine or dry
   sherry
½ teaspoon cornstarch
1 teaspoon salt
pinch of white pepper

Cut the chicken in long thin shreds.

Beat the egg white with the seasoning ingredients and add the chicken shreds, stirring thoroughly. Cut the peppers in long, thin strips.

Heat the oil in a wok, add the chopped onion and cook for a few seconds. Add the chicken and stir-fry for 5 minutes.

Remove the chicken with a slotted spoon and drain all but 1 teaspoon of the oil. Add the peppers and stir-fry for 3 minutes.

Return the chicken to the wok and stir. Cook for 2 minutes, then sprinkle with the soy sauce and serve.

Laver Pancake Rolls

(SERVES 2-4)
INGREDIENTS

¾ cup all-purpose flour
pinch of salt
1 egg
6 tablespoons water
corn oil, for shallow frying
4-6 pieces of laver (see NOTE
p. 85)

Sift the flour and salt into a bowl, add the egg and the water. Beat thoroughly to make a smooth batter of dropping consistency, adding a little more water if necessary.

Heat a little oil in a large pancake pan, add about one-fourth of the batter, tilting the pan so that the pancake coats it evenly. Cook for a few minutes until golden and then flip over and cook the other side. Repeat this until all the batter has been used up.

Broil the slices of laver for a few seconds. Place a pancake on top of each, roll up and serve.

Chinese Curried Macaroni

(SERVES 4)
INGREDIENTS

1 teaspoon salt
2 cups elbow macaroni
5 oz. boneless chicken
 breast, skinned
1 carrot
⅓ cup green beans
2 tomatoes
½ cup button mushrooms
¼ cup corn oil
3 garlic cloves, crushed
1 onion, minced
2 tablespoons Chinese curry
 powder (see NOTE p. 145)
¼ cup clear soup stock (see
 p. 261)
1 teaspoon salt
½ teaspoon white pepper

Bring a large pan of water to a boil, add the salt and throw in the macaroni. Cook for 8-10 minutes until the macaroni is tender. Drain well and then soak the pasta in cold water.

Dice the chicken, mince the carrot and green beans, cut the tomatoes in wedges and slice the mushrooms.

Heat the oil in a wok or skillet and add the garlic and onion. Stir-fry for 1 minute and then add the chicken, carrot, green beans, tomatoes, button mushrooms and curry powder.

Stir-fry for 2 minutes, then add the soup stock, salt and pepper. Bring to a boil.

Drain the macaroni and stir into the curry. Cook for 2-3 minutes until hot and serve at once.

銀耳甜湯

Sweet Fungus Dessert

(SERVES 4)
INGREDIENTS

1 cup (about 1 oz.) dried
　　white fungus (see NOTE)
3 tablespoons rock sugar (see
　　NOTE p. 114)
4 cups water
1 can (16 oz.) fruit cocktail

Place the fungus in a bowl, cover with warm water and soak for about 1 hour until it expands slightly.

Place the white fungus, sugar and the water in a saucepan, bring to a boil, lower the heat and then simmer gently for 30 minutes.

Off heat, let cool slightly. Add the fruit cocktail. Serve either hot or cold.

NOTE
Dried white fungus or silver ear fungus is available in most Oriental markets and can be kept for up to 6 months in a cool place.

炸芋酥餅

Deep-Fried Potato Patties

(SERVES 4)
INGREDIENTS

1 lb. potatoes
knob of butter
1 teaspoon salt
¼ cup chopped smoked ham
1 teaspoon sugar
pinch of pepper
1 egg, beaten
2 cups soft white bread
　　crumbs
corn oil, for deep frying

Cook the potatoes until tender and drain and mash them with the butter.

Stir in the salt, chopped ham, sugar and pepper and mix well.

Take large spoonfuls of mixture and mold them into balls in your hands. Dip in the beaten egg and then coat in the bread crumbs, pressing down lightly between your hands to form patties.

Heat the oil in a deep-fat fryer and deep-fry the patties for 2-3 minutes or until golden brown, turning occasionally. Drain on paper towels and serve.

冰糖甜藕

Sweet Lotus Roots

(SERVES 4)
INGREDIENTS

2 sections of lotus roots
  (renkon) (see NOTES)
8 black dates soaked
¼ cup rock sugar
2½ cups water

Peel the lotus roots and cut diagonally in large thick pieces (see small picture 1, right).

Place the lotus roots, the soaked dates and the sugar in a saucepan with the water. Bring to a boil, lower the heat and then simmer for 40 minutes.

Pour the contents of the pan into a large bowl and place in a steamer. Cover and steam over a low heat for 1 hour.

Serve hot or cold.

NOTE
Fresh lotus roots are sometimes available during the summer – look out for them in Chinese and Indian markets. When they are unobtainable, dried or canned lotus roots can be used instead. The lotus root will slightly discolor during cooking. If you prefer the whiteness of the lotus, place it in a bowl with 2 tablespoons distilled white vinegar and 1 cup boiling water for 3 minutes.

翡翠餃子

Emerald Dumplings

(SERVES 4)
INGREDIENTS

1½ lb. spinach
½ teaspoon salt
5 cups all-purpose flour
3 tablespoons clear soup
  stock (see p. 261)
¾ lb. ground pork
1 small Chinese cabbage
¼ cup malt vinegar
½ teaspoon chili oil

SEASONING
1 tablespoon ginger juice
1 tablespoon sesame oil
1 teaspoon sugar
1 teaspoon salt
½ teaspoon white pepper

Wash and trim the spinach, Chop into very fine shreds and add the salt, pressing the salt into the spinach to extract the green spinach juice.

Stir in the flour and sufficient warm water to make a soft dough. Knead slightly and then set the dough in a bowl. Cover with a damp cloth and set aside for 20 minutes.

Mix the seasoning ingredients with the soup stock in a large bowl. Stir in the ground pork and set aside for 5 minutes.

Scald the cabbage in boiling water for 5 minutes. Drain and soak in cold water until cold. Drain thoroughly, and chop very finely. Mix with the pork mixture to make a smooth, sticky paste.

Roll out the spinach dough on a floured surface to make a long ¾ inch-thick sausage. Cut the "sausage" in ½ inch sections and roll out each piece thinly. Place a spoonful of the pork and cabbage stuffing in the center. Bring the edges around and seal firmly, to make small dumplings.

Bring a pan of water to a boil and carefully add the dumplings. Boil for 2 minutes, stirring occasionally with a ladle. Add 2 tablespoons cold water. Cover, bring to a boil and cook for a further 4-5 minutes. Remove with a slotted spoon and serve with the vinegar and chili oil.

Scalded Abalone

(SERVES 4)

INGREDIENTS

1 lb. abalone (see NOTE)
2 tablespoons corn oil
1 scallion, minced
1 red chili pepper, seeded
    and finely sliced

SEASONING A
1 tablespoon finely grated
    fresh gingerroot
1 tablespoon sesame oil

SEASONING B
1 teaspoon rice wine or dry
    sherry
1 teaspoon salt
1 teaspoon sugar
2 tablespoons water

Rinse the abalone and soak in cold water for 30 minutes. Drain and scald in boiling water for 10 minutes.

Heat the oil in a wok, add the scallion and seasoning **A** and stir-fry for 1 minute. Add the abalone and cook for 1 minute.

Add the red chili pepper and seasoning **B**, along with the water. Cook for 1 minute and then remove the abalone with a slotted spoon and arrange on a serving platter. Spoon the sauce over the top and serve.

NOTE
If fresh abalone are not available, use thawed frozen or drained canned ones, in which case, follow the recipe from Step 2.

Spicy Clams

(SERVES 4)
INGREDIENTS

2 dozen cherrystone clams
¼ cup corn oil
8 garlic cloves, crushed
2 fresh red chili peppers,
  seeded and thinly sliced
1 scallion, sliced
1 tablespoon rice wine or dry
  sherry
black pepper

SEASONING
1 tablespoon light soy sauce
½ teaspoon salt
½ teaspoon white pepper
1 teaspoon sugar

Rinse the clams in cold water, discarding any with broken shells. Soak in cold water for 25-30 minutes.

Heat the oil in a wok and add the garlic. Stir-fry for a few seconds and add the chili peppers and then immediately add the scallion.

Drain the clams and tip into the wok. Cook over a high heat for 3 minutes, stirring and rearranging the clams with a metal spatula.

Add the seasoning ingredients and stir-fry vigorously for a further 2 minutes.

Spoon onto a serving platter and sprinkle with the rice wine and black pepper.

Stir-Fried Beef with Oyster Sauce

(SERVES 4)
INGREDIENTS

¾ lb. rump steak
6 oz. kale or Chinese
  cabbage
¼ cup corn oil
¾ inch piece fresh
  gingerroot, sliced
2 teaspoons sesame oil
½ tablespoon rice wine or
  dry sherry

SEASONING A
1 tablespoon light soy sauce
½ tablespoon rice wine or
  dry sherry
½ teaspoon white pepper
1 teaspoon cornstarch
1 teaspoon sugar

SEASONING B
3 tablespoons oyster sauce
½ teaspoon salt
½ teaspoon sugar
2 tablespoons water

Slice the beef against the grain in large thin pieces. Mix seasoning **A** in a bowl and stir in the beef slices. Set aside to marinate for 30 minutes.

Trim the roots from the kale or Chinese cabbage, place in a large bowl and cover with boiling water. Let stand for 5 minutes and then drain.

Heat the oil in a wok and when hot, stir-fry the ginger slices for a few seconds. Add the beef and cook over a high heat for 3 minutes. Discard the ginger.

Add seasoning **B**, including the water and stir thoroughly. Stir in the greens and continue to cook, stirring, for 2 minutes until wilted.

Add the rice wine and sesame oil and stir to mix. Serve immediately.

Stewed Shark's Fin with Mushrooms

(SERVES 4)

INGREDIENTS

6 Chinese dried mushrooms
1¼ lb. shark's fin, soaked (see NOTE)
2 tablespoons finely grated fresh gingerroot
¼ cup corn oil
3 scallions, sliced
½ cup chicken stock (see p. 149)
1 tablespoon cornstarch
fresh parsley, for garnish

SEASONING A

2 tablespoons ginger wine (see Glossary)
1 teaspoon white pepper

SEASONING B

2 tablespoons dark soy sauce
1 teaspoon sugar
1 teaspoon salt
1 teaspoon white pepper

Soak the Chinese mushrooms in warm water for 30 minutes. Drain and remove the stems then slice the caps thinly.

Place the shark's fin in a large saucepan with the ginger. Cover with boiling water and leave for 5 minutes.

Stir in seasoning **A** and bring to a boil. Lower the heat and simmer for 10 minutes. Drain thoroughly.

Heat the oil in a wok, add the scallions and stir-fry for 5 seconds. Add the sliced mushrooms and stir-fry for a further minute.

Add the chicken stock and seasoning **B**. Blend the cornstarch with a little cold water and stir into the wok. Bring to a boil, stirring, until mixture thickens and then lower the heat and simmer for 15 minutes.

Pour the sauce into a deep serving dish and arrange the shark's fin on top. Garnish with parsley and serve.

NOTE

Shark's fin is a great delicacy in China. It has little or no taste but adds a unique consistency to a dish. The best shark's fin is extremely expensive and takes 4 days to prepare. However a processed shark's fin which has been partially cooked and then redried is available from Chinese markets.

五香煮花生

Five-Flavored Peanuts

(SERVES 6-8)
INGREDIENTS

¾ lb. raw peanuts
2 star anise
2 tablespoons light soy sauce
1 tablespoon dark soy sauce
1 teaspoon rock sugar
½ teaspoon salt

Rinse the peanuts, drain, then soak in water for 4 hours. Drain again.

Place the peanuts in a saucepan, and cover with water. Add the star anise, both soy sauces, rock sugar and the salt. Bring to a boil and cook for 10 minutes, until the peanuts are soft. Drain and serve when cool.

Hot Pork Paste

(SERVES 6)
INGREDIENTS

1¼ lb. lean ground pork
3 tablespoons corn oil
lettuce, and chopped
   scallions, for garnish

SEASONING
1 tablespoon cayenne
1 tablespoon hot bean sauce
2 tablespoons sugar
3 tablespoons soy sauce
1 teaspoon salt
1 tablespoon ginger wine
   (see Glossary)

Mix the pork with the seasoning ingredients in a bowl.

Heat the oil in a wok or skillet and then add the pork mixture. Stir-fry over a high heat for 5 minutes.

Arrange on a bed of lettuce on a serving dish, and garnish with chopped scallions.

Two Kinds of Marinated Vegetable

(SERVES 4)
INGREDIENTS

¾ lb. Nappa cabbage
   preferably the stem end
½ cucumber
3 teaspoons salt

SEASONING A
1 tablespoon light soy sauce
1 garlic clove, crushed

SEASONING B
1 red chili pepper, seeded
   and finely sliced
1 tablespoon distilled white
   vinegar
2 teaspoons sesame oil
½ teaspoon white pepper

Slice off the stem of the Nappa cabbage and separate the leaves. Cut the stem end in thick diagonal slices.

Pare the cucumber and cut in thin shreds.

Place the two vegetables in two separate bowls and add 1½ teaspoons of salt to each. Marinate both for 20 minutes, stirring frequently.

Squeeze out any excess water, and then add seasoning **A** to the Nappa cabbage and seasoning **B** to the cucumber. Serve at once.

Sour Baby Shrimp

(SERVES 4)
INGREDIENTS

1 package (3 oz.) dried baby
   shrimp
⅓ cup distilled white vinegar
½ teaspoon rice wine or dry
   sherry

Rinse the baby shrimp in cold water and then soak in warm water for 30 minutes. Drain and dry thoroughly.

Dry-fry the shrimp in a wok over medium heat for 2 minutes. Spoon onto a serving platter.

Mix the vinegar and rice wine and serve, as a dipping sauce, with the baby shrimp.

油豆腐細粉

Pork Balls and Bean Thread Soup

(SERVES 6)
INGREDIENTS

1 package (10 oz.) bean curd
 threads
5 cups clear soup stock (see
 p. 261)
8 pork-stuffed meat balls (see
 NOTES)
6-8 fish balls (see NOTES)
2-3 teaspoons sesame oil

SEASONING
2 tablespoons preserved
 vegetable root or pickled
 cabbage, sliced (see
 NOTES)
2 teaspoons salt

Soak the bean curd threads in cold water for 30
minutes. Drain and cut in 5 inch pieces.

Place the soup stock in a large pan, add the pork
and fish balls and bring to a boil. Cook for 10 minutes
and then add the bean threads.

Cook for a further minute and then add the
seasoning ingredients. Bring to a boil and serve,
sprinkled with a little sesame oil.

NOTES
Pork meat balls and fish balls are available from
most Oriental markets and are usually sold in sealed
plastic packages.

Pickled cabbage is a red-root vegetable that has
been preserved in salt. It's sold in cans. Rinse before
use.

炸龍鳳腿

Mock Chicken Drumsticks

(SERVES 4)
INGREDIENTS

¾ lb pork tenderloin
2 boneless chicken breasts,
 skinned
3 tablespoons oil
1 can (3 oz.) water chestnuts,
 drained
1 celery stalk, thinly sliced
1 small carrot, shredded
½ tablespoon cornstarch
1 large sheet of chu-wang-
 yiu (see NOTE)
¼ cup all-purpose flour
corn oil, for deep frying

SEASONING A
2 teaspoons salt
1 tablespoon sugar
½ teaspoon five-spice
 powder

SEASONING B
3 tablespoons chili sauce
3 tablespoons ketchup

Using a sharp knife, cut the pork in fine pieces.
Very thinly slice the chicken and chop the water
chestnuts.

Heat the oil in a skillet and stir-fry the pork,
chicken, water chestnuts, celery and carrot for 1
minute. Add seasoning **A** and continue cooking until
the pork is lightly brown and the chicken no longer
pink. Mix the cornstarch with a little water and stir in
the mixture. Bring to a boil and cook for about 1
minute until thick.

Cut the chu-wang-yiu in four 4 inch squares. Place
on a flat surface and put 2-3 tablespoons of the pork
and chicken mixture in the center of each. Roll up,
molding the package into the shape of a chicken
drumstick.

Mix the flour with a little water to make a thick
paste and use a little of this to seal the packages. Coat
each of the packages in the remaining paste.

Heat the oil in a deep-fat fryer and fry the
"drumsticks" for about 7-8 minutes. Remove with a
slotted spoon and drain on paper towels.

Mix seasoning **B** and serve as a dipping sauce
with the "drumsticks".

NOTE
Chu-wang-yiu is a very thin dough, which when fried
has a deliciously crisp texture. It is available from
many Oriental markets.

Spring Roll

(SERVES 4)
INGREDIENTS

6 scallions
3 tablespoons corn oil
1 cup ground pork
¼ cup thinly sliced bamboo
    shoots
3 dried black mushrooms,
    soaked (see NOTES)
2 tablespoons cornstarch
2 tablespoons all-purpose
    flour
2 tablespoons water
about 15 spring roll wrappers
    (see NOTES)
corn oil, for deep frying

SEASONING

1 tablespoon shrimp paste
    (see NOTES)
1½ teaspoons salt
2 teaspoons sugar
½ tablespoon rice wine or
    dry sherry
pinch of black pepper

Trim the scallions, cut in fourths lengthwise and then cut in 3 inch sections.

Heat the oil in a wok. Add the pork, bamboo shoots, mushrooms and seasoning ingredients and stir-fry for 3-4 minutes over a high heat. Add the scallions and cook for a further 3 minutes, stirring.

Mix the cornstarch to a paste with a little water and stir in the pork and vegetable mixture. Cook over a moderately high heat until the mixture is thick and then remove from the heat and let cool a little.

Mix the all-purpose flour with the 2 tablespoons water to make a smooth paste. Arrange the spring roll wrappers on a flat surface and place 2 tablespoons of the filling in the center. Roll the "wrapper" up until semi-circular shaped and then brush the edges with the flour paste. Fold in the sides and continue rolling up.

Heat the oil in a deep-fat fryer and deep fry the spring rolls for 4 minutes or until golden. Drain on paper towels and serve.

NOTES

Soak the black mushrooms for 20-30 minutes in warm water, then remove stems and slice.

Spring roll wrappers are available in Oriental markets, and many large supermarkets.

Shrimp paste is available from Oriental markets. It should be used sparingly, as it has a very strong flavor.

Mixed Meat and Vegetable Broth

(SERVES 4-6)
INGREDIENTS

½ lb. spareribs
¼ cooked blood sausage
1 turnip
1 large carrot
1 large onion
½ inch piece fresh gingerroot
1 tablespoon rice wine or dry
    sherry
6¼ cups fish stock
6-10 fish balls (see NOTE
    on p. 371)

SEASONING

3 tablespoons sweet chili
    sauce
2 tablespoons shrimp paste
    (see NOTE above)
2 tablespoons corn oil
1¼ cups water

Roughly chop the spareribs in chunks and cut the blood sausage in 1 inch cubes, discarding the casings. Peel the turnip and cut in 1 inch cubes, thinly slice the carrot and cut the onion in wedges.

Place the ribs in a large Dutch oven with the ginger, rice wine and the fish stock. Bring to a boil, lower the heat and simmer for 30 minutes.

Add the sausage, turnip, carrot, onion and fish balls, bring back to a boil and lower the heat again. Simmer for about 1 hour, covered, until the vegetables are very tender.

In a separate pan, heat the seasoning ingredients along with the water until boiling. When ready to serve the broth, swirl in the seasoning sauce.

Steamed Eggs with Smelt

(SERVES 4)
INGREDIENTS

2-3 oz smelt
6 eggs
1 tablespoon melted
  shortening
⅓ cup clear soup stock (see
  p. 261)

SEASONING
1 tablespoon rice wine or dry
  sherry
1 teaspoon salt
½ teaspoon white pepper

Mix the seasoning ingredients and add the smelt. Let stand for 5 minutes.

Beat the eggs thoroughly.

Mix the shortening with the smelt and place them in a deep bowl with the eggs and the soup stock.

Place the bowl in a steamer, cover and steam over a high heat for 10 minutes.

Bean Curd Sheet Rolls

(SERVES 4)
INGREDIENTS

¾ lb. ground pork
4 water chestnuts
1 tablespoon dried baby
  shrimp, soaked (see
  NOTES)
5 Chinese dried mushrooms,
  soaked (see NOTES)
16 bean curd sheets
4 tablespoons corn oil
¾ cup clear soup stock (see
  p. 261)
4 tablespoons finely grated
  fresh gingerroot

SEASONING A
1 tablespoon rice wine or dry
  sherry
1 teaspoon salt
½ teaspoon white pepper

SEASONING B
½ teaspoon salt
1 tablespoon soy sauce
½ teaspoon white pepper

Mix the pork with seasoning **A** and let stand for 10 minutes.

Crush or mince the water chestnuts, mince the baby shrimp and chop the mushrooms in small cubes. Place together in a bowl, add the pork and work together to form a thick paste.

Soak the bean curd sheets in cold water until soft enough to handle. Dry on paper towels and set out on a flat surface.

Place 2-3 tablespoons of the pork mixture onto one sheet. Roll up from one corner, tucking in the left and right hand corners as you go.

Heat the oil in a wok and carefully add the bean curd rolls. Cook for 3 minutes and then add the soup stock, seasoning **B** and ginger. Simmer for 15 minutes.

Remove the rolls with a slotted spoon and arrange on a serving platter. Spoon the sauce over the top and serve.

NOTES

Soak the baby shrimp in warm water for 30 minutes.

Soak the dried mushrooms in warm water for 20 minutes and then remove the stems.

鹹　粥

Savory Congee

(SERVES 4)

INGREDIENTS

1½ tablespoons corn oil
1 scallion, chopped
5 oz. pork tenderloin, sliced
1 cup long-grain rice
3 tablespoons dried baby
   shrimp (see NOTE)
1 oz. dried fish
5 Chinese black mushrooms,
   soaked (see NOTE)
5 cups water

Heat the oil in a large Dutch oven. Add the scallion and sauté for 30 seconds. Add the pork and the rice and cook for a further minute.

Rinse the baby shrimp and dried fish in cold water. Remove the stems from the mushrooms and cut in small cubes.

Add the water to the pork and rice mixture and then add the dried baby shrimp, dried fish and the mushrooms. Bring to a boil, lower the heat and simmer for 35-40 minutes or until the rice is tender. Serve with assorted nuts.

NOTE
Soak the shrimp, fish and mushrooms in warm water for 30 minutes before use.

髮菜四素

Dish of Five Vegetables

(SERVES 4)
INGREDIENTS

1 oz. black moss seaweed
1 carrot
1 cup about ¼ lb. button
  mushrooms
8 baby corn cobs
1 cup snow peas
2 tablespoons corn oil
½ tablespoon cornstarch
½ cup clear soup stock (see
  p. 261)

SEASONING
1 teaspoon salt
1 teaspoon white pepper
2 teaspoons sugar
2 teaspoons sesame oil

Soak the black moss seaweed in cold water for 20 minutes. Drain.

Cut the carrot in thin strips, cut the mushrooms in halves or fourths, if large, and slice the baby corns in half lengthwise.

Place the carrots and baby corn cobs in a bowl and cover with boiling water. Blanch for 2 minutes, add the button mushrooms and snow peas and blanch for a further 3 minutes. Drain.

Heat the oil in a wok and add the carrot, baby corns, mushrooms and snow peas. Mix the cornstarch with a little cold soup stock and stir with the remaining stock into the vegetables. Cook for 5 minutes, stirring occasionally.

Add the black moss and seasoning ingredients and simmer over a low heat for 1 minute. Arrange the four vegetables on a plate and lay the black moss on top. Pour over the sauce and serve.

Oyster and Vegetable Medley

(SERVES 4)
INGREDIENTS

¼ lb. Chinese dried oysters, soaked (see NOTE)
1 tablespoon salt
2 tablespoons cornstarch
¾ cup water
3 tablespoons corn oil
1 egg, beaten
¼ lb. spinach
1 tablespoon peanut powder or ground peanuts

SEASONING A

¼ teaspoon salt
¼ teaspoon rice wine or dry sherry
2 teaspoons ginger juice

SEASONING B

3 tablespoons red bean sauce
1 tablespoon sugar
1 tablespoon soy sauce

Place the dried oysters in cold water with the salt and let soak for 30 minutes. Drain. Rinse the oysters in boiling water, and then soak again for 3 minutes. Drain thoroughly and pat dry.

Mix the cornstarch with the water, then mix with seasoning **A**.

Mix seasoning **B** ingredients with a little water. Heat 1 tablespoon of the oil in a small saucepan, add seasoning **B** and cook for 1 minute. Set aside.

Heat a further 1 tablespoon of the oil in a pan, and pour in seasoning **A**, tipping the pan to ensure it completely covers the base of the pan. Place the oysters on top, then pour in the beaten egg.

When the mixture has set, fold one half over the other. Add the spinach and the remaining oil, and cook for 2-3 minutes until the spinach is cooked. Remove from the pan and arrange on a serving dish, along with the peanut powder and seasoning **B**.

NOTE
Dried oysters are available from some Oriental markets. However, they tend to be quite expensive. If necessary halve quantities recommended here.

Thin Noodles with Oysters

(SERVES 4)
INGREDIENTS

10 oz. dried oysters (see NOTE above)
1½ tablespoons salt
1 package (10 oz.) thin egg noodles
¼ cup cornstarch
5 cups clear soup stock (see p. 261)
¼ cup sliced bamboo shoots
1 small carrot, sliced
3 Chinese mushrooms, soaked
¼ cup soy sauce
2 teaspoons salt
2 tablespoons chopped fresh parsley
½ cup black vinegar (see NOTE)
2 teaspoons white pepper
fresh parsley sprigs, for garnish

Place the oysters in cold water with the salt and let soak for 30 minutes. Drain. Rinse the oysters in boiling water, and then soak again for 3 minutes. Drain thoroughly and pat dry.

Separate the noodles and soak in cold water for 5 minutes. Drain.

Mix the cornstarch with a little of the cold soup stock. Place this and the rest of the soup stock in a saucepan. Bring to a boil, stirring constantly.

When the mixture has thickened, add the oysters, bamboo shoots, carrot, sliced Chinese mushrooms, soy sauce and salt. Bring back to a boil and boil for another 3-5 minutes.

Add the noodles, and boil for 3 minutes until they are just tender.

Add the chopped parsley, vinegar and pepper. Garnish with parsley sprigs and serve.

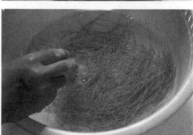

NOTE
Dark and rich, black vinegar is available from Oriental markets, but malt vinegar could be substituted if necessary.

Steamed Pumpkin with Rice Flour

(SERVES 4)
INGREDIENTS

1 small pumpkin or ½ large
  pumpkin
9 tablespoons corn oil
1 teaspoon salt
½ teaspoon pepper
2 scallions, chopped
8 tablespoons rice flour
3 tablespoons clear soup
  stock (see p. 261)

SEASONING
1 tablespoon light soy sauce
1 tablespoon oil
½ teaspoon salt

Peel the pumpkin and cut in large pieces.

Heat 8 tablespoons of the oil in a wok or skillet and stir-fry the pumpkin pieces for 5 minutes. Remove from the wok with a slotted spoon and toss with the salt and pepper. Set aside for 15 minutes.

Heat the remaining 1 tablespoon of oil in the wok, add the scallions and stir-fry for 1 minute. Remove and set aside for the garnish.

Mix the rice flour with the soup stock and the seasoning ingredients and coat the pumpkin pieces in this mixture.

Place the pumpkin in a deep bowl and set in a steamer. Cover and steam over a high heat for 30 minutes. Spoon onto a plate, garnish with the cooked scallions and serve.

五味冬瓜

Five-Flavored Winter Melon

(SERVES 4)
INGREDIENTS

2 lb. winter melon
3 Chinese dried mushrooms,
  soaked (see NOTES)
3 dried scallops, soaked
  (see NOTES)
2 small dried bamboo shoots,
  soaked (see NOTES)
3 tablespoons corn oil
2 teaspoons finely grated
  fresh gingerroot
1 cup dried shrimp
  (see NOTES)
½ cup diced smoked ham
½ cup diced lean pork
2½ cups clear soup stock
  (see p. 261)
2 tablespoons cornstarch

SEASONING
½ teaspoon salt
1 teaspoon sugar
½ teaspoon white pepper

Peel the winter melon, remove the seeds and dice in small cubes. Place in a large bowl, cover with boiling water and let stand for 5 minutes. Drain.

Remove the stems from the mushrooms and cut the caps in small cubes; slice the scallops thinly and finely dice the bamboo shoots.

Heat the oil in a wok or skillet and stir-fry the ginger for a few seconds. Add the mushrooms, scallops, bamboo shoots, dried shrimp, ham, pork and seasoning ingredients and stir-fry for 2 minutes.

Add the soup stock and stir to mix. Bring to a boil. Add the winter melon, bring back to a boil, lower the heat and simmer for 2 minutes.

Mix the cornstarch with a little cold water and stir into the soup. Simmer for 2 minutes until the soup has thickened and serve.

NOTES
Since dried food keeps very well, it means all these ingredients are available in this country too. In order to use dried food, it needs to be soaked first.
dried mushrooms – soak in warm water for 30 minutes
dried scallops – soak in cold water for 1 hour
dried bamboo shoots – soak in cold water for 30 minutes
dried shrimp – soak in warm water for 30 minutes

Banana Gelatin

(SERVES 4)

INGREDIENTS

1½ cups water
2 tablespoons unflavored
  gelatin
½ cup superfine sugar
4 bananas
3 tablespoons lemon juice
½ cup orange juice

Place ½ cup cold water in a bowl and sprinkle the gelatin over the surface. Let the gelatin soak for 5 minutes. Bring the remaining water to a boil, add to the gelatin and stir until the gelatin has dissolved.

Add the sugar, stirring until it has completely dissolved. Set aside for 10 minutes.

Slice the bananas and sprinkle with 1 tablespoon of the lemon juice to prevent them discoloring.

Mix the orange and remaining lemon juice in bowl and stir in the gelatin mixture.

Arrange half of the banana slices in a dessert mold, pour one third of the gelatin mixture over the bananas and place in the refrigerator for 5 minutes.

Add half of the remaining gelatin mixture to the mold, refrigerate for 5 minutes and then add the remaining gelatin mixture. Refrigerate for 30-60 minutes until set.

When the gelatin is set, place the mold up to the rim in boiling water for 5-10 seconds, and then invert the mold onto a serving platter. Decorate the dessert with the remaining banana slices and serve.

Pineapple Gelatin

(SERVES 4)

INGREDIENTS

1½ cups water
2 tablespoons unflavored
  gelatin
½ cup superfine sugar
6-8 pineapple rings
2 tablespoons lemon juice
½ cup pineapple juice

Place ½ cup cold water in a bowl and sprinkle the gelatin over the surface. Let the gelatin soak for 5 minutes. Bring the remaining water to a boil, add to the gelatin and stir until the gelatin has dissolved.

Add the sugar, stirring until it has completely dissolved. Set aside for 10 minutes.

Arrange the pineapple rings in a large dessert mold.

Mix the lemon and pineapple juice in a bowl and stir in the gelatin mixture. Pour over the pineapple rings and place in a refrigerator for 45-60 minutes or until set.

When the gelatin is set, place the mold up to the rim in boiling water for 5-10 seconds, and then invert the mold onto a serving platter.

MENU IDEAS

MENU 1
(SERVES 8)

Soup of Assorted Shreds
page 221

Five-Spice Chicken Pieces
page 77

Marinated Pork
page 101

Deep-Fried Shrimp with Black Sesame Seeds
page 57

Hot Beef
page 73

Paper-Wrapped Fish
page 41

Stuffed Green Peppers
page 126

Stir-Fried Spinach with Fresh Vegetables
page 189

Stir-Fried Rice Noodles
page 275

Crystal Beauty
page 259

MENU 2
(SERVES 6)

Chicken and Corn Chowder
page 81

Sautéed Shrimp
page 13

Sweet and Sour Fish
page 27

Assorted Shreds
page 131

Beef Slices in Sauce
page 73

The Farmer's Joy
page 229

Chicken with Sweet Rice
page 279

Fresh Fruit

MENU 3
(SERVES 4)

Shanghainese Thick Noodle Soup
page 271

Baked Creamy Clams
page 15

Crystal Paper-Wrapped Chicken
page 95

Barbecued Beef
page 113

Home-Town Style Snow Peas
page 225

Fried or Plain Boiled Rice
page 264

Fresh Fruit

MENU 4

(SERVES 4)

Mixed Meat and Vegetable Broth
page 373

Spicy Clams
page 363

Cantonese Fried Chicken
page 353

Hot Pork Paste
page 367

Steamed Pumpkin with Rice Flour
page 381

Fried or Plain Boiled Rice
page 264

Fresh Fruit

MENU 5

(SERVES 4)

Stewed Shark's Fin with Mushrooms
page 365

Stir-Fried Beef with Oyster Sauce
page 363

Mock Chicken Drumsticks
page 371

Two Kinds of Marinated Vegetable
page 369

Fried or Plain Boiled Rice
page 264

Sweet Lotus Roots
page 359

MENU 6

(SERVES 6)

Five-Flavoured Peanuts
page 367

Shredded Chicken and Pepper
page 353

Scalded Abalone
page 361

Spring Roll
page 373

Thin Noodles with Oysters
page 379

Dish of Five Vegetables
page 377

Fried or Plain Boiled Rice
page 264

Pineapple Gelatin
page 383

GLOSSARY

Abalone: A white-fleshed shellfish with a firm texture and a delicate scallop-like flavor.

Fresh abalone can sometimes be found in Californian markets, but there are laws governing the size and number that may be harvested, so the supply is quite limited.

Failing finding these, however, frozen abalone from Japan and Mexico are available from gourmet food markets. Canned minced abalone is also on sale; once opened it should be used straight away.

Dried abalone are also sometimes sold. However, since they need to be soaked for 4 days, they are probably more trouble than they're worth.

Abalone Mushrooms: *See Chinese Mushrooms*

Agar-Agar: A gelatinous seaweed used for making sweet or savory molds. Since it sets without refrigeration, it is particularly suited to hot climates like south China and Hong Kong where it is used a great deal. However, it is virtually tasteless and unflavored gelatin, or aspic are good substitutes.

Sold in most Oriental markets, it is normally only available in this country in dried form, either powdered or cut in strips. Keep in a covered container or wrapped in cellophane in a dry cool place, but not in the refrigerator, for up to 6 months.

Angled Luffas: Sometimes known as Chinese okra or silk squash, this vegetable is a member of the gourd family. It is a long, thin vegetable with deep ridges running along its length. It has a sweet flavor and is used for soups as well as stir-fries.

Available from some Chinese and Indian markets, it tends to be mainly around in the summer months. If unavailable, use cucumber.

Aniseed: Along with star anise, which has a similar flavor, aniseed is popular in Chinese cooking, adding a delicate licorice taste to sweet and savory dishes.

It is available whole, as tiny egg-shaped seeds, or in powdered form and can be bought in health food stores, Chinese delicatessens and some large supermarkets. If unavailable, use caraway seeds instead.

Bamboo Shoots: One of the most widely used vegetable in Chinese cooking, these fibrous, cream-colored shoots have a pleasant, slightly acid flavor and a firm texture.

Thanks to modern transport and greater demand, *fresh bamboo shoots* are now increasingly available from Chinese markets. Peel away the outer skin until you reach the firm heart. This can then be boiled whole or sliced or cut to slivers according to the recipe.

Canned bamboo shoots are widely available from Chinese stores and most supermarkets too. They either come ready sliced or in large 3 × 4 inch chunks. Drain and rinse in fresh water before using. Place any unused shoots in a dish, cover with fresh water and keep refrigerated for 3-4 days, changing the water daily to keep fresh.

Bean Curds: Made from puréed yellow soy beans, bean curd or tofu is used extensively in Chinese cooking. In many areas where meat is scarce or expensive, bean curd is an important source of protein and consequently there are many different varieties available.

Fresh Bean Curd: Comes in cakes about 3 inches square which can be cut to any shape. It has a fairly bland taste but when cooked with other ingredients, such as meat, fish or vegetables, acquires their flavors. It also adds extra protein, as well as an interesting consistency to a dish.

Fresh bean curd can be found in Chinese and Japanese markets. It is also sold in cans. Store in fresh water in a covered container for 2–3 days.

Dried Bean Curd: This too is sold in cake form, which is sliced or cut in strips and then fried, braised or stewed according to the recipe. An instant powdered form is also available. Available from Chinese supermarkets.

Dried Bean Curd Sheets: Comes in thin, stiff sheets and must be soaked in warm water for about 10 minutes before use. It can be cut in strips and used in soups, or used as a wrapper for small meat balls and rolls. Available from Oriental supermarkets.

Fermented Bean Curd/Bean Curd Cheese: Made by fermenting small cubes of bean curd in brine, chilis and wine. It is very salty, with a strong, distinct taste and while the Chinese often eat small quantities for breakfast with congee, it is mostly used for flavoring meat or vegetable dishes.

There are two types commonly available. The white fermented variety and the red Southern China one. Both are sold in jars or sealed packages and are available from Chinese markets. They will keep for months in the refrigerator.

Pressed Bean Curd: A firmer form of bean curd often used in vegetarian cooking. There are various types available. *Spiced bean curd* is seasoned with spices and soy sauce. It is also known as *fragrant dry bean curd*. It can be shredded to make noodles and added to soups or stir-fries. Available from Oriental markets.

Bean Sprouts: The young sprouts of mung beans, these are some 2 inches long, have a fresh flavor and a delicious crunchy texture which makes them a popular addition to stir-fries. Stir them into a dish just before serving, otherwise they will lose their crispness.

Fresh bean sprouts are widely available from Oriental groceries and some supermarkets. They should be white stemmed with pale yellow heads. Avoid any that appear to exude any brown juice since this means they are past their prime. They are best eaten on the day of purchase, but can be stored in a plastic bag in the refrigerator for up to a day. Canned bean sprouts don't have quite the crispness of fresh ones, but are still quite acceptable. These too are readily available from most supermarkets. Drain and rinse in cold water before using.

Bitter Gourd/Bitter Melon/Balsam Pear: Mostly light green to white in color, this gourd has an unmistakable bumpy skin and when cut open, reveals rosy-red seeds. As the name suggests, it has a rather bitter taste which finely complements rich pork dishes and it is frequently used in Chinese cooking, where it is a common vegetable. It is available from some Oriental and West Indian supermarkets and can be kept, refrigerated, for up to 2 weeks. If not available use *chayote* or summer squash or zucchini instead.

Black Bean Sauce/Black Bean Paste: Also known as *brown-bean sauce*, this thick paste made from small, black, salted soy beans is often used instead of soy sauce when a thicker sauce is required. It is very salty with a strong flavor and should be used sparingly. It is sold in cans or jars, either semi-whole or puréed. Buy from any Chinese market and keep unused sauce in a sealed container in the refrigerator for up to 2 weeks. *See also, Yellow Bean Sauce and Red Bean Sauce.*

Black Mushrooms: *See Chinese Mushrooms*

Black Moss: *See Seaweed*

Chayote: A pear-shaped vegetable with a similar texture to summer squash. Like squash it varies widely in size and shape, with the larger specimens being rather insipid. Therefore, look out for the smaller varieties. They come from the Caribbean, are widely available around the Gulf, and are becoming more popular elsewhere. If not available, use summer squash or zucchini instead.

Chili Peppers: These hot little green and red peppers are used frequently in Chinese cooking. There are many types, ranging from the hot to the unbearable, and beware of recipes advocating using 6-10 a dish. For Western palates it's best to play safe and use just one or two until you feel acclimatized to such fiery eating experiences! As a general rule, the smaller the chili peppers, the hotter they'll be. Besides making a dish very hot, chilis also add a distinctive flavor. They are normally finely sliced before adding to a dish with the seeds removed and discarded.

Fresh chilis are widely available. *Dried chilis* are lightly crumbled and used to flavor soups and stews. Available from health food stores and Oriental groceries.

Chili Oil: Made from small red chilis which have been slowly sautéed in oil, this oil can be very hot indeed and should be used sparingly. It is reddish in color and can be made at home. Sauté finely sliced chili gently in oil for 5 minutes until the oil is dark, using 1 chili to every 1 tablespoon oil.

Chili Sauce: Made from small chili peppers, this is a hot sauce used frequently in China as a condiment as well as 387 in cooking. It is available from Chinese and Western supermarkets and is most commonly available in bottles. It will keep almost indefinitely. *Sweet chili sauce* is not so hot and is a more popular condiment on Western tables. This too is widely available.

Chinese Cabbage/Nappa Cabbage/Celery Cabbage: A wide variety of cabbages are grown in China, where they are used in all sorts of dishes as well as in chutneys and pickles. The variety that is now commonly available in this country is, in China, known as the *pe-tsai*. A little like a large, pale Romaine lettuce, it has a thick white stem and pale yellow or green leaves and is also known here as Nappa cabbage. The leaves have a delicate savory flavor, while the stem is slightly sweet, similar to bean sprouts, with a crisp, celery-like texture. Celery cabbage is a good substitute.

Available from many markets, it will keep up to 2 weeks in the salad crisper of a refrigerator.

Chinese Curry Powder: A sweet smelling curry powder, not to be confused with Indian curry powders, which would give a dish a completely different flavor. Chinese curry powders are normally composed of anise pepper, cassia (cinnamon), chili, cloves, coriander seeds, fennel seeds, nutmeg, star anise and turmeric.

Available only from Chinese markets; store in an airtight container in a dry place.

Chinese Mushrooms and Fungi: Mushrooms and fungi are widely used in Chinese cooking, both in fresh and dried forms. Although they tend not to have a strong flavor, they are popular since they add a particular texture to a dish – a very important element in Chinese cuisine. Fresh Chinese mushrooms are difficult to find in the West, but there are a number of dried and canned varieties that can be bought.

These are normally only available from Oriental markets. Dried mushrooms should be soaked in warm water for 20-30 minutes before use, rinsing before and after soaking. Once soaked, remove and discard the stem which is very tough. Dried, the mushrooms and fungi will keep indefinitely, if stored in an airtight container. Once soaked, however, they should be used straight away.

Abalone Mushrooms/Oyster Mushrooms/Enok: Large and flat ear-shaped mushrooms with grey/fawn caps and soft cream-colored "bellies". They have an excellent flavor but need careful cooking as they can be tough.

Known in this country as oyster mushrooms or enok, they are available fresh mainly in winter from specialist groceries.

Chinese Mushrooms/Dried Black Mushrooms/ Winter Mushrooms: One of the most common mushrooms in Chinese cookery, these dried dark brown or black mushrooms are used in a whole range of Chinese dishes and add a chewy texture. You will find they come in varying thicknesses, the thick-capped ones being considered the best. The name, Winter Mushrooms, refers to the time of their harvest.

Cloud Ears/Wood Ears: Two common Chinese fungi which grow on the bark of trees. They are normally about 1½ inches in diameter, dark-brown, almost black, in color with crinkly skins. Although they have little flavor, they are popular since they add a slightly crunchy and firm texture to a dish and provide a contrast in color.

Silver Ears: A dried white fungi with little or no flavor but a delicate texture. Used mainly in sweet dishes, it should be soaked for 50-60 minutes before using.

Straw Mushrooms: Only available canned, these small conical mushrooms have a pleasant, delicate flavor a little similar to button mushrooms. Their texture is soft and

rather slimy. Drain thoroughly and rinse before using. If unavailable, use button mushrooms.

Chinese Sausages: Thin dried sausage links made of pork, beef or pork liver and duck. Steam before using in a recipe.

Available from most Chinese delicatessens, they will keep for a few months, wrapped in a plastic bag and stored in the refrigerator.

Chinese Spareribs: Not to be confused with American spareribs which are meaty and sold in slices, these spareribs are from the lower ends of the rib bones. They have very little meat on them but taste extremely good barbecued with Hoisin or barbecue sauce

Chinese Vinegar: A fermented rice vinegar, there are two principal types available, the *brown vinegar* and the *white vinegar*. Both are quite mild, with a slightly sweet taste. They can be found in Oriental markets, however substitute cider vinegar and distilled white vinegar respectively if preferred.

Cumin: A common Indian spice that is occasionally found in Chinese cooking. The dried seed is small and light brown in color, while the ground seed is olive green. Cumin has a strong, heavy aroma, adding a distinctive, pungent flavor to savory and sweet dishes.

Available from most supermarkets.

Dates/Red, Black: Dried dates that need soaking before use. The red dates are also known as *red jujubes*. Both should be soaked in cold water for 1-2 hours.

Available from some Chinese markets, but when not, substitute prunes.

Dried Black Beans: *See Fermented Black Beans*

Dried Chestnuts: Frequently used in Chinese cooking for their flavor and aroma, they are simply the fruit of the sweet chestnut. Dried, they are hard and crinkly and should be soaked overnight in cold water before using in a recipe.

Available from some health food shops, Oriental and Indian groceries.

Dried Duck/Dried Chicken: These are de-boned and pressed flat before being dried. They are used most frequently for flavoring stocks and soups and are available from most Chinese markets.

Dried Fish: Salted and dried in the sun, dried fish is used frequently both for flavoring other dishes or eating in its own right. Since dried fish will keep indefinitely, they are frequently exported from China and are frequently available from Chinese markets.

Dried Orange Peel: *See Orange Peel, Dried*

Dried Scallops: White scallops that have been dried in the sun, they have a sweet, slightly musty flavor. Available from good Oriental stores, they should be kept in a covered jar in a cool place.

Dried Shrimp: Small and orange in color, dried shrimp have been salted and dried in the sun and have a distinctive fishy smell and taste. They are available in several different qualities; in general, the larger they are the better. They should be soaked in lukewarm water for 30 minutes before using and then drained thoroughly.

The dry shrimp will keep indefinitely in an airtight container. Once soaked, however, use the same day.

Dried Squid: Highly regarded by the Chinese as a delicacy, dried squid has a strong distinctive flavor, quite different from the rather fragrant mild taste of fresh squid. Soak overnight in cold water before using.

Available only from gourmet groceries.

Fermented Black Beans: Small fermented soy beans commonly used in fish and seafood cookery. Since they are very salty, soak in cold water for 5-10 minutes. They are available in cans or jars and will keep 2-3 weeks if placed in an airtight jar in the refrigerator. *Dried black beans* can be used if canned beans are not available. They should be washed thoroughly and then marinated in brandy or rice wine for several hours.

Five-Spice Powder: Frequently used in all sorts of Chinese dishes, to many it summons up the taste and smell of China. As the name implies, it is made up of five ground spices – szechuan pepper, cinnamon, cloves, fennel seed and star anise.

Available from delicatessens, Chinese markets and some health food shops, it should be kept in a sealed container in a dry place. Like most spices it will keep for several months, but will gradually lose its fragrance and flavor and therefore should not be kept for too long.

Flours: There are many different kinds of flour used in China, made from grains, pulses and tubers. They are used for making the many types of noodles, for doughs and pancakes. They will normally be available from any Chinese and some Indian supermarkets. When not available, all-purpose flour can be used instead, or use the alternative listed below.
Cornstarch: This is a very common thickening agent in Chinese cooking. Arrowroot flour can be used as a substitute, but not all-purpose flour.
Potato Starch: Often added to batters to give more elasticity.
Rice Flour: Made from finely ground white rice, this is used in various batters and sweet dishes.
Glutinous Rice Flour: Made from glutinous rice, this has more elasticity than ordinary rice flour, becoming clear and sticky when cooked. It is used for certain sweet dishes, batters and dough.
Green Bean Flour: Sometimes known as *green pea flour*, this flour is made from ground mung beans. It is often light green in color, although can be white or pale pink as well. It is used for various dim sum and noodle recipes. If not available, arrowroot flour can be substituted.

Fuzzy Melons/Summer Melons: Looking a little like a cross between a cucumber and a zucchini, when young, these fruit/vegetables are covered with a silky fuzz which comes away under running water. The flesh inside is soft and white with white spongy seeds. These melons are available from Chinese markets.

Ginger, Fresh Root: A knobbly, pale-colored root, this is probably the single most important spice in Chinese cooking. It is almost always used with fish and seafood cookery and with many meats as well, such as beef, venison and pork. It has a sweet, fragrant aroma and adds a distinct almost citrus flavor and slight piquancy to a dish. It should be pared and then thinly sliced or grated. *Ginger juice* can be made by placing a few slices of fresh ginger in a garlic press and squeezing firmly.

Fresh gingerroot is available from many large supermarkets and will keep for 1-2 months if kept in a dry place. If it is not available, use ½ teaspoon ground ginger and 1 tablespoon lemon juice for every 1 tablespoon of fresh grated ginger.

Ginger Wine: An infusion of shredded ginger and Chinese rice wine, it is seldom available commercially, but can easily be made at home. If Chinese rice wine is unavailable, dry sherry can be used instead. To make 1 cup place 2 tablespoons finely sliced fresh gingerroot with the wine and let stand for at least 1 hour before use. It will keep indefinitely in the refrigerator.

Ginkgo Nuts: Small soft white nuts, a little larger than peanuts with a distinctive flavor. They should be blanched to remove the outer brown skin before use. Available canned from most Oriental markets. Canned nuts should be drained and rinsed before using.

Gluten Puff: Normally sold frozen in Chinese markets, it should be completely thawed before use. Canned glutens are also sometimes available, but take care that the sauce they come in complements the recipe.

Gourds: *See Bitter Melon*

Green Bean Flour: *See Flours*

Hoisin Sauce: Made with garlic, chilis, spices and soy beans, this brownish-red sauce is frequently used as a dip with pork and beef dishes. It is also commonly used with soy sauce in stir-frying. It has a strong, sweet flavor and should be used sparingly, otherwise it tends to overpower the rest of the meal.

Available from any Oriental and most large Western supermarkets, it is sometimes labeled Barbecue Sauce.

Jellyfish: Dried shreds of jellyfish are quite frequently used in Chinese cooking, giving the favored gelatinous texture to a dish.

Dried jellyfish can be bought from some Chinese stores. If not available, use shredded agar-agar or transparent vermicelli.

Laver: *See Seaweed*

Lily: *See Seaweed/Tiger Lily Buds*

Long Eggplants: Exactly the same vegetable as the short plump ones we're accustomed to, long eggplants are, in fact, common in China and are now occasionally available in gourmet food stores.

Lotus Leaves: Used only for wrapping food, lotus leaves impart a distinctive and delicate flavor to food during steaming. The food packages are usually served in their leaves, which are then unwrapped at the table.

They are sold in most Chinese markets, coming in cellophane packages or tied loosely with string. Soak for 20 minutes in warm water in order to soften them before using.

Lotus Root: A popular sweet in China, fresh lotus root is served simply chilled and sliced with a sweet apricot sauce. It is distinctive both in flavor and appearance, with a slightly musty taste and pale holey flesh that creates an attractive lace pattern when sliced.

Fresh lotus root, in 3 × 6 inch sections, can be bought from some Oriental markets. Canned lotus root is more commonly available from any Oriental foodstore. Soak dried lotus root overnight in cold water before using.

Lotus Seeds/Nuts: Used in a wide variety of dishes, both savory and sweet, these seeds from the lotus flower are ivory-colored and oval. They are available both dried and canned in syrup and if dried, should be soaked for 24 hours.

Luffas: *see Angled Luffas*

Medlar Leaves: A green vegetable with long thin leafy stems, resembling mint in appearance, but with a distinctive and unique flavor for which there is no real substitute.
Available from Chinese and some Indian markets.

Mustard Greens: A dark green vegetable with firm, pale green stems. It has a faint mustardy taste. Available year round, but at its best from June to October. Collard greens can be substituted when necessary.

Noodles: Many different types of noodles are eaten in China which are prepared from all sorts of flour. They come in a variety of thicknesses and shapes, tied into bundles or coiled into squares and rectangles. Today, more and more varieties are available to us, although for fresh noodles, it is necessary to visit a Chinese foodstore. Chinese dried noodles, however, can be bought from most large supermarkets.
Fresh Egg Noodles/E Mein: These large, yellow noodles are made of wheat and are either round or slightly flattened in shape. They should be rinsed and drained thoroughly before being fried and, like all fresh noodles, should not be kept for more than a day before using, otherwise they tend to become heavy.
Dried Egg Noodles/Mein Tsein: Thin dried yellow noodles, which are either round or slightly flattened. Used in soups and fried noodle dishes, they are sold in bundles or coiled into square packages and should be soaked first to separate the strands.
Rice Noodles/Ho-Fun: Made from rice flour, these are flat, opaque noodles, about ¼ inch wide. They are available fresh or dried and can be boiled or fried. Dried noodles should be soaked for up to 30 minutes to soften.
Cellophane Noodles/Bean Threads/Transparent Vermicelli: Glass-like opaque white threads made from mung bean flour. The noodles expand and become translucent upon soaking and are normally added to soups because they absorb large quantities of stock, giving them flavor and the soup substance. They should be soaked in hot water for five minutes before using. *Mung bean sheets* can be shredded according to the recipe. However, when not available, buy the packages of prepared noodles.

Orange Peel/Tangerine Peel, Dried: This dried peel is often added to soups and casseroles to give a distinct and pleasant orange-flavor. The best peel comes from large, brightly colored fruit. The peel is threaded onto twine and dried in the sun for a week. It normally comes in packages and can be bought from most Oriental stores. Soak for 20 minutes before use. Dried, it will keep indefinitely, if stored in an airtight container.

Oyster Sauce: Made from oysters and soy beans, this thick, salty sauce from South China is often used to flavor beef and occasionally vegetable dishes. Available from most Chinese markets, once opened it should be kept in the refrigerator.

Peanut Oil/Groundnut Oil: Although recipes in this book mostly call for corn oil, which is inexpensive and easily available, peanut oil is the type most favored by the Chinese and for special occasions it is slightly preferable. It is available from most supermarkets, groceries and health stores.

Peppermint Leaves: A member of the mint family, peppermint has deep green, crinkled leaves which are occasionally tinged with reddish brown. It has a pleasant aromatic bouquet and a strong menthol taste, but unless home-grown it could be quite difficult to obtain.

Plum Sauce: Made from plums, sugar, garlic, salt and chili, it adds a sweet, fruity flavor to various dishes and is often used when crisp-roasting meat and poultry. Sold in glass bottles or jars, it is available from most Chinese markets. It will keep indefinitely.

Potato Starch: *See Flours*

Preserved Vegetable: A turnip-like vegetable, preserved in brine and spices and with a very strong, salty taste. It is usually cooked with meats and vegetables to add flavor and saltiness to a meal. Look out for it in Oriental markets; it is normally sold in cans. Rinse in cold water before use.

Red Bean Sauce/Paste: Otherwise known as *sweet bean paste,* this thick sauce is mostly used as a dip or to brush on pancakes when serving Peking Duck. It is made from red beans, sugar and spices and is also used for sweet sauces or to accompany fish and seafood dishes. Keep covered in the refrigerator for up to 3 months.

Red Spinach: Not really red, but with red-tipped leaves, this Chinese spinach will add a red tinge to soups and casseroles. Regular spinach may be substituted.

Rice: A simple long-grain rice is probably the best choice for most Chinese dishes unless another type is called for. Unless it has been pre-rinsed, rice should always be washed in several changes of water. See p.264 for cooking long-grain rice.
Glutinous Rice: A round-grained rice used for puddings and certain savory dishes and stuffings. It becomes very sticky when cooked. Use short-grain rice when not available.

Rice Wine: A pale, rather sweet wine made from glutinous rice which is used frequently, both for marinades and in cooking. It is available from some liquor stores; dry sherry can be substituted if necessary.

Rock Sugar: Amber-brown sugar crystals used for desserts and candies and for glazing poultry. It is not as sweet as granulated sugar and needs dissolving in warm water before use. It is sold in Chinese markets and some delicatessens. It will keep indefinitely, stored in a covered container.

Salted Cabbage/Pickled Cabbage: Thin brownish-green pieces of the stem of Chinese cabbage, that has been preserved in brine. It has a savory, mildly salty flavor and a firm, crisp texture. Sold in jars, it can be bought from Oriental markets. Rinse thoroughly before use.

Salted Vegetable: *See Preserved Vegetable*

Seafood Sauce: *See Shrimp Paste*

Seaweed: There are several types of seaweed used in Chinese cooking, popular both for their flavor and texture. They are used generally in soups or stews and are normally only available from Chinese groceries.
Black Moss/Hair Seaweed: Fine dried black seaweed that is used in several traditional Chinese dishes. It is very fine and is known as hair seaweed as it is supposed to resemble Chinese hair. It should be soaked for about 40 minutes before use.
Laver: Sold in wafer-thin sheets, measuring about 8 inches square, this dark dehydrated seaweed is commonly

used for wrapping rice and vegetables. It has a slightly fishy fragrant flavor. It can also be deep fried. Fresh laver, a seashore treat, can be shredded and added to soups and salads. Dried laver is available from Chinese markets and Japanese stores, where it is called nori. It is sold in packages and resembles carbon paper.

Tiger Lily Buds/Golden Needles: These have a musty, slightly moldy flavor, which is very much an acquired taste. They are used to garnish various fish dishes and are occasionally used in pork and vegetable dishes. They should be soaked in cold water for 20 minutes before use.

Sesame Oil: A dark-brown, strong-tasting oil, used frequently in Chinese cooking as a seasoning. Made from sesame seeds, it gives food a distinct, slightly nutty flavor. Since it burns easily, it is never used by itself for frying but is sprinkled on stir-fried or deep fried dishes just before serving.

Widely available from large supermarkets and Oriental stores, it comes in convenient small bottles.

Sesame Paste/Sauce: A thick, sticky paste made from ground seeds. It has a strong, dry flavor and is used in several north and west Chinese dishes. Two types are normally available, the dark paste, which has been ground with the husks of the seed, and the lighter paste.

Available from Oriental markets and health food stores, where it is known as *tahini paste*, it comes mostly in jars and should be vigorously stirred before using.

Sesame Seeds: White sesame seeds are used frequently for sweet and savory dishes, often used to coat food before deep frying. They have a pleasant, nutty flavor and are available from health food shops, Chinese delicatessens and large supermarkets. They will keep indefinitely in an airtight container. Black sesame seeds have exactly the same flavor as the white and are normally used in cooking when a contrast in color is required. They are less widely available but can be bought from some Chinese markets.

Soy Sauce: The most familiar ingredient in Chinese cooking, soy sauce is used in savory dishes, almost without fail. Made from fermented soy beans, it is thin and dark brown in color with a rich, salty taste. There are two principal types available: *Dark soy sauce* is used with strong-flavored dishes, like beef and pork, while *light soy sauce* is used for more delicate food, such as seafood, poultry and vegetables. The lighter one is more generally served as a condiment at the table.

Shrimp Paste: Made from thousands of tiny shrimp, this strong-tasting sauce is used to add flavor to soups, noodles, vegetables and meat dishes. It is available either as a purée or as a more solid pâté. Both should be diluted in water before using. Surprisingly, it is not used in fish dishes. Available from Oriental markets.

Spring Roll Wrappers: Large paper-thin skins of rice flour dough, used for making spring rolls. They are sold in packages of 25 or 50 and if frozen, should be thoroughly thawed before using. They are becoming increasingly widely available. Keep unused wrappers in plastic wrap or covered with a damp cloth until ready to use, since once they have dried out, they break easily and become impossible to fold.

Star Anise: A highly scented eight-pointed star-shaped spice used mainly in braised dishes. It is one of the spices that make up Five-Spice Powder. Available from Chinese and Indian stores and gourmet food stores, it should be kept in an airtight container to preserve its aroma.

Straw Mushrooms: *See Chinese Mushrooms*

Szechuan Pepper: Tiny round spice with a reddish brown color, it goes into making Five-Spice Powder and is used, often with star anise, for red-meat dishes – especially those from the north and west of China. It has a very fragrant smell and can be used whole or ground. Available from most Chinese markets.

Taro/Dasheen: A dark brownish-red root vegetable, sometimes called dasheen, shaped a little like a turnip with a thick hairy skin. Inside, the flesh is creamy to dark reddish-brown with a flavor similar to a sweet potato. Popular in Chinese vegetarian cooking, it can be cooked in as many ways as the potato – baked, puréed, braised, deep fried, boiled or mashed. Like the potato, it needs to be cooked until quite soft.

Vinegar: *See Chinese Vinegar*

Water Chestnuts: Small round root plants, that can be halved or sliced and added to stir-fries and casseroles to give a crispy, crunchy texture and a fresh slightly sweet flavor. Fresh water chestnuts, occasionally on sale in Chinese markets, are sold in black-colored skins. These should be rinsed and the skin then peeled off. Canned water chestnuts are widely available on the other hand and simply need draining before use.

White Fungus: *See Chinese Mushrooms/Silver Ears*

Winter Melon: A large, torpedo-shaped melon, with a pale green to dark green skin and creamy white flesh. In cooking, the winter melon has more in common with squash than with summer melons. It should be cooked gently until very tender and it is used in soups and casseroles. It is sold in cans, but if not available, use summer squash instead.

Wonton Wrappers: Ready-made squares of rice-flour skins used for wrapping 'wontons' – small Chinese ravioli. They can be bought in packages of 20 from Chinese markets and some gourmet food stores and any remaining wrappers should be rewrapped securely or covered with a damp cloth otherwise the wrappers will dry out and become useless. They can be frozen. Thaw thoroughly before use.

Yellow Bean Sauce/Paste: Often used instead of soy sauce when thicker consistency is required. It has a similar consistency to Black Bean Sauce, but has added sugar, so is sweeter. It is also lighter and not quite so salty. It is used for making dips, dressings and some marinades and is available in cans or jars from most Oriental markets.

KEY TO VEGETABLES AND INGREDIENTS

Many of the vegetables illustrated here will be known to you; others are perhaps currently less identifiable. Not all of them appear in the recipes in this book, but you can use this guide to help you to identify the unknown vegetables you encounter during your forays into Chinese markets.

1. Head Cabbage
2. Mustard Greens
3. White Chinese Cabbage
4. Fennel
5. Watercress
6. Chinese Spinach
7. Chives
8. Chinese Chives
9. Lettuce
10. Brussels Sprouts
11. White Wormwood
12. Chinese Flat Cabbage
13. Pea Shoots
14. Chinese Cress
15. Stem Lettuce
16. Red Leaves
17. Sweet Potato Leaves
18. Asparagus
19. Chou-Tu-Fu (Bean Curd)
20. Lotus Leaf
21. Chinese Cabbage
22. Fuzzy Melon
23. Pickled Bamboo Shoots
24. Angled Luffa
25. Pickled Melon
26. Pickled Cowpea
27. Cedar Shoots
28. Sour Cabbage
29. Salted Vegetable
30. Taro (dasheen) stem

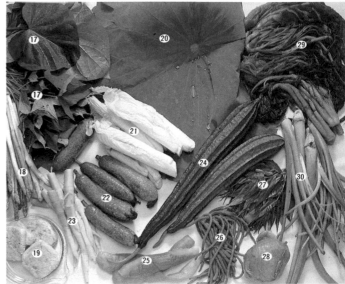

31. Mustard Flower
32. Kale
33. Celery
34. Rape Flower
35. Bitter Gourd (Melon)
36. Green-stemmed Flat Cabbage
37. Spinach
38. Eggplants
39. Bottle Gourd
40. Large Cucumber
41. Turnip
42. Green Oriental Radish
43. Kale Flower
44. Red Radish
45. Sweet Red Peppers (Bell Peppers)
46. Cucumber
47. Nappa Cabbage
48. Leek
49. Green Chili Peppers
50. Carrot
51. Garlic Stem
52. Medlar
53. Corn
54. Winter Melon
55. Water Spinach
56. Mustard Stem
57. Chinese Greens
58. *Ma* Bamboo Shoots
59. Garlic Flower
60. Lotus Root
61. Uzura Beans
62. Sponge Gourd
63. Taro (dasheen)

64. Chinese Mallow
65. Water-Bamboo
66. Basil
67. *Kuei* Bamboo Shoots
68. Green Bamboo
Shoots
69. Taro (dasheen)
70. Chinese Yam
71. Burdock (Gobo)
72. Tomato
73. Chinese Mushrooms

74. Pumpkin
75. White Yam
76. Bean Sprouts
77. Sweet Potatoes
78. Potatoes
79. Bur Clover
80. Rape (Field Mustard)
81. Broccoli
82. Cauliflower
83. Yam Bean
84. Snow Peas

85. Green Peas
86. Lima Beans
87. Green Beans
88. Baby Corn Cobs
89. Straw Mushrooms
90. Button Mushrooms
91. Jack Beans
92. Water Chestnuts
93. Kohlrabi
94. Bamboo Shoots

95. Abalone (Oyster)
Mushrooms
96. Arrow Head
97. Long-Stem
Mushrooms
98. Fungus
99. Chayotes
100. Seakale Beet
101. Fava Beans
102. Snap Beans

INDEX

395

飲且食兮壽而康

酥　夾　菊　夾　燒
車　肉　花　肉　餅
輪　小　酥　小　咖
蘇　燒　燒　燒　哩
卅　餅　餅　餅　餃
月　椰　　　椰　鮮
餅　絲　　　絲　肉
　　齊　　　齊　酥